Comparative Corporate Governance in China

With China already assuming its place as one of the world's biggest markets, both Chinese corporations and international corporations operating in China face the challenges of corporate governance. This insightful text explores a range of issues including: executive compensation, takeover markets, the securities market, insolvency issues, venture capital markets, and their role in corporate governance models.

Dissatisfied with the narrow focus on the board of directors and the takeover market, Yu enlarges the scope of corporate governance studies to cover both market forces and contractual mechanisms. Applying this approach, he examines how market forces and contractual arrangements can reduce agency costs in corporations in the United States, Germany, Japan and Hong Kong. *Comparative Corporate Governance in China* analyzes the political, social and economic factors that have shaped the changes in Chinese corporate law and securities regulation and makes the case that comparative corporate governance studies have significant policy implications for China's transitional economy.

Guanghua Yu is an Associate Professor in the Faculty of Law, University of Hong Kong and a Professor of Law in the School of Law, Southwestern University of Finance and Economics, PR China.

Comparative Corporate Governance in China

Political economy and legal infrastructure

Guanghua Yu

Routledge
Taylor & Francis Group

LONDON AND NEW YORK

First published 2007
by Routledge
2 Park Square, Milton Park, Abingdon, Oxon, OX14 4RN

Simultaneously published in the USA and Canada
by Routledge 270 Madison Ave, New York NY 10016

Routledge is an imprint of the Taylor & Francis Group, an informa business

Transferred to Digital Printing 2008

© 2007 Guanghua Yu

Typeset in Perpetua and Bell Gothic
by Keystroke, High Street, Tettenhall, Wolverhampton

British Library Cataloguing in Publication Data
A catalogue record for this book is available from the British Library

Library of Congress Cataloging in Publication Data
Yu, Guanghua.
Comparative corporate governance in China : political economy and legal infrastructure /
Guanghua Yu.
p. cm.
Includes bibliographical references and index.
ISBN 0-415-40306-5 (hard cover) – ISBN 0-415-40307-3 (soft cover) 1. Corporate
governance–China. 2. China–Economic conditions–2000– 3. Corporation law–China.
4. Securities–China. 5. China–Economic policy–2000– I. Title.
HD2741.Y825 2007
338.60951–dc22
2006028491

ISBN10: 0-415-40306-5   ISBN13: 978-0-415-40306-1 (hbk)
ISBN10: 0-415-40307-3   ISBN13: 978-0-415-40307-8 (pbk)

For my wife, son and daughter

Contents

CONTENTS

Preface

China has been in great transition since the end of the 1970s. It has gradually moved from a rigid planned economy with public ownership of the means of production toward a socialist market economy. Shaped by political, social, and economic factors, the enterprises have undergone significant changes. Macro changes in the economic system and micro changes at the firm levels have called for a general reform of the legal system as a whole, with a particular focus on the reform of corporate law and securities regulation.

While there is a wealth of literature on Chinese law, the discussions and debates on corporate law tend to be descriptive or not very relevant to the transitional Chinese economy. The importance of organizational economics and modern corporate finance has not been adequately dealt with by the existing literature on Chinese corporate law. Unsatisfied with the current body of work in this area, I have devoted a considerable amount of time and energy into the study of corporate governance issues from an interdisciplinary perspective in the last decade. This book to a large extent reflects my effort in using the agency theory to analyze the political, social and economic factors, which have shaped the changes in Chinese corporate law. The essays in this book indicate how the economic theories of organization and corporate finance clarify different facets of the agency problem of enterprises in China's transitional economy; further, the essays will suggest means of utilizing the political and legal system to address this fundamental problem.

Portions of this book have been presented at workshops and conferences at the law or business schools of Seoul National University, Academic Sinica of Taiwan, Melbourne University, Macquarie University, Canberra University, Beijing University, Tsinghua University, Renmin University, China University of Political Science and Law, and Zhejiang College of Finance and Economics. I thank the participants at these workshops and conferences for their substantial contributions.

Some of the chapters of this book are derived from articles that I have published previously. Chapter 1 is based on 'The Relevance of Comparative Corporate

Governance Studies for China,' 8(1) *Australian Journal of Corporate Law* 49 (1997). Chapter 2 is based on 'Using Western Law to Improve China's State-Owned Enterprises: of Takeovers and Securities Fraud,' 39(2) *Valparaiso University Law Review* 339 (2004). Chapter 4 is based on 'Takeovers in China: The Case against Uniformity in Corporate Governance,' 34(2) *The Common Law World Review* 169 (2005). Chapter 6 is based on 'Towards an Institutional Competition Model of Comparative Corporate Governance Studies,' 6(1) *The Journal of Chinese and Comparative Law* 31 (2003). I thank the copyright holders for permission to use the material.

Many have facilitated this project. I take the author's conventional liberty not to mention all but a few here. I am specially indebted to Professors Michael Trebilcock and Bruce Chapman of the Toronto Law School and former Professor George Triantis of the Toronto Law School for their insightful lectures in the past. My thanks also go to Ms Elizabeth Byun and Ms Evangeline Lam for their editorial assistance. My special appreciation goes to my wife, son, and daughter for their patience and understanding for the time that I denied them while writing and completing this book.

Guanghua Yu
Hong Kong
July 2005

Chapter 1

The relevance of comparative corporate governance studies

THE NATURE OF THE PROBLEM

Emphasis on the problem of separation of control and residual claims can be traced back to Adam Smith. Smith highlighted the potential pitfalls of company structures that separated management from ownership. He stated that:

> The directors of such companies being the managers rather of other people's money than of their own, it cannot well be expected that they should watch over it with the same anxious vigilance with which the partners in a private copartnery frequently watch over their own.[1]

He predicted that due to agency problems,[2] corporations that separated management from ownership would be unable to compete with organizational forms that allied ownership more closely with control. While he was correct in suggesting that serious agency costs would arise, he was wrong in predicting that the corporate form would fail. In their seminal work, Berle and Means examined the shareholding structure of modern US corporations and explained that the separation of ownership from control weakens the check on managerial power and makes convergence of interests between managers and shareholders more difficult.[3]

Sceptics such as Smith had noticed the potential problems resulting from the separation of residual claims and control in corporations. However, they neglected monitoring devices such as market forces and contractual mechanisms in alleviating such problems. It can be said that sceptics were either not interested in or have not paid any attention to comparative studies of monitoring devices. Recently, criticisms have been directed at these sceptics. Stigler and Friedland recognize the contribution of Berle and Means' work in that the maximizing of the present value of a firm should be modified to take account of the separate interest of the management.[4] However, they severely attacked the main theme of Berle and Means on two significant grounds. First, they claimed

1

that empirical evidence available at the time when Berle and Means wrote their book did not establish that different types of corporate control had an effect on profits. Second, the data also revealed no relationship between the compensation of corporate executives and the type of control.[5] However, I find that the analysis by Stigler and Friedland is far from satisfactory. With respect to the relationship between corporate profit and control, any static cross-sectoral analysis based on evidence on a particular point in time is simply unable to take into account the benefits gained from the growth of a corporation and the costs resulting from agency problems. I believe that ownership does matter.[6] With respect to the relationship between remuneration of corporate executives and type of control, the data used is again static. The effect on the labour market is not considered.

Furthermore, perquisite consumption is not confined only to salaries or bonuses. Luxury offices or hotel rooms and other activities such as reduced efforts should also be included. Stigler and Friedland, however, were clearly right in their criticisms that Berle and Means failed to pay any systematic attention to the operation of the economic system.[7] Within any economic system there exist monitoring devices which curb agency costs. Although Stigler and Friedland assumed the existence of such monitoring devices, they did not examine the economic implications of these monitoring devices.

Demsetz and Lehn launched similar attacks on Berle and Means' findings.[8] Their analysis on the separation issue is simple. They argue:

> If difference in control allows managers to serve their needs rather than tend to the profits of owners, then more concentrated ownership, by establishing a stronger link between managerial behavior and owner interests, ought to yield higher profit rates.[9]

However, they did not expect to find such a relationship and their view was confirmed by the data they collected.[10] I think that Demesetz and Lehn did not satisfactorily refute the thesis of Berle and Means. The finding that there is no correlation between the profit rate and ownership concentration does not mean that agency costs are not high in management-controlled corporations. As Demesetz and Lehn pointed out, the higher costs and reduced profits that would be associated with loosening of owner control should be offset by lower capital acquisition costs or other profit-enhancing aspects of diffused ownership if shareholders choose to broaden ownership.[11]

In the same article, Demsetz and Lehn also argued that share ownership concentration levels are inversely related to the aggregate size of the firm.[12] This relationship holds because as the value-maximizing size of the firm increases, the cost of acquiring a control block will also rise, deterring control accumulation. In addition, when the benefits from control transactions are smaller than the benefits resulting from share diversification, the latter will be chosen. It seems that Demsetz and Lehn did not consider comparative studies of monitoring devices. Otherwise, they may have found that their conclusion could not be applied to Germany and Japan. Roe pointed out that most of the biggest non-financial corporations in Japan and Germany are controlled by financial institutions.[13] I believe that comparative studies of monitoring devices guided by agency theories can explain the determinants of different monitoring devices in different places.

Despite the costs in the formation and growth of corporations, the economic functions of modern corporations indicate that the formation and growth of corporations also give rise to economic benefits. Under the conditions of shareholder profit maximization, the benefits resulting from the formation and growth of corporations include reduction of transaction costs,[14] risk diversification,[15] team work,[16] special knowledge of managerial experts,[17] and economies of scale.[18]

In this chapter, I assume these benefits (without proving them as the benefits connected with the formation and growth of corporations) normally exceed the agency costs. Deviation may occur when the management of a corporation makes mistakes or pursues its own interests in expanding the size of corporations. Competition between different sized corporations, however, sifts out the more efficient enterprises.[19]

My main purpose is to examine how monitoring devices such as market forces and contractual arrangements may reduce agency costs resulting from the separation of control and residual claims and also those agency costs connected with loan transactions and bond issues. Building on Jensen and Meckling's work, I discuss agency costs in section two. Then I will canvass the roles of various monitoring devices in alleviating agency costs. While there is a wealth of literature on agency theories, the literature on agency costs resulting from the separation of control and residual claims and the literature on agency costs related with loans and bond issues has been developed along separate lines. Although a particular method of financing determines the corresponding monitoring devices, a monitoring device may serve the purpose of controlling both the agency costs of equity financing and of debt financing. As the methods of financing corporate decisions through either debt or equity are not mutually exclusive, monitoring devices dealing with agency costs of both debt financing and equity financing could coexist.

In section three, I will compare special features of monitoring devices in Germany, Japan, the USA and Hong Kong. As monitoring devices can simultaneously affect both agency financing and debt financing, I conclude that monitoring devices in these countries are not static and countries can learn from each other, although it should be borne in mind that the adaptation of foreign laws is subject to local political and economic conditions. I will then demonstrate

3

in section four the relevance of comparative studies of monitoring devices for China's economic reform. In contrast to Roe, I believe that comparative studies of monitoring devices have significant policy implications.

AGENCY COSTS AND MONITORING DEVICES

Jensen and Meckling define an agency relationship in equity financing as a contract under which one person (the principal) engages another person (the agent) to perform some services on its behalf which involves delegating some decision-making authority to the agent.[20] In the corporate law context, the principals refer to shareholders and the agents refer to directors and managers. If the principals and agents are rational, there is good reason to believe that the agents will not always act in the best interests of the principals. This has been well documented by Berle and Means.[21] The divergence of interests will cause three types of costs – the monitoring expenditures by the principal, the bonding expenditures by the agent and the residual loss.[22]

The monitoring expenditures by the principals refer to the costs incurred by the principals to provide incentives for the agents through contract and to monitor the activities of the agents. The bonding costs are necessary because it is to the benefit of the agents to spend resources in order to guarantee that they will not take certain actions which will harm the principals or to ensure that the principals will be compensated if the agents take such actions.[23] The agents benefit from these expenditures as these costs serve the purpose of signalling to the principals that the agents are relatively good and reliable. Inefficient managers and directors are more likely to fail in corporations. Hence, it is less likely for them to make these promises. Therefore, bonding costs tend to alleviate the ex ante adverse selection problems.[24] The residual loss is inevitable as it is generally impossible for the principals or the agents to ensure that the agents will make optimal decisions from the principals' viewpoint at zero cost. Agency costs of equity financing may include lapses in managerial competence or effort, managerial entrenchment or empire building and excessive managerial compensation or perquisite consumption.

Similarly, there are agency costs in debt financing. The agency costs associated with the existence of debt claims for the corporation include the opportunity wealth loss caused by the impact of debt on the executives by the bondholders and the bond issuers or loan users, and the bankruptcy and reorganization costs.[25] The opportunity wealth loss refers to wealth transfer transactions that reduce efficiency. When the debt/equity ratio is very high, bond issuers and borrowers will have a strong ex post incentive to engage in risky activities which promise very high payoffs if successful but have a very low probability of success. If they do well, the bond issuers or borrowers capture most of the gain. On the other hand, if the riskier projects turn out badly, the creditors or bondholders bear most of the costs.[26]

Specifically, at least four types of wealth-redistributing transactions can be identified.[27] First, firm assets of the debtor or bond issuer are distributed to shareholders of the debtor or bond issuer. The most explicit form of wealth transfer is the distribution of firm assets to shareholders after debt has been issued. The distribution of firm assets to shareholders includes the payment of dividends or the repurchase of stock. The removal of assets decreases the expected value of the firm at maturity and devalues existing debt.

Second, wealth transfer transactions may be carried out by the subsequent issuance of debt of equal or higher priority. As the issuance of new debt of equal priority increases the amount of competing claims, the value of existing debt is reduced if the use of the new capital does not increase the present expected value of the firm at maturity by at least the amount of the new debt.[28] Existing creditors are also worse off if secured debt of higher priority is issued as this reduces the claims of the existing creditors if the new debt is not properly used.

Third, wealth transfer may take the form of increasing the risk of the assets of the borrower. After the issue of debt, debtors have the opportunity of switching to a riskier investment strategy that enables shareholders of the debtors to benefit from all the upside risk and participate in the downside risk only to the extent of their investment. In the transactions, creditors or bondholders must share in the downside risk up to the amount of their investment but cannot share in the upside benefits beyond the face value of their debt. The frequency of these wealth transfer activities increases when the debtor is close to insolvency. Finally, debtors may gorge valuable investment opportunities. Managers of the debtor have incentives to pass up valuable investment opportunities when profits from the investment would accrue to debt holders and not to their shareholders.[29]

Bonding costs refer to the promises made by the contractual parties to reduce adverse selection problems and moral hazard problems. For instance, the provision of firm-specific assets as security to the creditor is a type of bonding cost. In the case of the debtor not being able to pay the due debt, some valuable assets of the firm may be lost. Monitoring costs refer to the costs incurred by the creditor to check whether the debtor has misbehaviours which violate any contractual provisions and to check the management of the debtor's business. Since management is a continuous decision-making process, it will be almost impossible to completely specify the conditions without having the bondholders actually perform the management function.[30] In other words, unnecessary detailed provisions and continued monitoring of the debtor may result in some efficiency losses.

Bankruptcy costs include reduced claims, legal and liquidation or reorganization fees. Weiss estimates that bankruptcy costs for large corporations in the USA are approximately 3 per cent of the firm's assets at the time of bankruptcy.[31]

5

In addition to these direct costs, indirect costs include inefficient use of assets, loss of customers or suppliers, loss of warranties on the part of consumers before, during or after the process.

Agency theorists have adopted the concept of the nexus of contract in corporations developed by theorists of property rights.[32] In this way, agency theorists are able to analyse contractual arrangements between shareholders, directors, managers, and creditors without being hindered by the 'black box' (the artificial form of a corporate person) as discussed in neoclassical economics.[33] Within agency theorists, the individual agent is the elementary unit of analysis.[34] The key to understanding the agency problem is to recognize that parties to a contract bear the agency costs of the relationship. Therefore, self-interested maximizing agents have the incentive to minimize the agency costs in any contractual relationship.[35] Jensen and Meckling have argued, however, that the debtor (owner–manager) bears the entire wealth effects of the agency costs of debt and captures the gains from reducing them.[36] Jensen and Smith further explain:

> When bonds are sold, bondholders forecast the value effects of future decisions. They understand that, after issuance, any action which increases the wealth of the stockholders will be taken. Therefore, on average, bondholders will not suffer losses unless they systematically underestimate effects of such future actions. But the firm (and hence its stockholders) suffers losses, agency costs, from all nonoptimal decisions motivated by wealth transfers from debtholders. Therefore, by reducing these agency costs, contractual control of the bondholder–stockholder conflict can increase the value of the firm.[37]

I have difficulty accepting the argument that the debtor (owner–manager) bears the entire wealth effect of the agency costs of debt financing since misbehaviours of the debtor are fully anticipated at the time the debt is issued. In the first place, the distinction between ex ante adverse selection problems[38] and ex post moral hazard problems[39] is not clearly drawn. Creditors may be willing to incur screening costs in order to find good and worthy credit users. Both screening costs incurred by creditors and singling efforts made by the credit users are for the purpose of solving the adverse selection problem.

The ex post moral hazard is much more difficult to estimate. The claim that all future possible misbehaviours can be anticipated before the transaction excludes the uncertainty of the ex post moral hazard problem, hence, ex post adjustment. This seems to be inconsistent with reality where people conduct business on the basis of uncertain or imperfect information. Knight takes the view that profit derives from uncertainty.[40] In addition, it is difficult to argue that the debtor (owner–manager) bears the entire wealth effects of the agency cost of debt financing. If some creditors have less information on potential credit users, they will lose out on the market. If they extend huge loans to debtors who later become insolvent, these creditors suffer losses too. Although such creditors may shift some or all losses to other credit users, the result does not entirely support Jensen and Smith's argument. Shifting losses to future transactions and sustaining losses from credit transactions are different issues. Furthermore, not all losses can be spread to other credit users. Whether losses can be shifted depends upon the elasticity of the supply and demand curves. If the supply function of credit is positively sloped, borrowers do not bear the full incidence of increased costs.[41] Similarly, it can be proven that agency costs of equity financing are not entirely borne by agents such as directors and managers. Shareholders also bear part of the efficiency loss. A ready example is state-owned enterprises in socialist countries. Given the large number of these firms, the people of the country (in theory, the owners of these enterprises) bear the cost of having a very low standard of living. Part of the loss is obviously due to agents' deficiencies while another part of the loss can be attributed to collective action problems on the part of the owners.

Having defined agency costs, we will now examine monitoring devices which play the role of curbing these costs. As mentioned, there are many monitoring devices including market forces and contractual mechanisms. In the first place, the capital market exerts pressure to orient a corporation's decision process towards the interests of the residual claimants.[42] Whether this monitoring device is effective depends upon the efficiency of the capital market. Now it is generally accepted that stock prices quickly respond to publicly available information about the corporations. When a shareholder makes her or his initial investment, the price paid for securities of a corporation reflects the expected agency costs at that time fairly accurately. However, information costs money and foresight is not perfect, and managers may shirk or divert wealth from the shareholders after the fact. The unique nature of capital markets makes it possible for them to play a role in detecting and signalling unanticipated opportunism by managers when it occurs, and in this way the share price can discipline such conduct. By incorporating the consequences of management misconduct into such prices, capital markets furnish shareholders with a relatively unambiguous signal of corporate performance. So if the price of a corporation's shares increases faster than those of other similar corporations on the market, the investor can predict that the corporation is being well managed and monitored. However, if the share price of the corporation underperforms rivals, the spectrum of managerial incompetence or shirking is raised. If faced with the latter case, the shareholder has the option of selling his shares. Any sale of a company's share affects the share price in precise proportion to the total number of shares sold. Thus, the more shareholders selling their shares, the lower the price of the corporation's stock will be.

7

Not all the shareholders are willing or able to exit and another alternative is to voice their opinions.[43] The force of their voice depends upon the proportion of their shares relative to the existing shares of the corporation. For those corporations which have to rely on the stock market for future capital, the decrease in the price of its shares affects the cost of the firm's future capital. For other corporations which do not rely on the stock market for future capital, the market of corporate control, which we will examine later, may constrain the behaviour of the management.

External monitoring by a takeover market may also influence corporations because of the unrestricted nature of its residual claims.[44] Because the residual claims are freely alienable and separable from roles in the decision process, hostile bidders can circumvent the existing managers and gain control of the decision-making and approval process. The benefits of takeover transactions must be viewed both ex ante and ex post.[45] Ex ante, a regime with takeover markets makes incumbent managers more careful in aligning their interests with those of the residual claimants. Ex post, if managers do shirk and seek perquisite consumption, vigilant acquirers will respond quickly as the gains the acquirers expect vary in direct relation to the level of agency costs incurred by the shareholders of a given corporation. By displacing inefficient managers, the acquirers expect gains from such transactions although part of the gain is shared with the shareholders of the target corporation. When takeover transactions discipline managers, they also move productive resources to higher value users. Empirical studies in the USA support this position when the proper benchmark is used.[46] Further, defensive tactics by directors are likely to be harmful to the shareholders of the target corporation.[47]

Competition in product markets helps to control agency costs.[48] Under consumer sovereignty, if a corporation supplies a product that was popular with consumers because of quality, price, or style, then the corporation's market share will increase. If a corporation's product fails to capture an adequate market share, this will signal to the shareholders that they may need to discipline the managers. Although discipline of senior management is accomplished through the board of directors, shareholders can threaten to alter the composition of the board through their voting rights if the board refuses to discipline managers.

In loan transactions, failure of a company on the product market may result in default. If that occurs, the creditor will react quickly to exert its influence over the management of the borrower. Even if the creditor refuses to voice its opinion, the exit option of terminating further relationship with the borrower will send out signals to other stakeholders who may choose to exert their influence through voice.[49] While the product market is quite effective in forcing out inefficient firms in the process, the shareholders or creditors of a corporation may find the effect of this market comes too late ex post.

Directors and managers will pursue their own interests under constraints. However, collective action problems exist within the management.[50] Thus, the divergence of interests between principals and agents may be reduced by the operation of the managerial market. An unfaithful or indolent agent may be penalized through a reduction of salary or a demotion while a competent and diligent manager may be rewarded through a bonus or a promotion. With proper incentives, good managers and bad managers are distinguished over time. Bad managers may find difficulty finding suitable and satisfactory jobs elsewhere.[51] Bankruptcy and corporate control transactions provide additional warnings to managers who choose to shirk and purse perquisite consumption.

Of course, the effectiveness of this mechanism relies upon information on a manager's performance in isolation from his team. The managerial market also serves another important role in the control of divergence of interests.[52] To the extent that individuals within the firm aspire to replace managers above them, they may be motivated to closely scrutinize the performance of managers for misconduct that could lead to the removal of these incumbent managers by the principals of the corporation. In addition, monitoring activity by employees may be encouraged if the level of compensation received by employees is tied to their performance.[53] In this case, there is an incentive to detect and report managerial ineptitude that hinders the performance of the team as long as the number of individuals in the team is small.

In addition to these markets, the debt market has some influence in reducing agency costs of debt financing. In a model of repeat loan transactions, the bad reputation of the debt issuer who engages in wealth transfer transactions will increase future costs of raising capital on the debt market. No matter whether creditors or bondholders have taken precautions, if managerial costs of engaging in wealth transfer activities by the debtor exceed the marginal benefits of refraining from these activities, that debtor will not pursue these activities. Of course, the cost of bad reputation varies with the degree of future need of debt financing and the quality of information on the debt market. Thus, when the debtor corporation is close to or in insolvency, the constraint of the debt market becomes weakest.

Weak constraint of market forces on divergence of interests between principals and agents gives rise to contractual arrangements between these parties. It is these contractual mechanisms that check the misbehaviour of agents that I now turn to. Contractual arrangements which provide the creditor(s) with the right to influence or interfere with the debtor's business during the debtor's insolvency are quite normal. For instance, convertible bonds may serve the purpose of alleviating the problems of asset substitution and changing dividend policy after the debt is issued. This is so because the holders of convertible bonds may receive part of the benefits from the debtor's choice of either engaging in a higher risk project or changing the dividend policy. With convertible debt,

9

risk-increasing activities increase the value of the conversion option, and thus reduce the gains to debtors from taking higher-risk projects by transferring part of the gains to convertible bondholders.[54]

Another contractual arrangement in reducing agency costs of debt financing is requiring the debtor to provide security for its loans. Secured debt is able to reduce agency costs of debt financing connected with the moral hazard problem.[55] Once secured debt is established, creditors normally do not have to worry whether the debtor will change dividend policy ex post. As long as the debt is adequately secured, a change of dividend policy by the debtor after the debt is issued will not threaten the position of the secured creditors. Even if the debtor becomes insolvent, secured creditors can satisfy their rights by realizing the security. Secured debt may also eliminate the asset substitution problem if the debt is sufficiently covered by the security.[56] As secured creditors can realize their rights ahead of general creditors with relatively low enforcement cost, secured debt can reduce the cost connected with the asset substitution problem.

Backed by insolvency laws and the law on secured transactions, there are contractual provisions in secured debt arrangements which restrict the right of the debtor to dispose of the security once the agreement is reached. If the security is a firm-specific asset[57] of the debtor, the right of the creditor in exerting its influence over the debtor is considerable when the latter is not able to pay the due debt. It is because the disposition of the specific asset will exact a heavy loss on the part of the debtor.[58] Obviously, the threat of disposing of firm-specific assets will alleviate the ex post moral hazard problem.

Furthermore, secured debt may also alleviate the problem of debt erosion. As long as a creditor has perfected and registered its security interest, it is entitled to priority. Normally it is very difficult for the debtor to change the priority after the debt is issued, except by the provision of more senior secured debt to other creditors. Finally, secured debt can alleviate the problem of underinvestment.[59] This is because the benefits of a new project are shared by the debtor and its creditors. When the shareholders of the debtor and the existing creditors are unwilling or unable to provide an additional amount of capital for the project, unsecured debt is not very attractive to any potential creditor, as the new creditor has to share the benefits of the new project with the debtor and the existing creditors but bears all the cost for the failure of the new project. The secured creditor is safe unless the security is not able to cover the debt.

Still another contractual arrangement for the purpose of reducing agency costs of debt financing is for the creditor to hold a very large number of shares in the debtor's corporation. Generally speaking, a creditor may interfere with the debtor's business only when the debtor is not able to pay the debt fallen due. However, if the creditor is also the shareholder of the debtor's corporation, the creditor may voice its concern. When the creditor's shareholding is substantial, it may ask for the removal of certain directors of the debtor's corporation. The creditor's shareholding in the debtor's corporation may partially solve the problem of asset substitution and change of dividend policy after the debt is issued. Ex ante, the holding of shares in the debtor's corporation may deter wealth transfer activities depending on the proportion of the shares owned by the creditor. Ex post, the creditor may receive part of the benefits from the debtor's wealth transfer transactions as a shareholder.

Moreover, the creditor may penalize the responsible agents for wealth transfer activities if the shareholding of the creditor in the debtor's corporation is substantial. In addition, if the creditor is also the sole or substantial creditor, the underinvestment problem may be less serious. As the benefits of any further investment go to the creditors first, the creditor–shareholder has strong incentives to undertake the project. Finally, the debt erosion problem is alleviated if the creditor is a major shareholder of the debtor's corporation as incentives to prefer other creditors are minimized. The dual roles of creditor and major shareholder increase the quality of information of the debtor's corporation and thereby reduce agency costs resulting from debt financing. Long-term contractual arrangements between the debtor and its trade creditors through mutual shareholding may also reduce agency costs resulting from debt financing transactions. These contractual arrangements encourage mutual monitoring as long as the number of trade creditors is small.[60] The above contractual relations are also conductive to stable trade relations which encourage asset-specific investment.[61] In such corporate groups, both agency costs of equity financing and agency costs of debt financing have been reduced. Maintaining the efficiency and competitiveness of these groups is preconditioned on an efficient product market.[62]

In addition to these contractual arrangements which reduce agency costs of debt financing, other contractual arrangements may be more useful in curbing agency costs of equity financing. These contractual monitoring devices may coexist with market forces. I will discuss these devices in sequence. A vital contractual mechanism is the control of the decision-making managers both by a board of directors and by residual claimants (shareholders). Residual claimants generally retain approval (by veto) on such matters as board membership, auditor choice, mergers and new stock issues. Other management and control functions are delegated by the residual claimants to the board of directors.[63] The board then delegates most of the decisions regarding management functions and many decisions concerning the functions of internal agents, but it retains ultimate control over internal agents – including the rights to hire, fire, and set the compensation of top level decision managers.[64]

At the centre of the contractual mechanism adopted by the residual claimants to constrain managerial self-interest is the institution of shareholder voting. The right of shareholders to vote gives residual claimants the ability to determine the membership of the board of directors of the corporation. If managers choose to

11

shirk or divert from their responsibilities in order to maximize their own utility, the board has the right and responsibility to discipline and replace the management. Should shareholders be dissatisfied with the board's vigilance, they have the power to alter the composition of the board.

To many observers, including Jensen, internal contractual arrangements in corporations where shares are widely dispersed are too weak to force timely and efficient responses to excess capacity.[65] In the proxy context, Berle even claimed that the economists' view of proxy context was a wholly imaginary picture.[66] However, Dodd and Warner have made the point that, regardless of the proxy contest outcome, positive and statistically significant share performance is associated with the contest.[67] Others have doubts concerning the board of directors' ability to make independent judgments on firm performance as they are mainly selected by the management. But Rosenstein and Wyatt's study[68] of the wealth effects surrounding outside director appointments finds significantly positive share-price increase. These studies indicate that the board of directors has its role to play in checking managers' opportunistic behaviours. Moreover, there are also examples of board-initiated ousters of senior corporate executives of widely held corporations such as IBM, General Motors, American Express, and Manufacturers Life.[69]

The effectiveness of this internal mechanism depends not only upon the control of the decision-making agents but also upon the control of the decision-approval agents. As directors are few in number, their coordination is relatively easy. However, since directors are normally not substantial residual claimants either, they may also shirk. As such, continuing monitoring activities of these directors by shareholders is of pivotal importance to the reduction of agency costs.

The number of shareholders is much greater than the number of directors. To vote correctly to curb agency costs, shareholders need specific information. The greater the information that is available to shareholders concerning the performance of corporate agents, the more rational and effective their voting will be. While information is of considerable importance to shareholders, it cannot be generated without costs.[70] Each shareholder is willing to invest in information searching activities to the point where each additional unit of benefit derived is equal to each additional unit of cost spent. Unfortunately, collective action problems undermine the optimal level of information production because of the nature of widely dispersed equity holdings. As an investment by a shareholder for the generation of information cannot be fully internalized, information on corporate decision-making and decision-approval activities will generally be undersupplied.[71] A particular shareholder will reason that, since the benefits from an investment in information activities will accrue to all shareholders irrespective of their individual contribution, it is better to 'free ride' on the investment of other shareholders than to contribute oneself. The prisoners' dilemma indicates that if this is a rational strategy for one shareholder, it is equally rational for all similarly situated shareholders.[72]

While the collective action problem exists, not all shareholders are identical. Those with a relatively large stake in the corporation have more incentive to monitor the agents' conduct. As these shareholders may obtain proportionally more of the gains and shoulder more of the costs from an abnormally good or bad outcome, they will watch the agents more carefully. Furthermore, collective action problems may be overcome by the accumulation of shares and exercise of the attached votes as long as the law does not place severe restrictions. The managers' knowledge that they can be ousted by the exercise of these votes provides them with an incentive to maximize the wealth of the shareholders.[73]

Finally, contractual arrangements between the residual claimants and the management through compensation constrain agents' utility maximizing behaviours. Managers have incentives to maximize their own interests as they do not share a big proportion of the wealth effects resulting from their decisions. In addition, as their human capital is quite firm-specific and cannot be easily diversified, they are inclined to make conservative decisions. Salaries fixed at the beginning reduce ex post moral hazard costs to the extent that the present value of their future rewards will be strongly correlated with their past and present performance. In other words, if managers are concerned with the present value of their lifetime consumption and this depends on their current success of management, the former will not be enhanced by a track record of bad decisions or managerial slack.[74]

Compensation by salaries fixed at the beginning of the period, however, creates its own problems.[75] They include asset substitution, overretention and underleverage. The problem of asset substitution arises with fixed compensation at the beginning because the expected payoff increases as cash-flow risk and the probability of default decline. The problem of overretention exists as managers with fixed compensation have incentives to retain funds within the firm to increase the coverage on the fixed claims and perquisites. The problem of underleverage occurs because managers compensated with fixed claims have incentives to reduce debt and other claims on the firm, even when such reductions adversely affect firm value. The problems of fixed compensation lead to performance-based or accounting-based compensation through contractual arrangements.[76]

COMPARATIVE STUDIES OF MONITORING DEVICES

In this section, I will briefly discuss the key features of some of the monitoring devices in Germany, Japan, the USA and Hong Kong. I will show that, in addition to economic forces, politics and law also affect the forms and utilities of monitoring devices. If reform on the political front could be carried out, then one country can learn how monitoring devices can better achieve its economic purpose. As a matter of fact, there are signs that changes are taking place in some of these countries.

The role of universal banks in Germany

In Germany, banks are not prohibited from holding shares in non-financial corporations.[77] As such, banks are not only the major creditors in large non-financial corporations but also controlling shareholders. Generally speaking, debt financing plays a much more significant role than equity financing.[78] The historical and significant roles of banks in debt financing, without political and legal constraints, make it desirable for them to have the option of holding shares in the debtor corporations. This may be explained by the ex ante adverse selection problem and the ex post moral hazard problem faced by creditors. To solve these problems creditors have to screen and evaluate the debtor's investment project before a loan is extended. Once the loan is secured, however, the debtor may engage in wealth transfer activities. In one-shot transactions or in near insolvency cases, market forces are not effective in constraining opportunistic behaviours, leaving only contractual mechanisms.

In debt financing, creditors can normally intervene in the debtors' business only after default. As bankruptcy generally diminishes claims of general creditors, creditors prefer early exit if they do not have sufficient control of the debtor. If a creditor is also a major shareholder, it may deter wealth transfer transactions as previously explained. Ex ante, the creditor–shareholder may prevent wealth transfer transactions being adopted by the management. While Baums considers that the bank's representative on the supervisory board of the debtor corporation does not increase any further information, I feel otherwise.[79] The fact that the members of the supervisory board have to keep the information they receive in that capacity confidential does not mean that the bank is not better off. As long as the representative of the bank has used the information obtained by them through the supervisory board, bad corporate decisions can be prevented. In other words, through the bank's representative on the supervisory board the bank can intervene in a potentially damaging situation at a much earlier time.

Ex post, the creditor–shareholder may penalize managers. Significant shareholding in the debtor corporation makes voice more important than exit, otherwise the creditor–shareholder will suffer both equity and credit investment. Thus, it is not surprising to see that banks often take over the reorganization of corporations in distress.[80] Hence the role of majority creditor–shareholders of focusing on voice results in long-term contractual relations. This, in turn, encourages investment in firm-specific assets.

14

Some examples may illustrate the great influence of German banks on non-financial corporations. In 1986, Deutsche Bank, Dresdner Bank and Commerz Bank together owned 32.5 per cent of the shares in Siemens, 61.66 per cent in Daimler-Benz, 7.98 per cent in Volkswagen, 54.5 per cent in Bayer, 51.68 per cent in BASF, 63.48 per cent in Hoechst and 48.92 per cent in VEBA.[81] Among these banks, Deutsche Bank owned 17.6 per cent of the shares in Siemens, 41.8 per cent in Daimler-Benz, 2.94 per cent in Volkswagen, 30.82 per cent in Bayer, 28.07 per cent in BASF, 14.79 per cent in Hoechst and 19.99 per cent in VEBA. Although the three banks only own 7.98 per cent of the shares in Volkswagen, they can vote for 50.13 per cent of the shares.[82] This voting power comes from directly owned stock, investment corporations controlled by banks, and voting shares held by banks as custodians for their clients under the proxy system.[83]

Under the proxy system, banks need a special written power of authority to vote the deposited shares. Before a shareholder meeting, banks have to recommend to their customers how to vote, and have to ask for special instructions. In practice, giving such instructions is extremely rare. If a shareholder does not give the bank special instructions, the bank is to vote according to its recommendations. Generally, banks can vote their customers' stock on any matter. Further, banks are not restricted by a ceiling or cap equal to a percentage of the firm's stock capital. In its own shareholder meeting, however, a bank may only vote stock if the shareholders gives explicit instructions.[84]

I do not want to give the impression that banks directly control their borrowing corporations. German corporations are managed by a management board, which is monitored by a supervisory board. The management runs the corporations independently in its day-to-day business. The supervisory board screens and monitors the management board. Pursuant to German law, shareholders appoint 50 per cent of the members of the supervisory board in corporations with more than 2,000 employees.[85] Employees and labour unions appoint the other half of the members of the supervisory board. The supervisory board appoints the members of the management board. The managers' terms may not be longer than five years, except by extension by the supervisory board.

Empirical studies show that there is a significant involuntary 'fluctuation' of management board members not only in cases of serious problems within the corporations but also in less serious cases in which the supervisory board was displeased with the performance of individual managers or with the management board as a whole.[86] In addition the supervisory board determines the compensation of the members of the management board. Finally the supervisory board has the power to dismiss members of the management board if they have a reasonable cause.[87] The supervisory board also has the power and duty to check the annual reports and balance sheets of the corporation. Also, the supervisory

15

board can always ask the management board for reports. The board may also ask the management to obtain the approval of the board before important transactions, such as credits above a certain amount.[88]

People normally think that there may be a deadlock under the codetermination system as the employees and labour unions appoint another 50 per cent of the members on the supervisory board, but this rarely occurs.[89] There are two explanations for this. One is that employee representatives on the supervisory board do not intervene in purely business decisions. The other reason is that the shareholders are more powerful. The banker–shareholders could defeat employees by relying on two features of German corporate law. First, shareholders can, with a super-majority vote, send directions to the managerial board, bypassing the supervisory board; and second, the chair of the supervisory board is always a member of the shareholding side of the board and can cast the deciding vote in a tie.[90]

German banks are very active in appointing members to supervisory boards. In 1988, the managers of nine large banks held 94 seats on the supervisory boards of 96 (of the largest 100) corporations in the Federal Republic of Germany. The above figures refer to direct interlocks only where bank managers sit on the supervisory boards of non-financial corporations. They do not show other members who are also controlled by banks who sit on the supervisory board.[91] Normally, four or five banks effectively control the decision-making power of huge non-financial corporations. Few major banker–shareholders alleviate collective action problems. This, in turn, makes it easy to control the management board. Repeat screening and monitoring activities by few banks alleviates free-riding problems. Normally, one majority banker–shareholder plays a much more important role in a corporation in which it has a majority position and another bank as a majority shareholder does the same in another corporation. These few banks generally vote similarly on corporate decisions. As creditors of the corporation, they have, to a large extent, parallel interest vis-à-vis the management.[92] While a co-ordinated behaviour of these banks in the voting process has not been empirically determined, a government commission in its report of 1978 noted that 'the banks mostly vote in the same sense'.[93] Loan transactions require the banks to screen and monitor creditor users. Large shareholding in these debtor corporations significantly increases the power of the banks. As a consequence, both agency costs of equity financing and agency costs of debt financing have been properly controlled.

Aspects of Japanese corporate governance

The ownership of some of the large corporations in Japan has its own unique features. Large Japanese corporations typically belong to a 'keiretsu'. Within the keiretsu, there exist elaborate cross-holdings of debt and equity, a predominance of main bank lending, a high level of leverage, and a link between financial and trading corporations.[94] A main bank usually owns up to 5 per cent of the stock of the keiretsu's industrial corporations, which in turn own some stock in the main bank.[95] Generally, four other banks and insurers own blocks of stock in the industrial corporations, each roughly equal to 5 per cent of the outstanding shares, thus creating a latent five-holder coalition with 20 per cent of the outstanding stock.[96] Non-financial members within the group also hold shares in each other's corporation. For the six largest groups,[97] intragroup shareholdings ranged from 19 to 45 per cent in 1989.[98] Gerlach estimates that the shares of intragroup holdings for the 20 largest owners range from 33 to 74 per cent.[99] These numbers do not take into account any indirect shareholdings (that is, holdings by corporation A in corporation C through corporation B).

The high rate of shareholding in member corporations by a main bank and a few financial corporations is closely connected with the high leverage in these corporations. The corporations belonging to the financial keiretsu have on average more leverage than non-keiretsu members.[100] The holdings of member-corporation debt are strongly dominated by group financial institutions. Group banks extend loans to 98 per cent of all member corporations in their respective groups.[101] The main bank is normally the largest lender to core group members.

In addition to the cross-holding of debt and equity between financial institutions and other members, cross-holdings of equity are also closely related with intragroup lending through trade credits. Many members of the financial keiretsu transact with each other extensively on a long-term basis. In 1989, an average of 43 per cent of all bilateral relationships within the group involved some non-financial transactions.[102] Gerlach reports that Mitsubishi Aluminum sold 75 per cent of its output to other group corporations.[103] A large part of these intragroup transactions involves the group general trading corporation. The trading corporation has transaction relationship with virtually all group member corporations. In the Sumitomo group, the group trading corporation, Sumitomo Corporation, is involved in almost 90 per cent of all intragroup sales and purchases.[104]

My opinion is that the special features of the Japanese keiretsu can be explained by agency theories. The highly influential keiretsu corporations present serious potential agency costs of debt financing. There are two ways to address this problem. One is through detailed contractual restrictions and strict monitoring by the financial creditors. However, strict and continued monitoring activities may also cause efficiency losses to the borrowing corporation as it is impossible to specify the optimal choices in contracts in all cases without removing the decision-making authority from the management. When managerial discretion is severely constrained, some of the value of the expertise brought to the firm by the managers is also lost. Thus, lengthy and detailed provisions in agreements on credit transactions in Japan are normally not observed.

17

Another effective way of controlling agency costs of debt financing is to hold shares in the borrowing corporation. This, however, requires a sufficient proportion of shareholdings by the creditor. Legal constraints make such shareholdings difficult for financial creditors in Japan. After the Second World War, Japanese law allowed banks to own a maximum of 10 per cent of the shares in non-financial corporations. In 1977 the amended law mandated banks to reduce their shareholdings in non-financial corporations to less than 5 per cent within the next 10 years.[105] I argue that cross-holding in debt and equity within the keiretsu shows that private parties are persistent in devising institutions that circumvent, or minimize the effect of, political and legal constraints on economic activities.[106] Although Japanese banks initially were not allowed to own a sufficient proportion of shares in their borrowing corporations as the German universal banks did, they hold considerable shares in their borrowing corporations within the legal limits.

In addition, banks organized co-operative borrowing corporations within a group through cross-holding in equity. Although one of the reasons for establishing a keiretsu is to prevent possible takeovers by foreign corporations, banks also increased their power through indirect shareholdings. Empirical evidence is consistent with the agency cost explanation. The equity share of the bank in a particular group corporation normally increases with the size of the bank's outstanding loan.[107] Furthermore, the size of the bank shareholdings also appears to be positively correlated with the degree of leverage in industrial corporations.[108]

The cross shareholding between non-financial corporations is also consistent with agency cost explanation. Intragroup trade is correlated with intragroup lending through trade credits. The trade credits within the Sumitomo group contributed 18 per cent of gross financing of non-financing enterprises between 1970 and 1985.[109] Trade credits may result in serious agency costs to the creditor. Cross shareholding increases internal monitoring activities and facilitates the flow of information. Long-term relations solve the ex ante adverse selection problem. Mutual monitoring and cross shareholding make the threat of punishment of agents credible, reducing the ex post moral hazard problem.

Kaplan's study indicates that despite the virtual absence of takeovers, managerial turnover is very responsive to poor performance.[110] Kaplan and Minton report that when a corporation's stock market performance is poor but the corporation is not necessarily in financial distress, both the main bank and other keiretsu member corporations tend to appoint external directors to the board of the troubled corporation, but when the corporation has negative earnings, only the main bank sends external directors.[111] This combined use of debt and equity creates a state-contingent governance structure which alternatives between mutual and hierarchical enforcement.[112] Individual managers monitor each other through cross-holdings of equity and trade credit.[113] The reputation constraint and competition with other keiretsu and independent corporations on the product market strengthens mutual monitoring.

In addition to reducing agency costs in debtor corporations, cross-shareholding has other advantages. First, cross shareholding facilitates long-term trading relations. This, in turn, encourages investment in firm-specific assets.[114] Second, cross shareholdings reduce costs of adjustment and reorganization for corporations in distress. It is much easier to reorganize corporations in distress when the number of financial and trade creditors is very limited.[115] Hoshi *et al.* have found that when a corporation within the keiretsu is in distress, the production of that corporation increases. The reason is that banks continue to supply credit, and other trading members increase their supply and demand.[116] It cannot be denied that this type of corporate behaviour may maintain inefficient corporations. However, a high level of competition between different keiretsus and other independent corporations indicates that the efficiency loss is small, otherwise a particular keiretsu may not survive.

Why do Japanese banks, like German banks, play such significant roles in corporate finance and corporate governance? The answer seems to be related to law and politics. Like German law, Japanese law after the Second World War more or less restricted the stock market.[117] One might ask whether efficient corporate governance mechanisms only result from strong banks. The answer is no. A ready example is the USA.

Market oriented corporate governance features in the USA

In 1984, there were around 15,000 separate banks having 39,000 branches in the USA. On average, each bank only had 2.6 branches.[118] In 1991, the Gross National Product of the USA greatly exceeded that of Germany and Japan. However, the total assets of the ten largest banks in the USA were only 28.5 per cent of the total assets of the ten largest banks in Japan and 66.57 per cent of the total assets of the ten largest banks in Germany.[119] How can the relatively weak role of US banks in corporate governance be explained? Roe's political theory of corporate governance indicates that politics and law, to a large extent, restrict US banks in corporate governance.[120] Historically, American law confined national banks to a single location.[121] Branches of national banks could operate in a state only if state law permitted.[122] It is only recently that states have permitted out-of-state banks to open local branches.[123]

US banks are still not allowed to own equity in non-financial corporations.[124] The Bank Holding Act prohibits affiliation with insurers.[125] A bank holding company cannot own more than 5 per cent of the voting stock of any non-banking company and cannot otherwise control an industrial firm.[126] Bank trust departments are not prohibited from owning equity in non-financing corporations. However, no more than 10 per cent of a bank's trust funds may be

19

invested in the stock of any single corporation.[127] Under American law, a creditor in control of a debt corporation may be subject in bankruptcy to subordination of its loans.[128] Thus, even if banks could overcome diversification rules for their discretionary trust funds, they would fear the effect of control on their commercial loans to the same company if the company had a noticeable prospect of bankruptcy.[129]

Securities regulations make it difficult for banks to take active roles in corporate governance. To begin with, disclosure requirements place a heavy burden on controlling persons. When a 5 per cent shareholder group is formed, a filing must be made outlining the group's plans and revealing its ownership and sources of financing.[130] The burdensome disclosure of information by listed corporations on the stock market has been well documented.[131] Besides, a corporation may prefer to keep the information confidential. Proxy solicitation rules will be triggered if one institution contacts a sufficient number of others, making group action and coordination difficult.[132] In addition, in proxy contests, a shareholder who challenges management must bear most of the costs of a proxy campaign.[133] Further, securities regulations impose liability on controlling persons for illegal actions by the controlled corporation.[134]

In large competitive economies, shares are more likely to be dispersed when financial institutions are not permitted to play active roles in corporate governance. Without the involvement of financial institutions such as banks, other non-financial corporations are unlikely to be active as knowledge of managers in these corporations is quite firm-specific.

Widely dispersed shareholding in non-financial corporations requires alternative monitoring devices. Although the USA restricts the role of financial institutions in the corporate governance of non-financial corporations, it allows a relatively strong role for the stock market. As such, the monitoring devices of the capital market and takeover market are stronger in the USA than in Japan and Germany. The role of the capital market in corporate governance is to reflect the performance of corporations through their share prices. To those who need to raise capital, the capital market imposes a potential threat. Further, the takeover market imposes a threat on corporations that are not well managed. While the takeover market in the USA was relatively active in the 1980s, this market is at a low ebb. Public choice theories can explain this change. Populist sentiment has captured legislatures, and managers are the happy beneficiaries of a public opinion that helps insulate them from takeovers.[135]

The demise of the takeover market as a disciplinary device has directed people's attention to internal monitoring devices. Recently, reforms have been carried out to strengthen the role of the board of directors. This is mainly achieved by appointing more outside directors. While many have observed that internal forces in corporations whose shares are widely dispersed are too weak to force timely and efficient responses to excess capacity,[136] the board does play some role in corporate governance as discussed in section two. Further, hope also lies in the emergence of sophisticated investors, especially institutional investors who may have the incentives to pressure boards of directors to discipline their managers. The liquidity issue aside, active roles of institutional investors require some reform of the current regulations in the USA to allow them to hold more shares in non-financial corporations. Furthermore, resources are required to facilitate changes of the internal structures of these corporations as managers of these financial institutions may not be familiar with corporate governance issues in other corporations they have invested in.

While there are considerable differences concerning corporate governance in Germany, Japan, and the USA, similarities do exist. For instance, the product markets in these countries are very competitive. As discussed in section two, the competitive pressure on the product market is quite important in the context of disciplining managers within corporations. Although the labour markets are quite different in Japan and the USA, they achieve very similar objectives. In Japan, lifetime career, internal promotion and a thin labour market considerably constrain managers' opportunistic behaviours. If a manager in a large Japanese corporation is demoted or removed from their position, they suffer greatly as it might be very difficult for them to be reemployed in their previous position by the corporation again. The thin labour market makes it very hard for middle-aged managers to find suitable jobs in other corporations. In contrast, labour markets are more active and compensation packages are more flexible in the USA. These features are ideal for good managers. For bad or incompetent managers, the US model also makes it difficult for them to find suitable jobs elsewhere.

The shareholder control model in Hong Kong

In Hong Kong, large corporations which are of a purely commercial or business nature are usually listed or quite closely held. The shares held by the public in listed corporations are normally between 10 per cent and 25 per cent depending on the market value of the applicant.[137] Among listed corporations in 1988, corporations controlled by just four families accounted for over 36 per cent of the total market capitalization.[138] In the same year, the ten largest listed corporations accounted for more than 65 per cent of total market capitalization.[139] In addition to listed corporations, the vast majority of corporations are private in nature. Whether private or listed, Hong Kong corporations are typically paternalistic, centralized and flexible. Even the largest of them, although technically public, are rarely professionally managed.[140]

In these corporations, the founding members are in firm control. They normally include the chairman of the board of the directors. The other directors are closely related to the controlling shareholders or directors. In these family-controlled corporations, divergence of interests between the management and shareholders is kept to a minimum. In contrast, the major concern in family-controlled corporations in Hong Kong is the abuse of power by the majority shareholders. While this concern holds in small, private corporations, the problem is largely exaggerated in listed corporations.[141] The easy exit option available to small investors in these listed corporations and the reputation constraints on these family-controlled listed corporations are largely neglected. Evidence shows that the performance of stock prices in these corporations is far superior to those state-owned enterprises of China which are also listed in Hong Kong,[142] that is, Hong Kong corporations controlled by Chinese capital.[143]

The discussion of the basic features of corporate governance in Germany, Japan, the USA, and Hong Kong has several implications. First, comparative studies of monitoring devices show that in an economy where equity contributions are widely dispersed, the internal shareholder monitoring mechanism of controlling agency costs is relatively weak because of collective action problems. However, if the internal shareholder monitoring mechanism is relatively ineffective, market forces such as product market, managerial market and takeover market play important roles in reducing agency costs. The USA fits into this model. Conversely, if the internal shareholder monitoring is comparatively effective when majority votes are retained by controlling blocks, the takeover market and even the managerial market may not be very effective or relevant.[144] Hong Kong falls into this category. If natural persons are unwilling or unable to hold a controlling block, banks are the best alternative. Corporate governance in Germany and Japan roughly follows this line. If both the internal and external monitoring mechanisms are ineffective or lacking, then these economies cannot be efficient. Corporate governance in China's state-owned enterprises appears to fall in this category even after it recognizes the objective of maximizing shareholders' wealth. For the control of agency costs, it is not necessary that all the monitoring devices be equally effective.

Second, comparative studies of monitoring devices help us understand the determinants of monitoring devices. In addition, the method of financing, by equity or debt, is also relevant in the development of monitoring devices. Furthermore, the distribution of shares in corporations also affects the relative use of different monitoring devices.

Third, comparative studies of monitoring devices also indicate that the relative use of different monitoring devices is not static. Changes in economic conditions, law and politics, international trade and investment will affect corporate governance in a particular country. Attributing too much to cultural factors mystifies relevant issues and deters further studies. While recognizing the validity of theories of chaos and path dependence,[145] I believe countries can learn from others, especially those countries that are moving from planned economies towards market oriented economies.

Recent signs indicate that monitoring devices both in Japan and the USA are changing slightly. Anecdotal facts show that boards of directors are becoming more active than ever in the USA.[146] Moreover, the role of institutional investors is increasing in the USA. Although they normally do not send representatives to the boardrooms of the corporations, they have in recent years pressed the boards of poorly performing corporations to act up and improve their performance.[147] Changes have also taken place in corporate Japan. International pressure resulting from the liberalization of world trade and investment and domestic deregulation has significantly increased the role of equity financing in Japan.[148] The recent prolonged recession has put considerable stress on lifetime employment in Japan as the rate of job termination is increasing.[149] Derivative action against corporate managers also increased rapidly in the past few years.[150] All of these changes may erode, to some extent, the rational corporate governance model in Japan. If these changes continue, the role of market forces in corporate governance in Japan will become important.

THE RELEVANCE FOR CHINA

After discussing monitoring devices in Germany, Japan, the USA and Hong Kong, I now turn to look at policy implications for China. This is of particular importance to China as corporate reform calls for monitoring devices, market forces and contractual arrangements alike. It needs to be pointed out that drawing experiences from other countries is appropriate only after China has adopted policies which promote the maximizing of corporate profits for investors. To facilitate the discussion, I describe very briefly the nature of China's enterprises before its economic reform. I then provide a look at the evolution of the reform of enterprises in China. After examining the current monitoring devices and pointing out some defects, I finally canvass the relevance of comparative studies of monitoring devices for China.

Chinese enterprises before economic reform

From the formation of the People's Republic of China in 1949 until 1978 the Chinese economic system was based on a very rigid planned model. Within this economy, the means of production were owned mostly by the state, leaving a minor portion in the hands of enterprises, normally in collective ownership. The decision-making power for macroeconomic activities of the state and major activities of enterprises was concentrated in the hands of the state. Since currency–commodity relations remained, the market still existed. However, the basic means by which the various targets were realized were mandatory plans drawn up by the state hierarchy. As fiscal agents of the governments, banks only played the role of implementing governmental plans.[151]

23

Given that banks did not have to screen projects before the projects were undertaken and monitor the use of funds after the fact, constraints on enterprises were quite soft or nonexistent.[152] The enterprises immediately responsible for production had to follow state orders in all activities, including finance, management, sales, employment, wage policy and expansion, and enjoyed hardly any independence. As the economic benefits of enterprises were not linked with their performance, enterprises with significant profits had no right to dispose of their profits while enterprises operating with heavy losses were subsidized by the state. The Ministry of Finance distributed all budgetary allocations and collected all enterprise surpluses. Economic information was transmitted vertically between the higher and lower levels in the administrative system in the form of instructions and reports. Within this system, there was no role for the law of business organizations as known in Western countries. Insolvency was beyond any possible imagination.

The advantage of such a model was the employment of administrative power through highly centralized planning to facilitate extensive concentration of manpower, material and financial resources in sectors and areas to which the state had decided to give priority and where a high rate of capital accumulation was possible. But this highly centralized form of planned economy had its inherent flaws and drawbacks.

First, vertical management by administrative methods was substituted for enterprise management. Given the fact that freedom of contract and disposition of certain types of property, especially land and real estate were not recognized, efficient voluntary horizontal and vertical cooperation between enterprises was impossible, resulting in the misallocation of resources. Second, the level of government empowered to make plans and policies for enterprises' production targets was far too removed from the enterprises to secure the necessary information in time for making such decisions. The amount of work required to plan and guide enterprises was beyond any competent government, however benevolent and reliable. The information problem inherent in central planning was criticized by Hayek.[153]

The gist of Hayek's criticism was that the knowledge necessary for constructing a rational economic order never exists in a concentrated or integrated form, but is available exclusively as dispersed and frequently contradictory fragments in the minds of a multitude of separate individuals. In Hayek's judgement, knowledge of this kind, by its very nature, cannot enter into statistics and therefore cannot be conveyed to any central authority in statistical form. The price system, in contrast, effectively coordinates the separate actions of different individuals in an economy in which knowledge is widely dispersed.

Third, there were major defects in the systems of incentives. As appendages of state organs, the enterprises were subjected only to compulsory administrative instructions. For them, there was neither the internal motivating force of wealth maximization nor the external pressure of competition. Since economic benefits were not linked to their performance, the enterprises generally overstated their input requirements and understated the capacity of their outputs. Hence, this model eventually created a system that was very inefficient. Fourth, as employees were supposed to be working for the public good and not for personal interests, remuneration was not related to performance. As a result, egalitarianism was prevalent among employees of enterprises. Employees of state-owned enterprises were assured of their 'iron rice bowls', that is their jobs, and they were entitled to eat from the same 'big pot', that is, public assets in the state-owned enterprises.[154]

An evolution of enterprise reform

Recognizing the shortcomings of central planning almost exclusively based on public ownership of the means of production, China embarked on an economic reform in 1978. This economic reform began from rural areas where a contractual responsibility system was adopted. Except for some quotas on products such as rice, wheat, and oil seeds set by the state, farmers were able to determine the food to plant and were able to sell many agricultural products on the market. That system increased the role of the market as more and more agricultural products were traded on the market. Also as of 1978, urban enterprises were given more autonomy in managing their own affairs. They were allowed to retain part of their profits.

In 1984, the Central Committee of the Communist Party adopted the Decisions to Reform the Economic System.[155] The aim of the 1984 Decisions was to create an enterprise that was a relatively independent business entity. The General Principles of the Civil Law[156] further clarified that a state-owned enterprise acquires the status of a legal person provided the enterprise meets the legal requirements in asset amount, organizational charter and structure, premises and ability to meet civil obligations.[157]

The legal person of a state enterprise must meet its civil obligations with the assets the state has authorized it to manage.[158] To achieve the purpose of enhancing the efficiency of state-owned enterprises, the Enterprises Bankruptcy Law was enacted in 1986.[159] As will be explained later, this Bankruptcy Law was not strictly enforced in the 1990s.

On 13 April 1988, the Seventh National People's Congress adopted the Law on Industrial Enterprises Owned by all the People.[160] This Law specifies the nature, rights and duties of state-owned enterprises. According to this law, an industrial enterprise owned by all the people shall be a socialist commodity production and operation unit.[161] While the property of the enterprise shall be owned by all the people, the state-owned enterprise enjoys the rights to possess, utilize and dispose of the property which the state has authorized it to operate and manage.[162]

25

Before 1989, the judicial concept of the enterprise had incorporated the notion of a planned commodity economy. At that time, a measure of replacing earnings turned over to the state with taxes collected by the state was implemented in order to reshape the distribution relationship between the state and the enterprise through a uniform tax system.[163] Mandatory planning quotas were gradually decreased while pricing for commodities normally subjected to planning guidance was liberalized. A management responsibility system was adopted throughout China which enabled an enterprise's management to contract out state assets and to keep the earnings above the amount contractually owed to the state in order to provide money for expansion, reinvestment, higher wages and more fringe benefits for its employees.[164] In addition, outright grants from the fiscal budget were changed to interest-bearing loans.[165]

In the early 1990s, a consensus was reached among economists and legal scholars as well as some governmental officials that reform of the enterprise system must move towards a market oriented economy. In early 1992, Deng Xiao Ping, a retired senior Chinese Leader, visited southern China to promote further economic reform and to advocate the establishment of a socialist market economy in China. The Regulations for Converting the Status of Enterprises Owned by all the People adopted by the State Council in 1992 were intended to push the state-owned enterprises onto the market. Specified in the said regulations are 14 types of rights granted to state-owned enterprises, ranging from production controls, investment possibilities in other corporations and areas, the fixing of prices of products, to compensation schemes.[166]

Meanwhile, some state-owned enterprises started to adopt the form of limited liability corporations and joint stock corporations. That practice was based on the Opinions on the Standardization of Limited Liability Companies and the Opinions on the Standardization of Joint Stock Companies issued by the State Economic Restructuring Commission[167] in May 1992. It had then been generally recognized that corporations were an essential part of a modern enterprise system. Thus, the Company Law[168] was enacted in 1993 and this Law replaced the two opinions of 1992. In addition to provisions on governance and duties similar to fiduciary duties in Western laws, Article 5(2) of the Company Law provides that a company shall, under the macro-adjustment and control of the state and in accordance with the needs of the market, manage its business and organize its production independently for the purpose of increasing productivity and economic benefits and for the maintenance and appreciation of its assets. This provision virtually confirms that the objective of a corporation, whether state-owned or not, is to maximize the wealth of that corporation.

China has made significant progress in recent years to reform its financial system. Before 1979, there were only two banks in China. The People's Bank of China which engaged in domestic banking business and the Bank of China which dealt with foreign currency business. Beginning in 1979, China reconstructed the Agricultural Bank and the Construction Bank.[169] Based on a State Council's Decisions to Exercise the Function of Central Bank by the People's Bank,[170] the Industrial and Commercial Bank,[171] which was established in the 1980s, took over the commercial business from the People's Bank of China in 1984. Since then, the People's Bank became the Central Bank of China. The role played by the four specialized banks was significant. By the end of 1993, these four specialized banks accounted for 80 per cent of the total assets in China's banking sector.[172] Encouraged to act more like commercial enterprises, these specialized banks were, at least in theory, responsible for obtaining deposits, making profits and paying interest to depositors.[173] Enterprises were no longer given an automatic right to credit and banks were to allocate funds on the basis of enterprise profitability.[174]

The Law on the People's Bank of China legally confirmed that the People's Bank assumed the role of a Central Bank.[175] Soon after, the law on Commercial Banks was enacted.[176] This Law set out to achieve three main objectives. First, it was intended to push the four specialized banks onto the market and turn them into truly commercial banks. Second, banks were entitled to refuse any compulsory loan made by any outside person or unit.[177] Theoretically speaking, it is impossible for local governments to force these banks to accept loan requests. Third, the law is to regulate unhealthy conducts in the financial sector.

Continuing problems and analysis from a governance perspective

Despite enterprise banking sector reforms, performance of state-owned enterprises and banks remained poor in the 1990s. In 1987 losses incurred by state-owned, economically independent industrial enterprises amounted to 6.1 billion yuan.[178] Losses increased to 34.8 billion yuan in 1990 and to 45.2 billion yuan in 1993.[179] During the first four months of 1994, 50.1 per cent of these enterprises were running at a loss.[180] Although this improved slightly in the latter half of that year, 34.4 per cent of these state-owned enterprises were still running at a loss at the end of 1994.[181] Overstocking of products, chain defaulting, and poor management of funds was taking an increasingly heavier toll on the economic performance of enterprises. For instance, stockpiled products were valued at 412.4 billion yuan by the end of 1994.[182] Most of these losses resulted from medium to large-sized state-owned enterprises. In 1993, losses in the four basic industries, which include coal and electricity, accounted for more than 40 per cent of total losses. Continuously expanding production under low efficiency contributed to the high-speed development of the entire economy.

Despite the reforming efforts, performance of the banks remained poor in the 1990s. Overdue payments and non-performing loans remained high. While

27

official reports indicate that overdue payments and non-performing loans accounted for 15 per cent of all credit offered by banks in 1992,[183] unofficial estimates show that overdue payments and non-performing loans were close to 40 per cent of all outstanding loans.[184]

After a brief description of the poor performance of the state-owned enterprises and the state-owned banks, I now begin with an analysis of the causes of the inefficiency of state-owned enterprises from a corporate governance perspective. I believe that understanding the basic features of monitoring devices and the causes of inefficiency of China's state-owned enterprises is essential for proposing policy changes.

Before 1978, the product market was irrelevant as a monitoring device since state-owned enterprises were instrumental in fulfilling state-plans. Since 1978, the product market has developed rapidly and started to play the role of a monitoring device. On the whole, however, this product market requires much improvement. First, distorted prices resulting from a dual price mechanism exerted influence on the market from 1984 to the middle of the 1990s. While the prices of the majority of products on the market were determined by supply and demand on the market, the state still played a significant role in dictating prices of certain inputs such as oil and electricity. Since 1984 the state-owned enterprises producing such inputs had also been allowed to price a portion above production quotas according to market rates. Dual pricing of these products adversely affected the efficiency of the product market. Unequal external environment made it difficult to distinguish inefficient producers from those who are affected by unfair pricing.

Second, the difference of income tax regimes between domestic enterprises and foreign-invested enterprises has created another distortion. Foreign-invested enterprises are normally able to receive the benefits of tax holidays and reductions at the beginning of the first five years of their operation.[185]

Third, lack of comprehensive social insurance schemes, particularly in the 1980s and 1990s, and governmental intervention made it very difficult to strictly enforce the Enterprise Bankruptcy Law. This significantly weakened the discipline of the product market. Several factors contributed to the weak enforcement of the Enterprise Bankruptcy Law in the 1980s and 1990s.

To the central government, the exit of inefficient enterprises was not a purely economic problem.[186] On the political side, large-scale bankruptcies would affect political stability. Allowing a large scale of bankruptcies also contradicted the notion of a socialist economic system, a concept inserted in the Constitution of China. Article 7 of the 1993 Constitution states that the state-owned economy, that is, the sector of the socialist economy under the ownership of all the people, is the leading force in the national economy. The state ensures the consolidation and growth of the state-owned economy.[187] To the senior leaders of the Chinese Communist Party, considerable decrease of the state-owned sectors might undermine the political base of the Party's leadership. On economic grounds, forcing money-losing enterprises in financial distress to go bankrupt was not the equivalent to efficient resource allocation. The distorted prices up until the middle of 1990s might imply that some efficient enterprises lost money. In addition, chain defaulting among enterprises further complicated the issue. Efficient enterprises might have cash flow problems because they had difficulty collecting accounts receivable. Under these conditions, applying the liquidity test of insolvency was not necessarily a measure of efficiency.

To local governments, a large number of bankruptcies would affect their image of political achievements. Many unsuccessful projects were the result of lobbying efforts by local governments. Bankruptcies of these enterprises might indicate that their past promises were wrong. Furthermore, local governments could still claim credit from maintaining these enterprises. For instance, inefficient enterprises still added to the output statistics. Moreover, money-losing enterprises still paid certain types of taxes. Although these taxes might flow back to these inefficient enterprises in the form of subsidy, local governments could still claim these taxes from their localities.[188] Finally, inefficient enterprises could still give benefits to local officials.[189] These officials could obtain reimbursement from the inefficient enterprises for their 'entertainment' bills.[190]

As for local banks, state-owned enterprises were their main debtors. During the 1990s, 90 per cent of the working capital of most state-owned enterprises came from bank loans.[191] Among these, a very high percentage of loans were non-performing loans as previously discussed. To these banks, non-performing loans were still on their record of loans. Canceling non-performing loans, however, decreased the total loan balance, affecting their performance in the eyes of higher authorities.

Bankruptcy was also bad in the eyes of enterprises. Employees even in the 1990s did not expect their enterprises to go bankrupt. They did not even believe that their state-owned enterprises could go bankrupt. To them, unpaid wages and non-reimbursed medical bills would be paid by their enterprises sooner or later.[192] To senior managers, bankruptcy meant failure of their management and the end of their jobs. They might also discover that it would not be easy for them to find good jobs elsewhere in a market oriented economy.

All these factors explain why the number of bankruptcy cases dealt with by the courts was extremely low in the 1990s. From the date when the Enterprise Bankruptcy Law became effective on 1 November 1998, to the end of 1993, the courts in China only adjudicated 1,417 bankruptcy cases.[193] Exit barriers weakened the monitoring devices of the product market.

Finally, the efficiency of the product market has also been affected by fake products or products resulting from infringements of intellectual property rights. Because of the lack of awareness of the law by the Chinese people, products violating intellectual property rights are in large quantity on the market.[194] These products normally include computer software, electronic products, wine, beverage, etc. This also undermines the monitoring device of the product market. Obviously, China has to rationalize the price mechanism and strictly enforce intellectual property right law.

Comparative corporate governance studies reveal the importance of mutual monitoring and trading relations between members within a corporate group resulting from mutual shareholding. The function of this monitoring device depends very much on the efficiency of the product market. In an inefficient product market, it is difficult to distinguish between inefficient management and distortions caused by the product market. Therefore, the existence of an efficient product market constrains managerial behaviour by enhancing mutual monitoring.

Reducing collective action problems dictates that the number within a corporate group must be relatively small. If the number is quite large, free rider problems may be severe enough to undermine mutual monitoring. To encourage investment in firm-specific assets, the members within the group need to have trading or shareholding relations. In other words, there must be no competition between group members. Such relations are conducive not only to the reduction of agency costs resulting from debt financing but also to the decrease of agency costs caused by the separation between control and residual claims.

Unless the current laws of China are further revised, it is not possible for China to achieve the objective observed in Japan where the main banks play a significant role in corporate governance. Article 43(2) of the 1995 Commercial Banking Law provides, *inter alia*, that commercial banks are prohibited from investing in non-banking financial institutions and other enterprises within the territory of China.[195] Although the recent amendment gives the State Council limited room for change, the State Council has not made any significant reform yet. Therefore, if enterprises intend to establish a corporate group through mutual shareholding, no banks can be involved. As commercial banks cannot hold shares in other manufacturing corporations, Chinese banks cannot play the roles which Japanese or German banks have performed.

I am not able to find any economic rationales for prohibiting banks from owning shares in non-financial corporations. While American laws prohibit banks from holding shares in manufacturing corporations, the same does not apply to trust depart-ments within banks and bank holding corporations. It should be pointed out that American legislation has been criticized recently.[196] If the purpose of legislation in China is the protection of depositors, prudential regulation may achieve a similar purpose. Moreover, the primary task of corporate governance is to establish various markets and develop contractual mechanisms to reduce agency costs. In economies where efficient monitoring devices exist, the burden of proving that banks are not capable of making rational investments is on those who insist on the ban. If there are no other alternative monitoring devices, efficiency losses in non-financial corporations are inevitable given that banks and insurance companies are not allowed to hold shares in these corporations. Even if legally permitted, banks will not own shares in all corporations. They may simply refrain from holding shares in other corporations. The option, however, is desirable that banks may hold shares in some non-financial corporations, especially in those where the banks have provided a large amount of loans. Shareholding in these corporations provides the banks with the incentives to monitor the corporations. Those who oppose the development of the stock markets in China need to consider the impact of the laws on the role of banks in corporate governance. Simply assuming that banks can be effective monitors when there are no stock markets is not satisfactory. Under the current conditions, wealth maximizing banks will be quite reluctant to extend loans to corporations with a very high debt/equity ratio.

I have claimed that legal prohibition on banks from holding shares in non-financial corporations would cause efficiency losses when alternative monitoring devices do not exist. Now, I need to examine whether banks can be effective and efficient monitors if they were allowed to own shares in non-financial corporations under the current conditions in China. Given that inefficient state-owned corporations have to be subsidized through state-owned banks, commercial banks and policy banks alike, I believe that banks would not be efficient monitors. In other words, if banks are not able to exercise their creditors' rights, the shareholding of banks will not be very meaningful. Without a credible and efficient bankruptcy mechanism, neither state-owned enterprises nor banks will have any incentives to use resources efficiently.[197] Without the threat of bankruptcy, managers have little to fear about poor performance. Without the power to declare defaulting debtors bankrupt, banks are powerless to influence management.[198]

At this juncture, it is necessary to discuss the inefficiency of China's specialized banks which have been turned into commercial banks in the 1990s. The problem of China's dominant commercial banks[199] could be analysed by discussing some special characteristics of these banks. First, the location of branches of these banks parallels the location of local governments.[200] As discussed previously, banks were regarded as appendages of various levels of governments. They were quite instrumental in fulfilling state plans. Given the fragmentation of these banks, efficient allocation of resources on the national level was difficult as local governments frequently interfered with the loan-making decisions of local branches.

Second, the organization of these banks was quite similar to the bureaucratic administrative hierarchy of governments. In the past, a person without a ranking equivalent to that in the governmental hierarchy would not be qualified to occupy a parallel position in a bank. Seeking higher positions was the reflection of utility maximization of employees. Promotion, however, would not necessarily be related to performance. Other factors such as party loyalty and personal relations might be more important.

Third, these specialized banks had to provide not only commercial loans but also policy loans in the 1990s. These policy loans were mainly used to subsidize inefficient state-owned enterprises and to supply funds for some social welfare programmes such as unemployment insurance, retirement fund, disaster relief funds.[201] Despite the fact that three policy banks[202] were established in 1993 to separate policy lending from commercial lending,[203] these specialized banks still had to extend policy loans in the 1990s. In 1994, policy loans accounted for 20 per cent of the loans from the Commercial and Industrial Bank, 30 per cent of the loans of the Agricultural Bank, 15 per cent of the loans extended by the Bank of China, and 45 per cent of the loans provided by the Construction Bank.[204] Even after the enactment of the Commercial Banking Law, these banks still bear some of the burden of providing policy loans.

Fourth, these four specialized banks were traditionally separated in business transactions. This considerably restricted the loan options available to banks. Consequently, these banks, unlike Japanese Banks, were 'narrow-minded'. Although certain cross transactions were permitted in the early 1990s (for example, the acceptance of Chinese currency deposits by the Bank of China and foreign currency deposits by the Industrial and Commercial Bank) there remained a separation of functions between these banks. While the separation of functions made it difficult for these banks to diversify risks, they found it easier to monopolize their business within their respective areas. Under the conditions of soft budget constraints, monopolized positions caused managerial slack.

Because of the shortcomings, these banks became the focus of financial reform. The task of reforming these banks, however, was quite difficult and incomplete due to four main reasons. First, the monopolized positions of these specialized banks made financial reform difficult. As long as reform might reduce their benefits, the banks could work together to oppose the reforms.[205] On the other hand, it was much easier to adopt certain reform measures, such as decentralization of the banking sector, cancellation of the limits of loans, expansion of business scope of these specialized banks, because these measures were beneficial to the banks.

Second, the central government was indecisive in the 1990s. One of the concerns was the possible reduction of revenue of the central government. Business tax and profits submitted by these specialized banks has been the major source, accounting for one-sixth of the revenue of the central government.[206] As such, the central government was very cautious in choosing alternative reform measures. Another explanation for the slow reform was the fact that the current status of the banks was conducive to policy implementation. These specialized banks still assumed the role of providing policy loans. If the specialized banks were truly commercial and independent, they might not be willing to provide policy loans or provide loans to the enterprises desired by the central government.[207]

Third, local governments were not in favour of reforming these former specialized banks. Local governments used to give orders to the branches of these banks in their areas. They could request loans for new local projects from the banks. Further, they could ask that loans be supplied to money-losing local state-owned enterprises. Some local governments might use funds from the banks in case of a budget imbalance.[208] If the banks were turned into true commercial banks, local governments would be worse off. Given these factors, it was not hard to understand that the Commercial Banking Law could not always be strictly enforced.

Finally, money-losing state-owned enterprises opposed any change that might affect their position. For large money-losing state-owned enterprises, soft budget constraints implied that these specialized banks were, in the eyes of the state-owned enterprises, fund suppliers instead of creditors. Their position would be worsened if the banks became truly commercial banks. Profit maximizing banks would be less likely to continue their loans to corporations that were not earning money. Thus, reform was a threat to state-owned enterprises.[209] To small non-state-owned enterprises reform was in their favour. Under the conditions in the middle of the 1990s they suffered from credit squeeze in favour of large state-owned enterprises. Because of their small size, they were not able to utilize the stock markets in China. The Company Law requires a listed corporation to have a total capital of at least 50,000,000 yuan.[210] Furthermore, small non-state-owned enterprises were not important players affecting China's public policy.

Despite the resistance of various players in China, pressure on the state-owned commercial banks was mounting. Newly established small commercial banks challenged the traditional state monopolized banks. These newly established commercial banks were much more flexible and responsive to market needs. The internal control system of the small commercial banks was far better than that of these commercial banks. Past reform experience in China indicated that allowing the entry of private enterprises is far more effective than reforming the large state-owned enterprises. That implies that China should also adopt similar liberal attitudes towards the entry of private banks. In addition to the pressure of newly established commercial banks, competition from foreign invested banks has already increased new types of financial products and services. Moreover, the emerging stock markets in China have also undermined the role of the state-owned commercial banks as the markets provide alternative sources of capital.

Soft budget constraints and the legal prohibition against banks owning shares in non-financial corporations require the use of alternative monitoring devices.

33

The capital and corporate control markets are natural selections. Similar to our views, it is argued that if share prices reflect enterprise profitability, the capital market will channel investment funds to the most efficient enterprises as investors seek to maximize their returns.[211] It is further argued that capital markets create a market for corporate control. People believe that market mechanisms are more effective at rationalizing productive assets than the powers given to banks.[212] Furthermore, the creation of a stock market gives enterprises more financial autonomy since they no longer have to rely on the governments for funds. This also gives them more freedom to respond quickly to market opportunities, cutting through the regional, departmental and bureaucratic ties that continue to bind banks.[213]

Despite these possible benefits, the stock markets in China are artificially restrained. For instance, the delayed enactment of a Securities Law in the later 1990s was a deliberate effort on the part of the central government to discourage the speedy development of the stock market in China.[214] In China, the shares belonging to the state and state-owned enterprises are normally not traded on the Shanghai Stock Exchange or the Shenzhen Stock Exchange. Illiquidity of these shares and hostility towards the hostile takeover market in China has not only increased the cost of raising capital but also created obstacles in disciplining non-performing managers.

Present regulations not only show hostility to takeover transactions targeted at state-owned enterprises by private corporations but also make takeover transactions more expensive between any type of enterprises. Pursuant to the Tentative Regulation on the Administration of the Issuing and Trading of Shares (ITS),[215] when a legal person's direct or indirect holding of outstanding common shares in a listed company reaches 5 per cent of the company's total outstanding common shares, that legal person shall, within three working days report such fact in writing to the target company, the stock exchange and the China Securities Regulatory Commission (CSRC) and make an announcement.[216] In addition, any change of increase or decrease of the above acquired shares of such a legal person reaching 2 per cent will again trigger the reporting duty.[217] Above all, within 45 working days after any legal person's (other than a promoter's) direct or indirect holding of outstanding common shares in a listed company reaches 30 per cent of such company's total outstanding common shares, such legal person shall make an offer of takeover to all the shareholders of the target, offering to purchase their shares through cash payment.[218] If a takeover is made, the higher of the following two prices should be adopted as the offer price: (1) the highest price paid by the offeror for the purchase of such shares during the 12 months preceding the issuance of the takeover offer; or (2) the average market price of such shares during the 30 working days preceding the issuance of the takeover offer.[219] The high cost of complying with these provisions is obvious and the takeover market is thoroughly examined elsewhere in the book.

The managerial market used to be quite rigid and highly administrative in the 1990s. Similar to officials in banks, officials in China's state-owned enterprises had official rankings parallel to those in the army or the governments. Under that system, governmental officials and army officials were frequently assigned to state-owned enterprises to manage these enterprises whether they had expertise in management or not. They could be reassigned elsewhere if the need arose. Even if the enterprises they managed lost money, their jobs were secured. The worst scenario for them was to move to another state-owned enterprise or governmental agency.

Obviously, reform of that system is essential to China's enterprise reform. The market for managers needs to be developed to cope with the daunting task of moving the planned economy to a market oriented economy. On the market, the experience of management, the expertise in a specific industry, and the performance of managers all contribute to determining the level of compensation of managers. Simply stated, efficiency requires that good managers be rewarded while non-performing managers be penalized. As is discussed elsewhere in the book, a positive correlation between firm performance of listed corporations and remuneration has only occurred after 2002. Only in an efficient managerial market can managers be subject to both the incentives and the disciplines to efficiently manage their corporations. However, in the case of China, an efficient managerial market requires the existence of an efficient product market where poor corporate performers, whether state-owned or not, are driven out. That seems to be a thorny political problem which will exist for quite some time.

However, I am optimistic as an efficient product and efficient managerial market can be established gradually and applied both to non-state-owned enterprises and state-owned enterprises. Given the permission of free entry of private capital in China in the past, efficient exit of the failing state-owned corporations should also be possible. When the economy grows stronger, the markets as monitoring devices should provide better incentives and disciplines to managers in Chinese corporations. Globalization of trade and investment make it very hard for a country to maintain a large number of inefficient state-owned corporations as that country will not survive in a liberalized competitive world market.

CONCLUSION

In this chapter, I have pointed out the lack of attention to comparative studies of monitoring devices in the existing literature on Chinese law and economics. A broad perspective of comparative studies of monitoring devices should cover both market forces and contractual arrangements. Other things being equal, the more effective the monitoring devices, the lower the agency costs. Generally, all stakeholders benefit from low agency costs in corporations. While the literature on agency costs resulting from the separation of control and residual claims and on agency costs caused by debt issue are developed along different lines, I have tried to analyse both types of agency costs from a common agency perspective. I have briefly discussed the monitoring devices in the USA, Germany, Japan and Hong Kong. Comparative studies of monitoring devices help us understand the determinants of these devices. Politics and law play important roles in shaping the relevant monitoring devices. In addition, the method of financing, by equity or debt, is also relevant in the development of monitoring devices. Furthermore, the distribution of shares in corporations, and hence ownership, also affects the relative use of different monitoring devices. Comparative studies of monitoring devices also indicate that the relative use of different monitoring devices is not static. Changes in economic conditions, law and politics, and international trade and investment affect corporate governance models in a particular country although a total convergence of corporate governance models is unlikely. While recognizing the validity of chaos theories and path dependence, I believe countries can learn from each other, especially the countries which are moving from planned economies based on the public ownership of the means of production to market oriented economies. I have examined the case of China from an agency perspective. Various monitoring devices existing mainly in the 1990s have been analysed. After pointing out some inherent defects in the monitoring devices in China, I have proposed some policy initiatives. If reform in the political sphere can be pushed further, comparative corporate governance studies may provide useful policy guidance for China's future reform.

Chapter 2

The problem with the transplantation of Western law

INTRODUCTION

Since 1978, the Chinese government has tried various means, including the use of Western law, to improve upon the inefficiency of state-owned enterprises (SOEs). Despite its efforts, the poor performance of SOEs at an aggregate level has persisted.[1] What is less clear is the source of the poor performance. Peltzman posed the question: 'If a privately owned firm is socialized, and nothing else happens, how will the ownership change alone affect the firm's behavior?'[2] The question is further complicated as Atkinson and Halvorsen have pointed out that government in industry is often associated with the suppression of competition, making it problematic as to whether public ownership per se or the suppression of competition is driving poor performance.[3] Research in the property rights[4] and agency costs[5] tradition suggests that there will be performance differences between government and private ownership because of the broad menu of monitoring devices associated with private ownership. Alchian states the underlying premise: 'Behavior under public and private ownership is different because even with the same explicit organization goals, the costs-rewards system impinging upon the employees and the "owners" of the organization are different.'[6]

Kole and Mulherin found different results after studying a sample of nationalized enemy companies in which the US federal government held 35–100 per cent of the outstanding common shares for between one and 23 years during and following the Second World War.[7] Their study indicates that the performance of the government-owned companies was not significantly different than that of private-sector firms in the same industry. Hence, the interim government custodianship of the firms in their case does not have the effects normally attributed to government ownership. Kole and Mulherin's study has limitations, however. First, the firms in their sample were subject to interim custodianship by the US government rather than full-fledged government ownership. Second, the firms in the sample were eventually reprivatized. Third, Kole and Mulherin

37

do not have enough tools or evidence to measure the relative importance of the monitoring mechanisms such as comparative markets, monitoring shareholders, and external valuation faced by the government in their case.

Trebilcock has argued that, in addition to the lack of means to motivate or discipline agents in public organizations, public actors will pursue socially undesirable ends because of political self interest.[8]

This chapter focuses, from an agency perspective, on the Chinese SOEs, which provide non-public goods or services. Through explaining the difficulties of establishing various market mechanisms by utilizing Western law to improve upon the inefficiency of the SOEs, the article argues that China cannot well achieve the goal of using Western law to improve upon the inefficiency of the SOEs unless the state withdraws or considerably reduces its ownership in the large number of state-owned listed companies. This chapter proceeds as follows: in examining the reform of SOEs since 1978, section two provides a brief discussion of the political goal of controlling a large number of state-owned listed companies and presents empirical evidence of the structure of listed companies in the stock market. Section three examines the problems in establishing an efficient market of corporate control despite the transplantation of a Western type of takeover law. Section four discusses the widespread occurrence of securities fraud in the issuing of shares in listed companies. While focusing on the difficulty of enforcing Western type securities law to show the inefficiencies in the public provision of goods or services, the chapter also raises doubts on Minow's call for a public framework of accountability. If a public framework of accountability cannot be developed to deal with the abuse in SOEs, it is unlikely that such a framework will be very useful for private companies in market economies. While the contractual and market mechanisms which can be used to motivate or discipline agents in companies include the capital market, takeover market, product market, managerial market, shareholder monitoring, and creditor monitoring, this chapter only examines the takeover market and the capital market. The chapter concludes in section five that the political goal of maintaining the control of large SOEs in China makes it difficult to establish efficient market mechanisms or legal means to motivate or discipline agents in China's SOEs. The inefficient market or legal mechanisms adversely affect the performance of SOEs in China's transitional economy.

THE POLITICAL GOALS OF CONTROLLING THE LARGE SOEs

China has been under the control of the Chinese Communist Party (CPC) ever since the establishment of the People's Republic of China (PRC or China) in 1949. Under the leadership of the CPC, the Chinese economy from 1949 to

1978 was centrally directed under a very rigid system of state planning. Within this system, the state owned most of the productive resources, leaving a minor portion in the hands of enterprises (normally in collective ownership). The decision-making power for the macroeconomic activities of the state and major activities of enterprises were in the hands of the state. While the market still existed, since currency commodity relations[9] remained, the basic means by which the various targets were realised were mandatory plans drawn up by the state hierarchy. As fiscal agents of the government, banks only played the role of implementing plans.[10] Given that banks did not have to screen projects and monitor the use of funds after the fact, constraints on enterprises were quite soft.[11]

The enterprises immediately responsible for production had to follow state orders in many activities, including finance, management, marketing, employment, wage policy and expansion and enjoyed hardly any independence. As the economic benefits of enterprises were not linked with their performance, enterprises with significant profits had no right to dispose of their profits while enterprises operating with heavy losses were subsidized by the state. The Ministry of Finance distributed all budgetary allocations and collected all enterprise surpluses through the People's Bank of China. Economic information was transmitted vertically between the higher and lower levels in the administrative system in the form of instructions and reports. Having recognized the shortcomings of central planning where the means of production was almost exclusively based on public ownership, China embarked on an economic reform programme in 1978. This economic reform began in rural areas where a contractual responsibility system was adopted. Except for some quotas on products such as rice, wheat, and oil seeds set by the state, farmers were able to determine the food to plant and were able to sell many agricultural products on the market. That system increased the role of the market as more agricultural products were traded on the market. Also as of 1978, urban enterprises were given more autonomy in managing their own affairs. They were allowed to retain part of their profits. Reform measures also included permission for private investment by both domestic investors and foreign investors, liberalization of the economy through decentralization, and the establishment of market institutions.

While China has attracted worldwide attention for its economic reform and has achieved a very high rate of economic development, the CPC has maintained firm control of the reform process. To rule China, the CPC has always held firmly to the ideology of socialism. In the past, socialism was reflected by two key characteristics – the planned economy and public ownership of the means of production (productive resources). While the reform has done away with the planned economy and has considerably reduced the number of SOEs in the economy, the CPC has always insisted on the control of large SOEs. A brief review of the CPC documents will make that clear. While the Report of Jiang Zemin at the Fourteenth CPC National Congress in 1992 called for the establishment of a socialist market economy, it emphasized the dominant position of the system of state ownership in such a socialist market economy.[12] The Speech of Jiang Zemin at the Fifth Plenary Session of the Fourteenth CPC National Congress on 28 September 1995 reemphasized the importance of the dominant position of state ownership in China's socialist market economy over other elements of joint or private ownership.[13] This position is still reflected in Jiang Zemin's most recent speech at the Sixteenth CPC National Congress[14] and in the 1999 Constitution.[15] This dominant position of state ownership through the control of large state-owned listed companies serves important ideological purposes and is vital to the survival of the CPC in China. Unlike China, the full scope of privatization of SOEs in other former Eastern European countries has led to the collapse of the socialist regime in these countries. The following paragraphs will present some statistics on the poor performance of SOEs at the beginning of the 1990s and the structure of state ownership in most listed companies.

Although the reform of state-owned enterprises started in 1978, the performance of state-owned enterprises and banks remained poor in the 1980s and at the beginning of the 1990s. In 1987, the losses incurred by state-owned, economically independent industrial enterprises amounted to 6.1 billion yuan.[16] Losses increased to 34.8 billion yuan in 1990 and to 45.2 billion yuan in 1993.[17] During the first four months of 1994, 50.1 per cent of these enterprises were running at a loss.[18] Although things improved slightly in the later half of that year, 34.4 per cent of these state-owned enterprises were still running at a loss at the end of 1994.[19] Overstocking of products, chain loan defaulting, and poor management of funds have taken an increasingly heavier toll on the economic performance of enterprises. For instance, stockpiled products were valued at 412.4 billion yuan at the end of 1994.[20] Most of these loans were used by medium to large-sized state-owned enterprises.

Despite the reform of the financial sector, bank performance remained poor at the beginning of the 1990s. Overdue payments and non-performing loans were high. While official reports indicate that overdue payments and non-performing loans accounted for 15 per cent of all credit offered by banks in 1992,[21] unofficial estimates show that overdue payments and non-performing loans were close to 40 per cent of all outstanding loans.[22] The continuation of the dominant means of financing state-owned enterprises by loans from state banks would generate the political risks of bank insolvency if state-owned banks were not able to tighten the soft budget constraints of various loan users.[23]

Soft budget constraints and the legal prohibition against banks from owning shares in non-financial companies require the use of alternative means of financing corporate activities. The stock market was a natural selection. It is argued that if the share system is adopted, worker–owners will have greater incentives to improve the enterprise they work in.[24] The reformers believe that stock market mechanisms are more efficient at rationalizing productive assets than the intermingling of government administration and enterprise management.[25] Moreover, the creation of a stock market gives enterprises more financial responsibility since the worker–investors have to bear the cost of losses from the beginning.[26] China's company law and the stock market were, therefore, mainly designed to improve the performance of the inefficient SOEs.[27]

The statistical evidence is consistent with the goal of controlling large state-owned listed companies. A survey in May 1999 reveals that among the 862 listed companies on the two stock exchanges, state shares existed in 541 listed companies, accounting for 62.76 per cent.[28] Among the 541 listed companies, state shares account for 45 per cent of the total issued shares in these companies.[29] In 473 listed companies the state shareholder has either absolute or relative control[30] of the company, occupying 87.43 per cent of the 541 listed companies.[31] The state shares are mainly held by state asset administration bureaux, state investment companies or the parent companies of the state-owned listed companies.[32] To be sure, the percentage of state ownership is much higher as state ownership may be held by legal persons of other non-controlling state-owned companies.[33] In 70.79 per cent of the 541 listed companies, state shares range from 30–80 per cent.[34] In contrast to the traded shares held by individuals at the two stock exchanges, state shares and legal person shares of state-owned enterprises are not traded on the stock exchanges. Another piece of statistics shows that the percentage of traded shares owned by individual investors in most listed companies are only between 25–40 per cent.[35] The next two sections will explain how the political goal of controlling the large state-owned listed companies makes it difficult to establish an efficient takeover market and a primary stock market.

THE USE OF AN ENGLISH-STYLE TAKEOVER LAW

The takeover market, or the market for corporate control, is sometimes claimed to be able to discipline inefficient managers if they seek excessive perquisites or are not responsible or fail to improve the allocation of productive resources by employing synergistic practices to realize economies of scale or scope, and thus increase the revenue of the company. For this purpose, China has transplanted an English-style takeover law, hoping to allocate the productive resources in a more efficient way. The remaining part will explain whether the use of an English-style takeover law will well achieve the above goal.

China's early takeover transactions were regulated by the Tentative Regulations on the Administration of the Issuing and Trading of Shares (ITS).[36] In the ITS, provisions on takeovers are very similar to the Hong Kong Code on Takeovers and Mergers,[37] which was itself based on the London City Code on Takeovers and Mergers.[38] While there are only seven articles on takeovers in the ITS, the key provision is based on the London City Code.[39] According to this provision, within 45 working days after any legal person's (other than a promoter's) direct or indirect holdings of outstanding common shares in a listed company reaches 30 per cent of such company's total outstanding common shares, such legal person shall make an offer of takeover to all the shareholders of such company, offering to purchase their shares through cash payment.[40] The more recent Securities Law slightly modifies this 30 per cent threshold. Pursuant to the Securities Law, if an investor acquires 30 per cent of the shares of a listed company through a stock exchange and continues to purchase such shares, that investor shall make a takeover offer to all the shareholders of the listed company unless exempted by the securities regulatory authorities.[41] If a takeover is made, the higher of the following two prices should be adopted as the offer price: (1) the highest price paid by the offeror for the purchase of such shares during the 12 months preceding the issuance of the takeover offer; or (2) the average market price of such shares during the 30 working days preceding the issuance of the takeover offer.[42] I will call this provision the mandatory purchase provision and further discuss it later.

A few other provisions are related to fair treatment of minority shareholders and are much easier to justify. For instance, all the conditions contained in a takeover offer shall apply to all the holders of the same types of common shares.[43] If the total number of shares that the maker of a takeover offer prepares to buy is less than the total number of shares for which the offer is accepted, the offeror shall purchase shares from the offeree shareholders on a pro rata basis.[44] In the event of a change in any of the main conditions of offer after a takeover offer has been issued, the offeror shall promptly notify all offerees.[45] The notice may be made in the form of a press conference or newspaper announcement or by other means of dissemination. During the term of a takeover offer and for a period of 30 working days thereafter, the offeror may not purchase the shares in question on any conditions other than those set forth in the offer.[46]

Still other provisions are related to disclosure and the facilitation of potential competing takeover offers. If a legal person holds, pursuant to the disclosure provision, directly or indirectly, more than 5 per cent of the common shares of another listed company, a public announcement shall be made and a written report disclosing the fact shall be sent to the listed target company, the relevant stock exchange and the China Securities Regulatory Commission (CSRC) within three working days from the date of acquisition.[47] In addition, any change of at least 2 per cent, whether it be an increase or a decrease, in the holdings of the aforementioned acquired shares of such a legal person will again trigger the reporting duty.[48] The Securities Law has raised this 2 per cent threshold to

5 per cent.[49] When this threshold is triggered, such a legal person shall not directly or indirectly buy or sell shares of the target company within two working days from the date the announcement is made and report submitted and before the submission of the report.[50] According to another provision for the purpose of facilitating takeover offers, the takeover offer period, calculated from the date the offer was issued, shall not be less than 30 working days.[51] Offerors shall not withdraw their takeover offer during the offer period.[52] Furthermore, the offeree shareholders have the right to withdraw their acceptance during the offer period.[53] As will be discussed later, the political goal of maintaining control over the large state-owned enterprises makes the disclosure provision and the provision for facilitating competing takeover offers irrelevant in the 1990s.

The mandatory purchase provision was adopted in the United Kingdom in 1968[54] and later widely spread to many other countries and regions such as Australia,[55] Germany, Portugal, Italy, and Switzerland.[56] The takeover law in the USA does not have such a provision. The rationale behind the provision is the equality of treatment of minority shareholders. If an acquiring company pays a premium to the majority, block or some shareholder(s) in a target when purchasing their shares, the acquiring company shall also be required to extend the same premium to the minority shareholders in the target company. An introductory provision in the London City Code reflects that policy concern. The provision stipulates that the Code is designed principally to ensure fair and equal treatment of all shareholders in relation to takeovers.[57] This rationale, however, is based on an unrealistic assumption that whatever the law, the number of takeovers will not be reduced. While others[58] also made a similar point, it is empirically difficult to verify this claim. To do so requires the collection of two sets of evidence at the same time in the same country. One set of evidence shows the number of takeovers under a regime with mandatory purchase provisions and the other set reveals the number of takeovers under a regime without mandatory purchase provisions. As at any particular time a country normally only has one set of rules, the goal of using empirical evidence to directly assess the mandatory purchase provision is impossible to achieve. Assessing the mandatory purchase provision at different times in the same country is affected by other factors. For instance, despite the adoption of the City Code in the United Kingdom in 1968, the larger number of takeovers in the 1970s and 1980s than in the 1950s is affected by the factor that the economy in the United Kingdom in the 1950s and early 1960 was only just starting to recover from the Second World War. Inter-country comparisons of the number of takeovers between the USA and the United Kingdom are affected by other factors. For instance, in the USA, the shareholding structure is far more widely dispersed. Limited evidence does indicate, however, that the small number of takeovers in the USA in the 1990s[59] is possibly affected by the state anti-takeover law enacted in the 1980s.[60] Similar to the mandatory

43

purchase provision, the anti-takeover law in most states of the USA appears to increase the costs of takeovers.

Before proceeding to an evaluation of the mandatory purchase provision, it is necessary to discuss the motivations of acquiring companies in taking over target companies. The transfer of a controlling interest in a given company will take place in two types of situations. First, an acquiring company may believe that the target company in question can be managed in a more efficient manner and will thus generate more profit as the incumbent managers are indulging in excessive perquisites or are not working hard.[61] Second, the acquiring company may be able to employ synergistic practices to realize economies of scale or scope after the takeover to increase profits.[62] In both of the above cases, the transfer of control will be efficient at a price between the ceiling price of the present value of the future income stream generated by the acquiring company and the floor price of the present value of the future income stream of the firm as it is currently being operated by the target management. While abuse of minority shareholders may occur in some takeovers, this can be safeguarded by the general corporate law on the protection of minority shareholders and on penalties being imposed on looters.[63] Empirical evidence to a large extent supports the theories of disciplining inefficient managers and of synergy effects.[64]

Despite the overwhelming evidence that target shareholders make abnormal investment returns in takeovers, the mandatory purchase provision mainly takes the ex post view that once a takeover takes place, the gains[65] from takeovers should be shared equally by all the shareholders in the target. I will evaluate this mandatory purchase provision by using both the autonomy value and the welfare value. Neither criterion can justify this premium sharing provision. On a Nozickian rights-based approach, a distinction is made between threats and offers.[66] Threats reduce the possibilities open to the recipient of an offer whereas offers expand them. From that perspective, takeovers would seem properly to be viewed as offer rather than as threat to minority shareholders in the target company when the assets under the incumbent management are not efficiently utilized. The possibility of having a new management team indicates that take-overs increase target shareholders' possibilities relative to their position prior to their interaction with the acquirer. Even the threat of takeovers disciplines managers in a potential target company.

Despite the conclusion that takeover transactions enlarge shareholders' contractual possibilities and despite the overwhelming empirical evidence that shareholders of target companies receive abnormal returns resulting from takeover transactions, an enormous body of academic writing has focused on the problem of coercion in takeovers, particularly in partial bids.[67] Coffee notes that demonstrated examples of coercion remain as rare as confirmed sightings of the Loch Ness monster.[68] The ex ante Nozickian rights-based approach provides hardly any justification for the mandatory purchase provision. If takeovers enlarge the opportunities of the target shareholders as they are considered as offers rather than threats, mandatory purchase provisions cannot be justified. Even from the perspective of the remaining target shareholders, mandatory purchase provisions may reduce their contractual opportunities as the heavy burden of the provision on the acquirer could result in few takeovers ex ante. Ex post, mandatory purchase provisions may be viewed as offers to particular offeree shareholders in the target as they can choose either to sell their shares to the acquirer with the premium or to remain in the target and expect the improvement of the target by the acquirer. Mandatory purchase provisions, however, are certainly threats to the shareholders in the acquiring company. If takeovers through control transactions do not create third party effects of coercion on the remaining shareholders in the target it is not clear why the freedom of contract between the acquirer and part of the shareholders in the target should be restrained at the expense of the minority shareholders in the acquiring company by a mandatory purchase obligation.

It is often argued that the absence of the rule would permit the acquirer to put pressure on those to whom private or market offers are made to purchase shares which will give the acquirer control.[69] The following statement describes this: 'I offer you an attractive price for your shares. If you do not accept it now, you may lose the benefit of the offer and, in addition, find that your shares have declined in value because I will be prepared to make only a lower offer (or not at all) once I have obtained control of the company.'[70] In a jurisdiction where two-tier bids are outlawed and assuming takeover transactions are efficient in most cases, it is not clear why the share price will decline significantly. In other words, the above statement is purely arbitrary. Further, the pressure generated by takeover offers can be dealt with by the requirement of independent advice to shareholders, provisions on the minimum offer period and shareholders' withdrawal rights to facilitate takeover auctions.

It is also argued that permitting the acquisition of control over the whole of the company's assets by purchasing only a proportion of the company's shares would encourage transfers of control to those likely to exploit the private benefits of corporate control rather than make the most efficient use of the corporate assets.[71] The above statement is neither supported by empirical evidence nor consistent with corporate law. I have already provided empirical evidence that most takeovers enhance efficiency. Further, corporate law never prohibits the control of corporate assets by having a controlling proportion of shares. Therefore, the mandatory purchase provision cannot be supported on this ground. For instance, after any possible 'going private' transaction following the mandatory purchase, the target is still entitled to go public again. Any abuse of the rights of minority shareholders can be protected by the general corporate law. Obviously, the mandatory purchase provision cannot permanently ensure that shareholders in the target are not abused.

The autonomy value provides little support for the mandatory purchase provision. The welfare value would also object to the mandatory purchase provision. Mandatory purchase provisions increase the cost of acquiring the control of target companies. The harmful effects of the mandatory purchase provision are obvious. In the first place, mandatory purchase provisions may reduce the number of offers by making targets more expensive to acquire. According to the economic law of demand, the higher the price, the lower the demand from purchasers. Lower demand in the context of takeovers means fewer takeovers, hence, possibly a reduction of wealth in society. Second, the philosophy of sharing the gains from takeover transactions contained in the mandatory purchase provision reduces the return of investment on the part of the acquirer. The inability of acquirers to appropriate the full value of their investment will lead them to undertake too few takeovers. This is the classic public good problem.[72] The proper management of an inefficient target company is a public good to all the shareholders of the target. Grossman and Hart have pointed out that there are significant costs in ensuring that directors/managers act in the interest of the shareholders.[73] If one shareholder (acquirer) devotes resources to improving management, then all the shareholders benefit.[74] The mandatory purchase provision exacerbates the externality problem by allowing the remaining shareholders of the target company to share equal gains from takeovers. This severe externality problem indicates that it cannot be assumed that a company which is not being run in the interests of shareholders will always be vulnerable to a takeover bid. The declining number of takeovers in the 1990s in the USA after the adoption of anti-takeover legislation in most of the states warrants public attention. An antidote to this externality problem is to exclude the remaining shareholders in the target from sharing equal gains[75] resulting from takeovers ex post, and is hence an argument for abolishing the mandatory purchase provision at least at the low threshold of 30 per cent or to allow them to share the premium at a discount of the control transfer premium.

The support of either a higher threshold of mandatory takeover offers or the sharing of a low premium in takeover offers can be found in the takeover laws of many countries. The Swiss law permits shareholders, by provisions in the company's constitution, to raise the triggering percentage from one-third to up to 49 per cent or to display the obligation entirely.[76] Article 187(4) of the Portuguese Securities Code also permits the constitutions of unlisted companies to raise the mandatory bid threshold to 50 per cent.[77] Austrian law sets the takeover price at the higher of either the average market price of the securities in the preceding six months or 85 per cent of the highest price paid by the acquirer for the shares in the previous 12 months.[78] Swiss law goes even further by requiring only that the offer be at not less than the higher of the market price when the bid is made or 75 per cent of the highest price paid for the shares by the acquirer over the previous 12 months.[79]

46

To understand how the imported takeover law adjusts to China's local conditions, we need to understand the ownership structure of the listed companies on the two stock exchanges. As discussed previously in section two, the development of China's corporate law and the establishment of the stock market at the beginning of the 1990s were closely related to the reform of the state-owned enterprises.

The shareholding structure in most listed Chinese companies examined in section two makes it impossible for an acquiring company to accumulate control through buying shares on any stock exchange. So far, there has been no successful acquisition of control of a listed company by purchasing shares on the stock market. To acquire sufficient percentage of shares in a target listed company, instead, requires the purchase of part of the non-traded shares owned by the state or other companies. This makes the negotiated takeover the preferred method of takeover in China. Under this method, an acquiring company negotiates with a majority or block shareholder and enters into a share transfer agreement with that shareholder in the target listed company.

Negotiated takeovers in China, however, have to overcome some procedural and legal hurdles. On the procedural side, acquiring state shares or legal person shares of state-owned enterprises requires approval by the relevant authority. Article 29 of the Provisional Measures on the Administration of state-owned Shares of Joint Stock Companies provides that the transfer of state-owned shares needs the approval of the State Asset Administration Commission and the provincial government.[80] Transferring more than 30 per cent of the state-owned shares in a listed company requires the joint approval of the State Asset Administration Commission and the State Economic Restructuring Commission.[81] The approval procedure is consistent with the goal of the government to maintain control of the large state-owned enterprises on the stock market.

In addition to overcoming this procedural hurdle, negotiated takeovers have to comply with the requirement of the mandatory purchase provision, which is central to the London City Code. The cost of following such a mandatory purchase provision is well recognized by regulators in China.[82] The practice of dealing with negotiated takeovers and the adjustment of the English-style takeover law to the Chinese takeover market reflect the concern that strictly following the mandatory purchase provision is inefficient.

The first negotiated takeover took place in 1994 under the early takeover regime. Hengtong Investment Ltd (Hengtong) was incorporated in Zuhai in 1981.[83] Focusing on real estate development, Hengtong has also developed into areas of shipping, communications, textile and electronic products. To market its electricity meters in Shanghai, Hengtong planned to acquire a property development company in Shanghai. Search efforts revealed that Shanghai Lingguang Ltd (Lingguang), which produces glass and electronic components, was a suitable target. Lingguang issued 33.8 million shares in total. Among all the

47

issued shares, Shanghai Construction Ltd held 55.26 per cent of the shares on behalf of the state while individual investors and legal person investors accounted for 32.55 per cent and 11.89 per cent of the shares respectively. Shortly before the transfer of control, the price of the shares of Lingguang was trading around 13 yuan per share on the secondary market. Hengtong's motivations in acquiring a controlling block of Lingguang shares were twofold: (1) mainly to rely on Shanghai Construction Ltd's connection with the property market in Shanghai, and (2) partly to take advantage of Lingguang's technology. The deal was encouraging news to Lingguang and Shanghai Construction Ltd based on the information available then as Lingguang was short of funds to carry out ambitious development projects. An agreement was reached among Hengtong, Shanghai Construction Ltd, and Lingguang to transfer 35.5 per cent of the shares held by Shanghai Construction Ltd to Hengtong at the price of 4.3 yuan on 28 April 1994. Transferring more than 30 per cent of the shares of a target, however, triggers the mandatory purchase provision. To avoid the high cost of mandatorily purchasing the rest of the Lingguang shares, Hengtong applied to China Securities Regulatory Commission (CSRC) for an exemption from the mandatory purchase requirement. The CSRC granted its permission mainly on the ground that the transferred shares were non-trading state-owned shares.[84]

The Hengtong case raises a number of questions. Could the CSRC approve the transfer price of 4.3 yuan when the shares held by individuals and traded on the secondary stock market were around 13 yuan? Is the significant discount on the controlling shareholding able to ensure that the productive resources of the target would move towards a more efficient purchaser? Another question is the legal ground that the CSRC gave the exemption from the mandatory purchase obligation when the ITS contains no legal provision which could confer that discretion to the CSRC. The lack of legal provisions of course did not constrain the CSRC when the rule of law is not deeply entrenched in China. Finally, should China follow the US approach by exempting transfer of control through an agreement under the need for a protection test[85] if it is well recognized that the cost of following the English mandatory purchase provision is too high?

Later development of the takeover law partially addressed the issues which arose from Hengtong. The Securities Law[86] modifies the mandatory purchase provision and deliberately gives the CSRC the discretion to exempt acquirers from following the mandatory purchase requirement if they acquire shares through any stock exchange.[87] The modified mandatory purchase provision now provides that if an investor holds 30 per cent of the issued shares of a listed company and continues to buy such shares through a stock exchange, the investor shall make a takeover offer to all the shareholders of the target listed company.[88] The Securities Law seems to make a difference with respect to negotiated takeovers. Article 89 of the Securities Law stipulates:

48

In the case of takeover by agreement, the acquirer may execute the equity transfer by entering into an agreement with shareholders of the target company as prescribed in laws and administrative regulations.

When a listed company is taken over by agreement, the acquirer must, within three days after the agreement is reached, submit a written report on the takeover agreement to the State Council's securities regulatory authority and the stock exchange, and make an announcement.

The above article seems to be based on the need for the protection test in US securities regulations on the grounds that sophisticated investors do not need the protection of law when selling shares.[89] It is relatively clear that the article does not expressly compel the acquirer to make an offer to all the shareholders in a negotiated takeover. Nor does the article require the acquirer to obtain approval from the CSRC for such a negotiated takeover except for compliance to the reporting and announcement requirements. The article seems to recognize the high cost of the mandatory purchase provision and the need for a corporate control market to improve the inefficient state-owned listed companies. This article, however, has not been used in that way. The CSRC's position is that, whatever the method of acquiring control, the mandatory purchase provision must be complied with unless it has granted the acquirer an exemption. This position is consistent with how negotiated takeovers are normally performed in China. By the end of 2000, all the 121 negotiated takeovers had followed the pattern of Hengtong in that an exemption was obtained from the CSRC.[90]

As discussed previously, most of China's state-owned enterprises on the stock market are not very efficient. A study has found that there is a negative correlation between firm performance and the percentage of state-owned shares.[91] Empirical evidence in another study also suggests that takeovers in China are largely efficient compared with the status of many companies before the takeover although the market could be more efficient overall if ideological issues were properly dealt with.[92]

The inefficiency of the state-owned listed companies and the need for an active takeover market to facilitate the reallocation of productive resources requires that China modify the English-style takeover law in the Chinese takeover environment. This objective has led the CSRC to reconsider its position on negotiated takeovers. In 2002, the CSRC issued the Procedures on the Administration of the Takeover of Listed Companies (Takeover Procedures).[93] While the Takeover Procedures reaffirm the position of the CSRC that, whatever the method of acquiring more than 30 per cent of the shares in a target listed company, the mandatory purchase requirement must be complied with unless exemption from the CSRC is obtained,[94] the Takeover Procedures have provided numerous grounds upon which the CSRC is prepared to grant an exemption.

49

Among the exceptions some are related to debt restructuring and insolvency reorganization. For instance, an exemption will be given if the transfer of shares is applied for on the basis of a court ruling and results in the percentage of shares held or controlled by the purchaser exceeding 30 per cent of the listed company's issued shares.[95] An exemption will also be provided if a bank engaging in normal business has acquired more than 30 per cent of the issued shares of a listed company but the bank has no intention or taken no action to actually control such a listed company and has made arrangements to transfer the excess shares to non-affiliated parties.[96] The exemption on insolvency is provided to an acquirer which is taking over a listed company in financial distress in order to rescue it and has proposed a feasible restructuring plan.[97]

Other exceptions are based on the ground that no shareholder in a target listed company has received any takeover premium. An example is where an acquirer has accumulated more than 30 per cent of the shares of a listed company resulting from the company's issuance of new shares.[98] Another exception is if the acquisition of more than 30 per cent of the issued shares of a listed company is caused by the reduction of the company's capital.[99]

In the past, the CSRC frequently gave exemptions if the administrative transfer of state-owned shares had caused the transferee to hold or control more than 30 per cent of the issued shares of a listed company. This exemption is still kept.[100] Finally, the Takeover Procedures have added a catch-all provision, giving the CSRC the discretion to exempt the mandatory purchase provision if the CSRC considers it necessary to meet the needs of the development and changes of the securities market and the need to protect the legitimate rights and interests of investors.[101] The transfer of control through administrative means as practised in the past has made the mandatory purchase provision largely irrelevant. If the catch-all provision is also liberally used, the mandatory purchase provision will also be made partly irrelevant.

The discussion of the adjustment of the English-style mandatory purchase provision clearly shows that application of the provision in China is path dependent. The political goal of maintaining control of the state-owned listed companies has completely changed the rationale of using such a provision. The past socialist system of public ownership of the means of production created interested parties which controlled both the political and economic resources. These interested parties will try to protect their vested rights and interests. An easier way of continuing their control is to maintain the control of the large state-owned listed companies to serve ideological purposes. The insistence of this political goal requires a different way of using the law of takeovers. I echo the view of Art and Gu that China's developing securities market can be properly understood only in the context of its underlying motivation, by carefully avoiding the mistake of assuming that adoption of Western-style structures and laws implies movement toward Western goals.[102]

If we take the ex ante efficiency view discussed previously, the adjustment of the imported takeover law is very positive in the sense of achieving the primary goal of improving the large number of inefficiently run state-owned listed companies. Another positive use of the English-style takeover law is the adoption of the position of non-frustration on the part of the directors in a target listed company when facing a takeover offer.[103] Article 33 of the Takeover Procedures provides that the decisions made, and measures taken by the directors, supervisors and senior management of the target company with respect to the takeover offer made by an acquirer may not prejudice the legitimate rights and interests of the company or its shareholders. More specifically, the said article prohibits the adoption of measures of issuing new shares or convertible bonds, the repurchase of its own shares, the amendment of articles of association, and the signing of contracts, which could have a major effect on the company's assets, liabilities, rights, interests or business outcomes except in the ordinary course of business, after an acquirer has announced its takeover intention.

In the USA, whether the board of directors or the shareholders should be given the ultimate power to decide whether the corporation should be sold to a bidder that offers to buy all of the corporation's shares at a substantial premium above the current stock market price is very controversial. Easterbrook and Fischel argue that the management should remain completely passive in the face of a takeover bid.[104] Their argument is based on the assumption that most takeovers are efficient in that they discipline incumbent managers in the target. When incumbent managers are facing a takeover bid which tends to remove them, it is unlikely that their action of defeating the takeover will be for the best interest of the corporation.[105] Bebchuk argues that, once mechanisms to ensure undistorted shareholder choice are in place, boards should not be permitted to block offers beyond the period necessary for putting together alternatives for shareholder consideration.[106] In contrast, Lipton argues against a regime of shareholder voting with no board veto.[107] According to Lipton, there are significant costs to corporations in being managed as if they were constantly for sale.[108]

The Delaware General Corporation Law (DGCL) takes a middle ground. The DGCL gives the board of directors a central role in corporate decision-making,[109] but it also requires stockholder assent for many fundamental transactions.[110] The DGCL is, however, silent on the most contentious question in the debate: in what circumstances, and to what extent, are directors empowered to prevent shareholders from accepting a tender offer? The Delaware judicial view also follows the middle ground. While in principle, Delaware case law holds that the purpose of the corporation is to maximize the wealth of its stockholders,[111] Delaware decisions also give directors substantial authority to deploy the powerful weapon of a poison pill[112] and to block takeover offers that appear to be in the best interests of the current array of stockholders.[113] The

Delaware courts, however, have subjected defensive measures to a heightened form of judicial review under which directors must prove the reasonableness and good faith of their actions.[114] The result is a regime in which directors are given substantial authority to forge corporate strategies while leaving room for stockholders to vote down management-preferred directors and to use the election process to avail themselves of a tender offer.[115]

The adoption of the English-style mandatory purchase provision at the beginning of the 1990s has educated regulators in China relatively well on other parts of the London City Code. When the CSRC issued the Takeover Procedures in 2002, it again chose the English position of non-frustration over the Delaware type of takeover law on the proper role of the target board when the target is facing a takeover offer. The choice is largely satisfactory for China. There are at least two reasons. First, Delaware law is very complicated. At this stage, regulators and judges in China are still not sophisticated in takeover law. To expect them to administer the Delaware type of takeover law when even the judges in other parts of the USA are not able to do it well is likely to be counterproductive. Second, directors in the USA are subject to greater constraints by very strict fiduciary duties, derivative suits and various market mechanisms which are not available in China.[116]

While the adoption of the English-style takeover law and the adjustment of the law in China are in the right direction, negotiated takeover transactions have a serious defect. As discussed previously, only shares held by individuals in listed companies are traded on the two stock exchanges. State shares and legal person shares of state-owned enterprises are not traded on the stock exchanges. This raises the issue of pricing the control block of state-owned shares. In the Hengtong case, the control block was priced at 4.3 yuan per share when the shares traded at the stock exchange were around 13 yuan per share.[117] The Opinions Concerning the Exercise of State-owned Shares in Joint Stock Companies[118] dictate that the lowest transfer price of state-owned shares is the net asset value per share.[119] In Hengtong and all the other cases before 2004 when the control block of state-owned shares was transferred, the price of the shares of the block was several times lower than the price of the shares traded on the stock market. In a few cases, even the requirement of the lowest transfer price of net asset value per share was not followed.[120] The practice of negotiated takeovers in China also provides an indication as to why the mandatory purchase provision, which is central to the London City Code, is not followed in China. The mandatory purchase provision is based on the premise that the acquirer has to extend the same premium to all other shareholders if it buys shares at a price higher than the market price from the majority, block or some shareholders, who are more likely to get the benefits because of their position. This ensures the equality of treatment of all shareholders in the target. In China, when the control block is priced at a much lower price than the market price of other shares traded on the stock market, the mandatory purchase provision has lost its rationale. Obviously, the CSRC and the Government are more interested in the facilitation of the reallocation of the productive resources of state-owned listed companies. The interest of the minority shareholders is to a large extent ignored. This again leads to the conclusion that the political goal of maintaining the control of state-owned listed companies has made the imported law considerably irrelevant. While not following the mandatory purchase provision can be justified on efficiency grounds, cheap transfers of control blocks in China has left minority shareholders with inadequate protection.

In the USA and United Kingdom, the concern of takeover law is to ensure the minority shareholders a premium over the market price if the acquirer gains control by offering the outgoing shareholder(s) in the target a price higher than the market price. Because of the benefits of control, the price of the controlling block is normally higher than the price of the shares of a target on the secondary market. The higher price of the controlling block is a basic market mechanism to protect the minority shareholders in that only those who are able to manage the target better can obtain control given the constraints. There might be mistakes in prediction or judgement on the part of the acquirer and the effect of a takeover may be disastrous. The market in the long run will correct the mistake. The cheap transfer of control in China, however, is not able to ensure that acquirers are necessarily better than the existing target management. Furthermore, the discounted share price of the control block creates serious risks of exploitation of minority shareholders. Recently, the State Asset Administration Commission and the Ministry of Finance jointly issued the Provisional Measures on the Administration of the Transfer of State-owned Shares in January 2004 (Provisional Measures).[121] The Provisional Measures now permit but do not compel the use of auctions or biddings in takeovers in addition to negotiated takeovers. Similar to other administrative rules, however, these Provisional Measures are more interested in ensuring that the state-owned assets are not depleted in low priced transfers of control to private enterprises rather than liberalizing the control of SOEs.

While auctions and biddings in takeovers will alleviate the problem of cheap transfers of control in listed companies in China, the move towards an efficient takeover market requires a radical reform over the large-scale exits of state-owned enterprises in many sectors of the economy. state-owned enterprises are unlikely to be efficient. As Trebilcock has persuasively argued, there are inadequate means to motivate the agents in state-owned enterprises and there are inadequate means to discipline such agents in state-owned companies compared with the means available to private-sector firms.[122] If the governments are not pursuing the political goal of maintaining the control of the large listed companies, it is more likely to have a competitive takeover market where private-sector companies are able to join the competition in acquiring control

53

over some large state-owned listed companies. The involvement of private-sector companies will significantly increase opportunities for takeovers of inefficiently run state-owned listed companies. The recent case where two foreign trans-national companies bid for control over Harbin Brewery on China's takeover market provides a very good example.[123] In that case, not only was the price of takeover 50 times the earnings of Harbin Brewery in 2003, but also the competing bidders were making a takeover bid for 100 per cent of the shares in the target company. It must be acknowledged that this was a very exceptional case. Only when the governments are serious in exiting from most listed companies will the regulators pay more attention to the protection of rights and interests of the minority shareholders in listed companies in China. To realize the goal of achieving efficiency through corporate law in general and takeover law in particular, the Chinese government must abandon the concept of controlling the state-owned listed companies for the purpose of political control. Only then can the law of takeover fully realize its efficiency goal of disciplining inefficient managers and realizing synergy gains. Currently, the use of English-style takeover law does not satisfactorily achieve the goal of improving upon the inefficiency of SOEs.

WEAK ENFORCEMENT OF THE LAW ON SECURITIES FRAUD

In a market economy, private companies compete for scarce financial resources. They obtain capital either through retained earnings or from the capital markets through new equity or debt investment. In a relatively efficient capital market, the cost of capital formation is lower for companies with strong corporate governance than for com-panies with weak corporate governance. Competitive discipline requires a company not to waste resources; if it does, retained earnings will disappear and new investment will not be forthcoming. An efficient capital market not only requires the law to deal with abuse but also requires the credibility of the threat of using the law to deal with abuse.

In contrast, state-owned enterprises do not face a 'hard' budget constraint.[124] Rather, governments have access to capital through their taxation powers and may use those monies to fund operations, even if those operations would not survive in a private setting.[125] Megginson and Netter have pointed out that the risk of using the taxation powers is present when governments supply goods and services directly or through the vehicle of SOEs.[126] The lack of discipline upon the SOEs in the capital market is another reason why SOEs are far less motivated and efficient than private companies.

As discussed in section two, China's stock market was mainly designed at the beginning of the 1990s to solve the inefficiency of SOEs. That is why the state-owned listed companies dominate the two stock exchanges.[127] This section will explain that China's SOEs enjoyed the privilege of using the stock market as another form of the soft budget constraint. As long as SOEs do not have to compete with other private-sector or foreign companies for capital on the stock market, it is unlikely that they will have the same motivation to maximize profits. When the stock market is also used to achieve the political goal that the governments will maintain the control of the large SOEs in many sectors of the economy, it is unlikely that the Western style of securities regulation will be strictly enforced. This section will also explain that if a public framework of accountability cannot be developed to deal with abuses in state-owned companies, it is doubtful whether such a system can be developed in a cost effective way to curb abuses in private-sector companies on the market.

CASES OF SECURITIES FRAUD

Chengdu Hong Guang Industrial Ltd (Hong Guang)

In 1996, Hong Guang applied to the China Securities Regulatory Commission (CSRC) for the listing of its shares.[128] Despite the fact that the corporation suffered a loss of 103 million yuan, the corporation claimed that it had a profit of 54 million yuan. Falsification of its profit record also occurred in 1997 and 1998 after its shares were listed. In addition to covering the huge losses it suffered, Hong Guang used 34.3 per cent of the capital raised (140 million yuan) to buy and sell shares on the stock market by itself and through a securities company. As speculative trading by state-owned enterprises and listed companies was prohibited,[129] the speculative trading of shares was carried out through the opening of 228 individual trading accounts. As a matter of fact, Hong Guang only used 16.5 per cent of the capital for the projects described in the prospectus. Most of the capital raised was actually used by the company to pay its debts to banks both at home and abroad. After investigation, CSRC confiscated the illegal trading profits of 4.5 million yuan derived from speculative trading, imposed an administrative fine of one million yuan, and permanently prohibited the chairman of the board of directors, the general manager, and the deputy financial officer from assuming senior officer positions in listed companies or securities institutions. Subsequently, the Intermediate People's Court of Chengdu sentenced these three people for a jail term of three years or less.[130] While this was the first case where criminal liability was imposed on responsible persons in listed companies, the court refused to hold a trial for the claim of civil liability. Even though the fraud would be a clear case of tort of deceit in well-developed common law juris-dictions and civil liability can also be grounded on Article 77 of the Provisional Regulation on the Administration of Issuing and Trading of Shares[131] and Article 63 of the Securities Law,[132] the Court justified its decision on the ground that the loss suffered by investors was not necessarily caused by the fraud.[133] It is not clear whether criminal liability would have been imposed had the responsible persons not used the raised money for speculative trading (a purely personal act compared with the raising of funds for the company).

Energy 28

Energy 28[134] falsely claimed to have a profit of 16 million yuan at the time of its application for share listing and a total profit of 211 million yuan during the three years thereafter. Furthermore, the company changed the use of funds as specified in the prospectus in 1996 and in the documents for additional issue of shares in 1997. The CSRC imposed an administrative fine of 1 million yuan on the company, 50,000 yuan upon the chairman of the board of direc-tors, and 30,000 yuan upon three other directors. There were neither criminal proceedings nor civil lawsuits instituted in this case.

Sanjiu Medical and Pharmaceutical Co. Ltd (Sanjiu)

During an investigation conducted by the CSRC in June 2001 the CSRC discovered that the controlling shareholder of Sanjiu improperly used a total of 2.5 billion yuan of the funds of Sanjiu, accounting for 96 per cent of the net assets of Sanjiu.[135] The board of directors and the supervisory board of Sanjiu did not prevent the use of such a large amount of the listed company's funds by the controlling shareholder for a connected transaction. Except for public criticism by the CSRC, no shareholders' action was taken against the con-trolling shareholder in this case. Lack of clear provisions on derivative actions by shareholders makes it very difficult for individual shareholders to sue the wrongdoers who violate provisions in either the Company Law or in the Articles of Association of Listed Companies.[136] Improper use of funds by listed companies also occurred in Hubei Meierya Co. Ltd (Meierya).[137] In that case, the controlling shareholder improperly used the amount of 368 million yuan belonging to Meierya, accounting for 41 per cent of the net assets of Meierya. It does not appear from the report that either the board of directors of Meierya or the shareholders of Meierya legally authorized the use of fund.

These cases in China provide strong evidence that managers are not working for the best interests of the residual claimants. They had cheated the investors of money at the time of listing via falsification of the profit records (the case of Hong Guang). The strategy of using a false profit record is also adopted for the purpose of subsequent distribution of shares after the company has become a listed company (the case of Energy 28). The controlling shareholders' abuse of the funds of the listed company in the case of Sanjiu and Meierya shows the lack of consideration on the part of controlling shareholders for the interests of the minority shareholders. A Chinese way of vividly describing the cheating of capital suppliers by the insiders (managers and controlling shareholders) is 'quanqian' (circling money).

The Chinese government has tried to get rid of the problem of the soft budget constraint in that the state-owned banks cannot tighten the credit provided to SOEs. This has created problems for those SOEs which are not well-managed. The use of the stock market is expected to provide the necessary funds so that some symbolic large state-owned listed companies can survive while subjecting them to some stock market disciplines. From an agency perspective, when managers and directors in SOEs are not motivated to pursue the clear goal of profit maximization and are not subject to hard budget constraints if their companies are not efficiently run, they will seek personal gains. The above cases have provided good examples. The cases also reveal another important point that the political goal of maintaining some symbolic large listed SOEs requires the continuous supply of capital. If the past problem was that state-owned banks could not tighten the credit on inefficient SOEs, the current problem is that the governments cannot tighten the supply of capital on the stock market. If capital markets cannot penalize inefficient SOEs because of political concerns, it is unlikely that corporate law and securities regulation including civil remedies will be strictly enforced. The evidence that the courts are more willing to impose criminal penalties on higher level managers in state-owned listed companies than civil compensation provides some support of my argument. I will canvass this issue further in the next part.

Weak enforcement of securities regulation

Since the establishment of the Shanghai Stock Exchange in 1990 and the Shenzhen Stock Exchange in 1991,[138] the stock market in China has developed relatively quickly. By the end of 2000 there were 1,211 corporations listed domestically and internationally.[139] In December 2000, 30 per cent of the capital of corporations was raised on the stock market as compared with the 10 per cent figure in 1993.[140] The capitalization of the stock market is 57 per cent of the gross domestic products.[141] This is very puzzling considering the weak protection of minority shareholders. The high savings rate and lack of alternative investment channels explain why the stock market in China could develop quickly even though investors were frequently cheated. Measured by the criterion of whether corporations assure a reasonable return to the suppliers of capital, the corporate governance system in China requires considerable improvement.

The weak protection of minority shareholders is caused by several factors. In the first place, criminal prosecution is rarely instituted for misrepresentation cases. Although the Company Law[142] and the Provisional Regulation on the Issuance and Trading of Shares (ITS)[143] do not contain clear provisions on criminal liability for misstatements in disclosure documents, the Decision on the Punishment of Crimes in Violation of the Company Law (Decision)[144] provides that if a company issues shares or corporate bonds with a falsified prospectus, subscription forms, or corporate bond distribution documents, thereby raising huge amounts of capital and causing serious consequences or other serious events, the persons directly responsible shall be sentenced for a term of less than five years and/or subject to a criminal penalty of 5 per cent of the amount raised.[145] A similar provision was subsequently incorporated into the 1997 Criminal Act.[146] Despite such a clear provision and numerous cases of misrepresentation, the first case where criminal liability was imposed on three directors occurred only in 2000.[147]

Second, the civil liability regime is not only poorly framed but also enforcement is weak. Compared with the relatively clear provisions on criminal liability, there are only a few major provisions on civil liability. Article 77 of the ITS stipulates that anyone who violates the ITS and causes losses to others shall bear civil liability according to the law.[148] Since four types of misconduct, covering misrepresentation, insider trading, market manipulation, and fraud committed by securities intermediaries against customers are regulated by the ITS, it is very difficult for judges who are not sophisticated and do not have law-making power to apply such a vague provision to deal with civil liabilities when capital users or intermediaries deliberately or negligently mislead investors through disclosure documents. Because of this reason, Article 77 of the ITS has not been used to hold any defendant civilly liable for misrepresentation. The Securities Law[149] provides in Article 63 that if the prospectus, documents of offer of corporate bonds, financial or accounting reports, listing documents, annual reports, mid-term reports or ad hoc reports distributed by the issuer or distributing securities company contain a falsehood, misleading statement or major omission and thereby cause investors to sustain losses in the course of securities trading, the issuer or distributing securities company shall be liable for damages and the responsible directors, supervisors and/or the managers of the issuer or distributing securities company shall be jointly and severally liable for damages. While Article 63 catches issuing companies and underwriters both for negligent statements and fraudulent statements made in these relevant disclosure

58

documents, Article 202 provides the ground for civil liabilities in connection with fraudulent misstatements produced by intermediaries. Article 202 provides, among other things, that 'if a professional organization that issues documents such as audit reports, asset valuation reports or legal opinions for the issuance or listing of securities or for securities trading activities' provides false certification and causes losses to investors, the professional organization shall bear liability.[150] The article further stipulates that if the fraud results in losses to investors, the intermediary shall bear joint liability. There are at least two problems with Article 202. First, fraudulent misrepresentation is difficult to prove in practice. A better approach is to add negligent misrepresentation as grounds for holding the intermediaries civilly liable. Second, there is no need to always hold the intermediaries jointly liable for damages as provided at the end of the article. They should also be independently liable to pay civil damages for their own negligence, particularly when the issuer has no fault. Leaving aside the problems in Article 202, the civil liabilities for negligent misrepresentation provided in Article 63 are relatively clear. By the end of 2002, however, there had not been a single case where an issuer had borne civil liability despite the large number of cases of negligent or fraudulent misrepresentation.

In the Hong Guang case discussed previously, the First Intermediate People's Court of Chengdu in the Province of Sichuan sentenced several directors to three years' imprisonment or other criminal penalties.[151] Investors in this case also instituted civil actions, claiming for damages on the grounds of misrepresentation. The first person who brought a lawsuit was Jiang.[152] The District People's Court of Pudong, however, did not accept his case, explaining that the case did not fall within the scope of acceptance.[153] Civil lawsuits were also instituted in several courts in the similar case of 'Yin Guang Xia'.[154] While many courts refused to accept cases of misrepresentation, a court in Wuxi originally planned to entertain a similar lawsuit.[155] Shortly after the acceptance of the case by the court in Wuxi, the Supreme People's Court instructed all courts not to accept civil cases related to securities fraud, insider trading and market manipulation.[156] Upon receiving the Notice, the Wuxi Court suspended the treatment of the case. The Notice of the Supreme People's Court invited a great deal of criticism over that matter.[157] Four months later, the Supreme People's Court circulated another notice to the lower courts, instructing them to accept civil suits related to misrepresentation in disclosure documents.[158] In this subsequent Notice, the Supreme People's Court conditioned the acceptance of civil lawsuits upon investigation and punishment of the wrongdoer by the CSRC.[159] Further to that, even though the 1991 PRC Civil Procedure Law contains provisions that allow it,[160] the Supreme People's Court states that no class actions should be allowed as class actions are not deemed 'appropriate' in securities cases.[161] Although the Supreme People's Court subsequently issued a relatively detailed judicial opinion,[162] up to the end of 2004, there had been no

59

court judgment requiring an issuer who had committed securities fraud to pay large sums of damages to hundreds and thousands of small investors.

In addition to the weak enforcement of criminal and civil provisions, lack of shareholders' remedies is another factor contributing to the weak corporate governance system in China. Neither the Company Law nor the Securities Law contains any provision which gives the shareholders the right to bring actions derivatively against corporate directors or managers for their wrongful activities. Evidence in the USA shows that lawsuits are more common in firms more likely to need monitoring and that the probability of CEO turnover increases after a lawsuit is filed.[163]

Japan's experience is also helpful. In October 1993, Japan's Commercial Code was revised to reduce the fees required to file a derivative lawsuit.[164] Since then derivative lawsuits have increased by five times.[165] Japanese managers have also heightened their awareness of their duties to corporations and their shareholders.[166] Law reform in China is also necessary in order to facilitate shareholders' derivative actions. This is particularly so when most of the listed companies in China are majority-controlled. Among the 1,124 listing companies in April 2001, 79 per cent of the listed companies were controlled by a shareholder who owned more than 50 per cent of the shares.[167] In 65 per cent of the listed companies, the state shareholding dominates.[168] This further indicates that insiders control most of these listed companies. Without the threat of derivative actions, the interest of minority shareholders is unlikely to be well protected.

Still another factor contributing to the weak protection of minority shareholders is the low quality of certification by intermediaries. When companies which raise capital cannot be trusted, third party certification plays an important role in solving the adverse selection problem.[169] Third parties here include investment banks, accounting firms, and securities counsel. The principal role of securities intermediaries is to vouch for disclosure quality and thereby reduce information asymmetry in the securities markets.[170] The system of third party certification works well, however, only when the securities' intermediaries are subject to constraints. Some of the constraints include self-regulation, a licensing system, civil liability to investors, and criminal liability.

The role of self-regulatory organizations in China is currently too weak to curb serious securities fraud. The licensing system works better in China. The CSRC administers the licensing system. For securities companies (investment banks), a licence from the CSRC is required in order to carry out underwriting of share issues. Qualified accounting firms still need a licence jointly issued by the CSRC and the Ministry of Finance in order to do securities-related accounting. Over the last few years, the CSRC suspended the licenses of and penalized many securities companies and accounting firms. Due to the limited resources of the CSRC, however, many wrongdoers are unlikely to be caught. Under these circumstances, criminal liability and civil liability are needed to deter false certification. By the end of September 2002, there had not been a single case where an accounting firm or underwriter had been subject to criminal liability. As far as civil liability is concerned, holding accounting firms liable requires fraudulent misrepresentation to have taken place.[171] Since it is difficult to prove the intention of cheating, imposing civil liability on accounting firms will be far more difficult. Securities underwriters may also bear civil liability for misrepresentation as specified in the Securities Law.[172] In addition to the duty of verifying the truthfulness, accuracy and comprehensiveness of disclosure documents, securities underwriters are also responsible for determining the prices of shares distributed. Although it is relatively easy to find fault with securities underwriters as negligent misrepresentation or important omission gives rise to civil liability under Article 63 of the Securities Law, there is not a single case where a securities underwriter has been sued. The logic is simple. If issuers have rarely been held liable for the losses suffered by hundreds of thousands of investors, how can securities underwriters be held civilly liable for the losses suffered by investors? When securities intermediaries are not subject to adequate constraints, the role of third party certification is considerably weakened.

Section two has pointed out that China's stock market and the relevant laws were initially designed to improve upon the inefficient SOEs. If, at the time of enterprise reform, various governments knew that the SOEs were not efficiently managed and yet they urged these enterprises to go to the stock market for capital, it is unlikely that violations of imported Western-type of securities regulation will be heavily penalized. Strict enforcement of civil liability provisions is inconsistent with the political goal of the governments to maintain some symbolic large SOEs in key sectors of the economy as many SOEs would be denied the benefit of using the supply of capital on the stock market and became bankrupt. This explains the phenomenon of the soft budget constraint on China's capital market. It also partly explains the weak enforcement of the law, which is a cause of the defect of market institutions in China.

Some may argue that the weak enforcement of securities fraud law is no different compared with the weak enforcement of law in China in general. While this argument may be true to some extent, the government is under less political pressure to enforce cases of violation of intellectual property law or cases of violation of tax evasion. The weak enforcement of cases of securities fraud stands on a different ground. Others may argue that if there are political hurdles in enforcing the civil remedies against state-owned listed companies, there should be cases of applying the civil remedies against non-state-owned listed companies for securities frauds. This argument, however, would put the courts in a terrible position of discriminating between state- and non-state-owned listed companies and is unlikely to be adopted by the courts.

61

A public framework of accountability

While recognizing the benefits of privatization, Professor Minow has also pointed out some concerns.[173] One of the concerns is that privatization can undermine a value as basic as guarding against the misuse of public funds.[174] According to Minow, a shifting mix of public and private providers of education, welfare, and prison services requires a system of public accountability:

> Privatization of public services soared precisely when major corporations engaged in unfettered private self-dealing and one major religious group reeled from scandals, cover-ups, and mounting distrust among the faithful. The coincidence in timing should be all the reminder anyone needs of the vital role of public oversight and checks and balances.[175]

Professors Trebilcock and Iacobucci have already pointed out the fundamental problem with Minow's article.[176] Their view is that it is inadequate to move directly from making observations about flaws in private markets to drawing conclusions about the importance of maintaining public sector influence in various settings.[177]

The cases discussed in this section provide an interesting test ground. If a public framework of accountability works well, such a system should be relevant to Chinese SOEs in which governments are heavily involved. I will briefly discuss in the context of China why a public framework of accountability does not work well or cannot be easily established. As most listed SOEs in China only provide non-public goods, it is unnecessary to discuss in detail non-instrumental values like democracy, equality and pluralism.

Accountability in the public framework means being answerable to authority that can mandate desirable conduct and sanction conduct that breaches identified obligations.[178] More specifically, accountability includes the use of contracts when working with private enterprises to deliver social services. At a minimum, a public framework of accountability for these activities would disclose the facts surrounding the contracting process to the public.[179]

The distribution of shares of SOEs in China involves contractual arrangements with intermediaries, the disclosure of underwriters and the nature of the issuers. In order to issue shares to the public, issuers are required to contract with accounting firms and securities companies, both of which are mainly SOEs. When acting as securities underwriters, securities companies must examine the truthfulness, accuracy and completeness of the public offer documents.[180] If they find that such documents contain any falsehoods, misleading statements or major omissions, they may not carry out the sales activities.[181] Issuers are also required through contracts to have the financial and accounting reports of the company for the last three years verified by accounting firms.[182] Furthermore, issuers are required to disclose detailed information about themselves to the

CSRC and the public.[183] Despite these contractual arrangements and legal requirements, securities fraud in disclosing false or misleading information to the public persists as discussed.

Minow's second model of public accountability imposes constitutional obligation upon governments.[184] At least, these constitutional values are meant to guard against self-dealing or other conflicts of interest that arise when private parties are entrusted with public duties.[185] As part of the provision of non-public goods or services is carried out by SOEs in China, various rules against self dealing or other conflicts of interest are available. These rules include Party discipline, criminal liability and civil liability. Party rules require that members of the Chinese Communist Party (CPC) shall not seek special interest or privilege except within the scope of law or policy.[186] Violations of CPC rules may result in warnings, serious warnings, removal of the offender's position within the CPC, putting the violator onto a monitoring list while keeping CPC membership, and expelling the violator from the CPC.[187] To be sure, in a country always ruled by one party, the loss of party membership is a significant and real cost. In addition, the criminal law penalizes managers and directors whose misconduct relates to bribery,[188] competition with the company[189] and seeking gains for their own self interest or for friends.[190] Moreover, company law also prohibits or restricts self-dealing or conflicts of interest transactions.[191] Despite all these rules, connected transactions between parent companies and subsidiaries or between associated companies of SOEs are very frequent, harming the interest of minority shareholders. Statistics show that 84.6 per cent of the listed companies carried out connected transactions in 1997.[192] While personal gains-seeking in conflicts of interest transactions will be heavily penalized,[193] connected transactions between associated companies of SOEs rarely attract legal liability. This again shows the failure of public accountability relating to public involvement in the provision of goods and services in China.

A third model of accountability advocated by Minow is administration.[194] While it is not easy to specify the content of administration, the term requires the collection of information so that providers of goods or services can be properly chosen, assessed, and monitored.[195] The Chinese situation shows that Minow's approach is unlikely to be successful. In the early to mid-1990s, the Chinese government specified a quota[196] for the distribution of shares by issuers to ensure the quality of issuers and to control the speed of development of the stock market. To get a quota, potential issuers had to apply to provincial governments or ministries under the State Council for approval.[197] The locally selected companies then were to obtain further approval from the CSRC, which also consulted the then State Economic and Trade Commission and the State Development and Planning Commission.[198] Despite the heavy involvement of various governmental agencies, abuse of the process is widespread as discussed in the early part of this section.

The fourth legal model for public accountability advocated by Minow is democracy.[199] Democracy involves both the processes and values committed to governance by the people.[200] Disclosure of relevant information, accompanied by periodic occasions for the expression of public views on certain decisions and the standards set and used to assess them, would enhance democratic values.[201] While China never adopted any Western democratic form of government, the concept and system of socialism reflect a value of rule by the people. In a rigid socialist country, the means of production are all in the hands of the state. Employees or people in general are the masters of the country and its enterprises. Rational passivity and free-rider problem, however, lead people into the direction of irresponsibility. The vehicle of SOEs was originally intended to serve better the people who are the residual claimants of SOEs. The reality, however, does not reflect well the socialist ideal.

The wide spread of securities fraud in China's listed SOEs reveals the failure of a system of public accountability. It is a puzzle why a public framework of accountability along the lines advocated by Minow does not work in China or cannot be developed to better deal with the waste of public resources in SOEs. Trebilcock and Iacobucci also doubt whether public accountability mechanisms work to discipline public actors.[202] They conclude that the features that undermine the market often undermine the public provision of goods or services as well.[203]

If a public framework of accountability does not work well in the public provision of goods by using the vehicle of the SOE, it is doubtful whether such a public framework works to discipline private actors. At the very least, the imposition of legal accountability or other constraints on the private sector may entail costs in terms of reduced competition, innovation, and flexibility which may negate any advantage of private sector over public sector provisions.[204]

CONCLUSION

This chapter uses the example of takeovers and securities fraud to examine why the imported western style of takeover law or securities regulation cannot be fully enforced in China. The political goal of maintaining the control of a large number of state-owned listed companies appears to be a significant contributing factor, explaining why China cannot fully utilize the benefits of Western law in the establishment of a market oriented economy. If China wants to compete successfully in a globalized economy, the Chinese government has to consider seriously the issue of whether the government should withdraw or considerably reduce its ownership in the large number of state-owned listed companies. The two examples of takeover and securities fraud can be extended to other areas to show that the institutional defects in state-owned companies do not provide

64

adequate means to motivate managers and directors in these companies to work for the best interest of their companies nor does it provide adequate means to discipline the managers and directors if they do not work for the best interest of the companies they serve. During the transition from a planned economy to a market oriented economy, corporate governance is an important matter, particularly after China's accession to the WTO, within which China has to compete with other developed nations under similar background rules.

Chapter 3

The proper role of government in building a venture capital market

INTRODUCTION

The Coase theorem shows that under the condition of zero transaction costs,[1] the choice of institutions does not affect the ultimate outcome of economic activities between contractual parties. However, in the real world where transaction costs are not zero, different institutional arrangements would affect the results of transactions in different ways. Hence, it is important to take the arrangement of institutions seriously. Studies on institutional arrangements demonstrate that institutional arrangements could affect the benefits and costs of interested parties by changing their transaction costs through contractual arrangements. But what is institution? North tells us that institutions include any form of constraints worked out by human beings to reduce the uncertainty of human activities.[2] His concept of 'institution' includes formal constraints such as constitutions, laws and contractual arrangements, and informal constraints such as customs and traditional values. Obviously, governments play a crucial role in shaping institutions since it is the governments that create constraints such as the constitution, law and regulation.

Different institutional arrangements shape the performance of venture capital markets in different ways. There are two examples – the stock market oriented venture capital market in the USA and the bank oriented system in Germany and Japan. A venture capital market is a special investment system with its own regulations, infrastructure and specific contractual arrangements, etc., in which high and new technological enterprises in seed, start-up or other firms in early stages raise capital that cannot be raised from the traditional market, and in which venture capitalists who join the management of the portfolios expect to get a high return or be able to easily withdraw the capital from the portfolios. As developing venture capital markets can help promote the innovation and commercialization of high and new technology and improve a nation's competitiveness in the international market, the Chinese government has made serious efforts to accelerate its development of the venture capital market. As institutional arrangements would affect the outcome of transactions, a natural question is how the Chinese government should develop the proper institutions to speed up the development of its venture capital market.

This chapter discusses the economic significance of developing venture capital in China in section two. Section three provides a comparative study of the two major different venture capital systems in the world. Section four argues why an actively developed stock market is crucial to the development of venture capital markets. Based on the analysis of section three, section five uses the Wenzhou informal financial markets to show the negative effects of direct governmental investment in the venture capital market by the Chinese government. Section four explores further steps the Chinese government should take in developing its venture capital market.

ECONOMIC SIGNIFICANCE OF DEVELOPING A VENTURE CAPITAL MARKET

Venture capital investment involves complicated contractual arrangements between entrepreneurs and venture capitalists and between venture capitalists and fund providers. As there are very few restrictions imposed on venture capital investment in developed Western countries, it is difficult to clearly define what 'venture capital' is. Black and Gilson define venture capital as investment by special venture capital organizations in high-growth, high-risk, often high-technological firms that need capital to finance product development or growth and must, by the nature of their business, obtain this capital largely in the form of equity rather than debt.[3] In Chinese official documents, the following description is provided:

> Venture capital refers to investment acts whereby equity capital, management and consultancy services are provided mainly to high growth venture enterprises in the science and technology sector in the hope that medium to long term capital gains can be reaped through an equity transfer after the enterprise has developed and matured. The establishment of a venture capital mechanism . . . ; is conducive to accelerating technological innovation and the transformation of technological achievements. Such a system should be capable of integrating the promotion of technological progress carried out by firms in the economy with the financial support offered by the financial institutions. Its main components include investing entities, investment targets, means of capital withdrawal, intermediary service organizations, and a supervisory system.[4]

67

While a thorough understanding of the contractual relationship between fund providers and venture capitalists as well as between venture capitalists and entrepreneurs is essential for a better understanding of venture capital investment, this article does not try to explain these contractual relations, as other authors have thoroughly discussed them.[5]

Efficient venture capital markets can improve innovation and risk tolerance, which are the main elements of adaptive efficiency. Economists pay attention to adaptive efficiency in institutional change. North states:

> adaptive efficiency is concerned with the kinds of rules that shape the way an economy evolves through time. Adaptive efficiency also focuses on the willingness of society to acquire knowledge and learning, to induce innovation, to undertake risk and creative activity of all sorts, as well as to resolve problems and bottlenecks of the society through time.[6]

Venture capitalists focus on the entrepreneurs who can lead changes. Many entrepreneurs have made their innovations outside the confines of established enterprises or beyond the boundaries of existing industries.[7] As risk undertakers and catalysts, venture capitalists play a unique role in the process of creating societal wealth and an evolving economy[8] which, in turn, supports innovation. Obviously, facilitating venture capital markets enhances adaptive efficiency.

Since efficient venture capital markets can improve the adaptive efficiency of enterprises through investment in the start-up firms, they play a very important role in the growth of start-up firms. The importance of venture capital in the process of nurturing entrepreneurs and the establishment and growth of start-up firms is now widely accepted.[9] China also intends to improve its venture capital market. During the past few years, scientific and technological development in China has significantly contributed to the development of the national economy. However, the weak ability to convert the research results of science and technology into actual productive forces, the low degree of commercialization of high and new technology research results and the small number of high and new technology industries with their own intellectual property rights remain basically unchanged.[10] Major scientific research institutions still are affiliated with administrative organs, without an interlinked relationship with the national economy; qualified personnel exist largely in the scientific research institutions, but are relatively few in other entities.[11] Such conditions often hinder the innovation and commercialization of high technology. Under the increasingly severe competition on the international market, the lack of one's own technological innovation capabilities makes it difficult to ensure sustainable national economic development and national economic security. The establishment of a venture capital market and the promotion of commercialization of high and new technology research results are necessary for the implementation of the strategy of making the country prosperous through scientific education.[12] However, Chinese enterprises often encounter difficulties obtaining funding and financing. Yet, at the same time, banks in China have felt the burden and pressure resulting from the huge amount of unused household savings.[13] An efficient venture capital market can help solve the gap of capital shortage in nurturing enterprises while reducing the banks' pressure derived from the unused household savings.

The success of the US venture capital market actually helps the USA solve similar problems. In the USA venture capitalists have, to different extents, financially aided such firms as Microsoft, Intel, Lotus and Yahoo. These hi-tech enterprises are now household names that are known internationally. About 80 per cent of the high technological enterprises that are the mainstay of the US economy have been nurtured by venture capital. With their outstanding economic performance, these high technological enterprises, supported by venture capital have been the foundation stone of the New Economy of the USA.[14]

The success of the US venture capital market has drawn considerable attention and has been imitated by many other countries. Now venture capital has developed rapidly not only in North American but also in Europe and Asia.[15] In Japan, the government officials and other related circles call for the creation of a more active venture capital market to improve the international competitiveness of Japan.[16] To know how to improve the development of the venture capital market in China, it is useful to first look at the current venture capital models in the world. The next section examines the characteristics of the two major models of venture capital in the world.

COMPARATIVE STUDY OF TWO DISTINCTIVE VENTURE CAPITAL MODELS IN THE WORLD

In comparison to the venture capital markets of Japan and Germany, the venture capital market of the USA is far more developed. At the end of 1994, 591 venture capital funds in the USA had total investments worth US$34 billion.[17] In contrast to the USA, in Germany there were only 85 venture capital institutions with total investments of US$5.5 billion.[18] In the same year, 120 venture capital institutions in Japan had a total investment of US$10 billion.[19]

The fund structure of the US venture capital institutions greatly differs from that of Japan and Germany. In the USA in 1994, pension funds accounted for 46 per cent of the venture capital funds, endowments and foundations 21 per cent, banks and insurance companies 9 per cent, private individuals and families 9 per cent, other corporations 9 per cent and others 2 per cent.[20] In the same year, German venture capital organizations received the majority of their capital from

69

banks (55 per cent), insurance companies (12 per cent), other corporations (8 per cent), private individuals and families (8 per cent), government agencies (7 per cent) and others (10 per cent).[21] During 1993 and 1994, 24 per cent of the funds of venture capital in Japan came from banks, 15 per cent from insurance companies, 33 per cent from other corporations.[22]

Examining the above data will reveal that in Japan and Germany, the major fund providers of venture capital are banks. Because of the close relationship between banks and venture capital institutions in Japan and Germany (so-called bank oriented market of venture capital) venture capital investment in these two countries is more conservative than in the USA. In the USA in 1994, venture funds invested most heavily in software (20.75 per cent of total disbursements), medical and healthcare-related industries (14.4 per cent), consumer-related industries (10.5 per cent), telephone and data communication (10 per cent), and biotechnology (9.2 per cent).[23] In the same year, only 11 per cent of the funds of new venture capital went to high technological industries in Germany.[24] Venture capital funds of Japan in 1994 mainly went into the manufacturing, wholesale and retail sales and the service industries.[25]

Compared with Japan and Germany in which banks are the most important players for venture capital investment, the stock market plays a more important role in the financing of venture firms in the USA by creating a good exit for venture capital funds (stock market oriented venture capital). Between 1991 and 1996 there were 1,059 venture-capital-backed initial public offerings (IPOs) in the USA, as well as 466 firms exiting through the acquisition of the venture-capital-backed firms.[26] According to German data in 1995, venture funds exited from 264 venture-capital-backed firms through different ways. Among the 166 venture-capital-backed firms, venture capital exited through buy-back by entrepreneurs.[27] The exit of venture capital in the other 74 firms was by sale of the venture firm. Only 12 firms exited through IPOs,[28] and only one occurred on the domestic market.

In contrast, NASDAQ in the USA is nine times as big as a similar market in Japan.[29] In 1995 the number of IPOs in Japan was only one quarter of the number in the USA.[30] Further, in the USA, the start-up to IPO process takes 4–7 years on average; in Japan, similar process takes around 20–29 years.[31] Although there may be a difference in the data, a sanguine estimate is about 17 years.[32] In addition, 92 per cent of the companies whose shares are traded on the OTC market in Japan are 15 years old or older, and only 1 per cent of such firms are less than ten years old in Japan; in the USA, 42 per cent of the firms whose shares are traded on NASDAQ are less than ten years old.[33]

Venture capital investment in Japan was very conservative. First, Japanese venture capital investment companies did not take large equity stakes in their portfolio firms. A Japan Fair Trade Commission survey of 72 venture capital investment companies showed that 27 firms (38 per cent of the total) did not own more than 10 per cent of the equity of any firm in their portfolios,[34] 5 per cent of the companies owned more than 10 per cent of the stock of one to ten portfolio companies.[35] Second, Japanese venture capital investment firms preferred to provide loans for the venture firms. In 1993 loans to 715 firms accounted for 58 per cent of total venture capital disbursements. Equity investment only represented 42 per cent of the total disbursements.[36] Third, only 16 per cent of all Japanese disbursements invested in early stage financing. The majority of venture capital disbursements went to relatively mature industries.[37] In contrast to the disbursement of venture capital in Japan, about 37 per cent of the US new venture capital disbursements were invested in seed, start-up and other early stage firms.[38]

The above comparison shows that the venture capital market in the USA has fortunately developed to encourage adaptation and innovation; by contrast, the venture capital markets for innovation in Japan and Germany are constrained. Gilson and Black explain that bank oriented systems lack an institution (a developed stock market) crucial to the incentive structure at the heart of the entrepreneurial process.[39] Milhaupt has a similar view that an actively developed stock market is crucial to the development of a venture capital market. Furthermore, he finds that there are five key traits of the active venture capital market in the USA which are at least loosely linked to the stock market orientation but not found in Japan's bank-centred system. The five traits are: the existence of large, independent sources of funding, liquidity, highly developed incentive structures, labour mobility, and risk tolerance.[40] Based on this thorough analysis, Milhaupt concludes that the development of active venture capital markets may require not only an active stock market but also the concomitant legal and social practices found in a stock market oriented corporate culture. The following section discusses the significance of a developed stock market, which provides different options of exit for venture capital to an efficient venture capital market.

THE SIGNIFICANCE OF A DEVELOPED STOCK MARKET

A developed stock market is essential to an efficient venture capital market because it can provide a better way of exit for venture capital.[41] Why must venture capital exit from the portfolio firms? Its withdrawal is determined by the special capacity of venture capitalists. Venture capitalists provide portfolio firms with capital, assistance of management and monitoring of the operating process of the firms[42] as well as the reputation capital for third parties.[43] The non-capital service provided by venture capitalists is much more important to the early stage venture firms. With the increased experience of the management of the portfolio companies, the enhanced skills, and the establishment of its own

71

reputation, the importance of the non-capital service provided by venture capitalists would decrease.[44] This requires that the non-capital service provided by venture capitalists should be put into other early stage portfolio companies when the venture firm has succeeded. Because the non-capital service provided by venture capitalists is highly connected with the capital service of venture capitalists, the withdrawal of non-capital service often is accompanied by the exit of the capital controlled by venture capitalists. As a result, venture capitalists can utilize their comparative advantage by providing their non-capital service and capital service together in a cyclical way.[45] On the other hand if the portfolio firm fails, the high liquidity can reduce the loss of venture capitalists.

Generally speaking there are four different methods for venture capital fund to withdraw from the portfolio venture firms. They are: bankruptcy, buy-back by entrepreneurs in venture firms, sale of venture firms, and initial public offerings of venture firms. To know why a developed stock market can provide a better exit and is crucial to venture capital investment, let us first look at how the four exit mechanisms operate.

Liquidation

In a venture capital market, it is not uncommon for portfolio firms to fail. Bankruptcy is the way for venture capital funds to exit when portfolio firms fail. Shareholders normally cannot get any assets from the bankrupt enterprises. Since the intangible property in the portfolio firms takes the skills and knowledge of venture entrepreneurs as a significant asset, it is impossible for the shareholders to get much of the remaining assets. However, precisely because the intangible property in the portfolio firms takes up a large portion of the whole assets, the portfolio firms normally cannot obtain loans from banks or other creditors. Williamson has the view that the leverage of debt to equity should be positively correlated to the liquidation value of the assets.[46] To creditors, high liquidation value means that the consequences of debtor default are less serious. High liquidation value is also positively correlated to the tangible assets of the debtor enterprise. Shleifer and Vishny show that it is difficult for the enterprises with more firm specific assets to get loans.[47] This is so because firm specific assets reduce the liquidation value. To venture firms with high expenditure of research and development, their assets often are firm specific property. So it is frequently difficult for venture firms to get loans.

Myers points out that, if the value of the enterprise is dependent on the investment in future optional projects, it is not easy for such enterprises to receive loans[48] because the substitution of investment projects afterwards may make creditors worse off. If the enterprise succeeds, what the creditors get is only the fixed return. When the enterprise fails, however, the creditors would suffer from the down side. The asymmetry of risks and expected return determines that creditors are often not willing to provide credit to high and new technological enterprises with high risks. Even though creditors can demand a much higher rate of interest through negotiation, a high rate of interest can cause liquidity problems in the operating process of the enterprise and affect its development as well as aggravate the risk of asset substitution.[49]

The above analysis explains why it is difficult for seed or start-up venture firms to get large numbers of loans other than from venture capitalists. Venture capitalists can sometimes obtain some of the remaining assets in the liquidation process, partly because venture capitalists can participate in and monitor the management and decision-making through some kinds of contractual arrangements, and partly because venture capitalists enjoy senior creditor status by holding convertible bonds. Another reason why venture capitalists are able to obtain some assets from the venture firms is because venture capitalists often ask entrepreneurs of venture firms to have some investments in the firms in order to achieve incentive alignment.

Buy-back by entrepreneurs

Compared with bankruptcy, venture capitalists often achieve higher returns from the exit of buy-back by entrepreneurs. When signing the finance and management contracts between venture capital institutions and venture firms, entrepreneurs in venture firms often require the equity buy-back provisions from venture capitalists. Where the venture firm succeeds, venture entrepreneurs can buy back the shares held by venture capitalists according to the agreed price. Such provisions often meet Pareto efficiency and normally make the two parties better off. To venture capitalists, what they receive is the highest expected investment return. Because venture capitalists accumulate the experience of financing and provide suggestions on management, their relative advantages would be reduced when the venture firms become mature.[50] Therefore, venture capitalists withdraw the capital from successful enterprises and reinvest in other enterprises with enormous developing potential.

Venture capitalists like this way of exit through buy-back. Venture entrepreneurs would also like to buy back the shares held by venture capitalists so that they can control the successful enterprises. The ex post strategy of exit of venture capital makes possible the transfer of much decision-making power to venture capitalists unmatched by their smaller equity holding. Although the exit strategy of buy-back has its many advantages, it is unsuitable for very successful enterprises. It is very expensive for entrepreneurs to buy back the shares of venture firms with great developing potential owned by venture capitalists. Most entrepreneurs of venture firms may not have enough money to buy back the shares from venture capitalists.

Selling venture firms

Selling venture firms is another exit means for venture capital. In some cases, it may be the most efficient exit method. For example, sometimes it is better for small enterprises to innovate, but allocate production and sales functions to big existing enterprises. Milhaupt takes the view that innovating in big existing enterprises is not always conducive to adaptive efficiency[51] because innovation in big enterprises is closely related to the existing industry, market, and the culture of enterprises. However, once the innovative technology is developed in small enterprises, it is better to carry out production and sales in big enterprises. Big existing enterprises often have the advantage of economies of scale in production and sales. Under such conditions, selling the early-stage enterprises to big existing enterprises would create 'synergy effects'. Part of the returns brought by the 'synergy effects' would be realized by the early stage firm through the higher sales price of the venture firm.[52]

Although selling venture firms has its own advantages, it normally means for venture entrepreneurs that they will lose the control of the successful venture firms that they have developed. Many entrepreneurs were willing to take the high risks of failure and voluntarily offer the control and monitoring rights to venture capitalists when they obtain the venture capital fund mainly because they would obtain the control of the enterprise after the enterprise becomes successful. In addition, to venture capitalists and venture entrepreneurs the return from selling the venture firms to a third party is far less than that from initial public offerings. An empirical study in the USA showed that liquidating venture firms results in 80 per cent investment loss to venture capitalists; selling venture firms often brings 15.4 per cent annual investment return to venture capitalists; initial public offering normally gives rise to 59.5 per cent annual investment return to venture capitalists.[53] Obviously, selling venture firms is not the best option either to venture capitalists or to venture entrepreneurs.

Initial public offerings

Among the four exit options, initial public offering is the most attractive one to venture capitalists and venture entrepreneurs. To venture capitalists, the exit strategy of IPOs gives them the highest investment return. From the perspective of the contractual relationship between venture capitalists and venture entre-preneurs, it is of significant importance for venture capitalists to withdraw their investment in the invested firms in order to reinvest in other new firms or other markets.[54] First, venture capital fund providers need to measure the skills of the different venture capitalists through some specific ways to decide to whom the new funds should flow. The different returns of the exit options provide the best comparison. IPOs also provide the necessary condition for venture capital fund providers to make an investment in good venture capital funds. Second, venture capital providers need to compare the return of venture capital with the return of alternative investment to decide whether to invest in the venture capital market or not.[55]

To venture capitalists, whether they can bring the venture firms into the IPO stage is highly relevant to whether they can attract more capital in the future. Because there exist economies of scale in venture capital fund management, the amount of funds to manage is very important to venture capitalists.[56] Portfolio investment to diversify risks also requires that venture capitalists hold enough venture capital. Empirical studies show that on a macro level, the number of IPOs is directly related to the amount of capital invested in the venture capital market.[57] If the number of IPOs increases in a particular year, venture capital funds increase next year. The same is true on a micro level. If one venture capital fund cannot bring any venture firm into the IPO stage, it is difficult for the venture capital fund to get new sources of venture capital. Hummer-Winblad is a good example.[58] Hummer-Winblad established the first venture capital fund in 1989. Although in 1999 they spent about half a year marketing their second fund, it was very difficult for them to raise new capital because the institution had no record of bringing venture firms onto the IPO market. However, when they successfully put Powersoft into the stage of IPO in 1993, Hummer-Winblad raised a fund of US$60 million in just a few months.

To venture entrepreneurs, the listing of venture firms not only significantly increases the price of their shares but also helps them regain control of their venture firms. In general, venture capitalists' control of the venture firms disappears after the venture firms' initial public offering.[59] The implicit self-executing contractual arrangements between venture capitalists and venture entrepreneurs, which return the control over the venture firm to venture entrepreneurs after the firm succeeds, makes it easier for entrepreneurs to surrender a great deal of control power to venture capitalists when the venture firm raises capital at the early stages. If venture entrepreneurs do not consider the control over the venture firm important after its success, it is difficult to imagine why they were willing to run the risk of the failure of the venture firm and take the risk of being removed from the management after they offered much control power to venture capitalists during the early stages of receiving finance.

The importance of IPOs to the venture capital market fully explains that a fully developed stock market is crucial for the development of an efficient venture capital market. Stock markets and venture capital markets mutually contribute to each other. Because a developed stock market plays a very important role in the USA venture capital market, the venture capital market in the USA is considered to be a 'stock market oriented' model of venture capital. The Chinese government is trying to further develop its stock market to improve the venture capital market.

75

DEVELOPING A VENTURE CAPITAL MARKET

The emerging legal framework for venture capital

It has been concluded in section three that different venture capital systems have different outcomes. This again shows that in the real world, where transaction costs are not zero, different institutional arrangements would affect the efficiency outcome of transactions in different ways. The question is, to achieve the objective of establishing an efficient venture capital market in China, which kind of venture capital model should be adopted? Put it another way, which model is appropriate to China – stock market oriented or bank oriented venture capital?

The intention of the Chinese government to develop a stock market oriented venture capital regime was reflected by governmental policies and regulations between 1985 and 1999. In 1985, the Chinese Communist Party formulated the Decision on Reforming the Science and Technology Regime.[60] The Decision provides, among other things, that the development work on high and new technology, which tends to change rapidly and has high risk, may be supported by venture capital.[61] In 1991, the State Council promulgated the Provisional Measures on Certain Policies Regarding the State High and New Technology Development Zones.[62] Article 6(3) of this Provisional Measures provides:

> Relevant departments may establish venture capital funds within the high and new technology industry development zones to develop high and new technology with high risks. These relatively matured high and new technology industry zones may permit the establishment of venture capital investment companies.[63]

In 1995, the Chinese Communist Party and the State Council jointly issued the Decision Concerning the Acceleration of the Development of Science and Technology.[64] Paragraph 33 of the Decision re-emphasized the need for developing a venture capital investment regime.[65] The policy of emphasizing the development of venture capital later found expression in the Law Concerning the Promotion of Conversion of the Results of Science and Technology.[66]

In November 1999, the Chinese government issued a more specific document entitled 'Establishing a Venture Investment Mechanism Several Opinions' (Several Opinions). The Several Opinions provide:

> The objective of establishing a venture capital market in China is to promote the development of high and new technology; to realize the commercialization of research results; to enhance the contribution of scientific and technological progress to economic growth and, through the creation of a favorable external environment, to encourage enterprises to actively become

involved in technological innovation and scientific and technology venture activities; and to facilitate adjustments of the industry and the upgrading of product composition.[67]

The above policies and laws indicate that China has planned to establish a venture capital regime that encourages adaptation and innovation. As previously discussed, a stock market oriented system can better encourage adaptation and innovation than a bank oriented system does with respect to venture capital. It seems that adopting a stock market oriented system in China is a positive way towards the construction of a venture capital market. Moreover, banks in China have difficulty channelling funds of venture capital not only because venture capital has very high risks but also because they are burdened by bad debts.[68] When the Law on Commercial Banks still prohibited or discouraged banks from owning shares in borrowing companies,[69] a bank oriented venture capital market would not have provided powerful incentives for banks to monitor the borrowing venture firms. This is so because if the venture firms were very successful, the lending banks could only receive the normal fixed return. On the other hand, if the borrowing venture firms are not successful in taking high risks, the banks involved tend to suffer from the downside losses. Obviously, a bank oriented venture capital regime under the current conditions is not able to solve the moral hazard problem of asset substitution. Similarly a bank oriented venture capital regime under the current regime is not able to make the best use of the convertible bonds instrument, which is a key condition of a successful venture capital investment regime.

The Several Opinions set out a conceptual framework within which China's growing hi-tech industries can develop by using venture capital funds attracted from a variety of sources, and aim at establishing a capital market system beneficial to the withdrawal of venture capital by share transfer, share buy-backs and domestic and overseas listing. The Several Opinions indicate that a Chinese individual can buy shares in a private (as opposed to publicly listed) company or fund in which the individual concerned has no interest other than as an investor. This conceptual framework shows that the Chinese government has no intention to establish a bank oriented venture capital market but to establish a stock market oriented venture capital market.

As China is still a transitional economy, the government still plays a very significant role in the economy. With respect to venture capital, the focus of governmental policy received very positive responses, mainly from governments both at the national level and at the regional level. At the national level, the Ministry of Finance and the State Science and Technology Commission established the China New Technology Venture Capital Investment Ltd in 1986.[70] To facilitate borrowing, the Ministry of Finance and the State Economic Trade Commission also established the China Economic and Technology Investment

77

Guarantee Ltd with an equity capital of RMB 500 million in 1994.[71] The State Science and Technology Commission, the Science and Technology division of the Ministry of the National Defence, and the Merchant Shipping Group Ltd also jointly established the China Science and Merchant High-tech Ltd in 1989. More venture capital investment companies, however, were established at the provincial level in the 1990s. The relatively large ones include the Shenzhen High-tech Venture Capital Investment Ltd, the Beijing Science and Technology Venture Capital Investment Ltd, the Guangdong Science and Technology Venture Capital Investment Ltd, the Shanghai Science and Technology Investment Ltd, and the Jiangsu High-tech Investment Ltd.[72] Just as in the swift development of China's stock market, governmental involvement in venture capital investment sped up the development of China's venture capital market. The rapid development of the venture capital market, however, has its own problems. As discussed elsewhere in the book, state-owned enterprises are more likely to pursue non-wealth maximizing goals.[73] Furthermore, compared with private enterprises, there are fewer means available to motivate managers in state-owned enterprises and there are fewer means to discipline managers in state-owned enterprises. Still another problem is the lack of adequate resources of governments as there are other competing projects or needs.

While the lack of experience and the necessary infrastructure may explain the inefficiency of state-owned venture capital companies, the role played by the Wenzhou informal financial market shows the vitality of the private sector in Wenzhou's economic development despite having similar conditions as the rest of China.

Private sector financing in Wenzhou

China's economic reform policy has provided the necessary conditions for the development of a private sector. During the expansion of the private sector, however, the financing of projects of private firms by formal financial institutions accounted for a very small proportion. Among the gross industrial products of 1985, 1990 and 1995, the state-owned sector accounted for 64.8 per cent, 54.6 per cent and 33.97 per cent respectively while the contribution of the private sector was 35.14 per cent, 45.4 per cent and 66.03 per cent respectively.[74] Despite the fact that the private sector was getting more important in the economy, the private sector firms in the above three years only received 5.44 per cent, 5.48 per cent and 2.7 per cent of the loans from state-owned banks.[75] Because of serious capital shortage constraints faced by private individuals and firms, the informal financial market naturally developed. Among the various informal financial markets, the informal financial market of Wenzhou provides the best example of the vitality of the private sector in China's economic development.

Wenzhou is located in the southeastern part of Zhejiang province. It has jurisdiction over nine counties and is well known for its dense population and lack of farming land.[76] Since Wenzhou does not have adequate natural resources such as coal, oil and ore, it is not a good place for energy production. Thus, light industry is more suitable for Wenzhou. It is because of some of the above reasons that the people there usually participate in business instead. Like other regions in China, the development of the light industry of Wenzhou was seriously constrained while the economy was still a planned economy. As Wenzhou is also very close to Taiwan, a potential 'war zone', the state made very little investment. From 1949 to 1978, the state only invested RMB 560 million in Wenzhou.[77] As a result, the state-owned sector was very weak in Wenzhou.

The economy of Wenzhou developed very rapidly after the initiation of China's economic reform policy in 1978. Compared with the Pearl River Delta where there is heavy foreign investment, and the southern part of Jiangsu province where considerable economic contribution is made by township and rural enterprises, the development of the Wenzhou economy relies more on individuals and private firms. In spite of the low amount of investment by the state between 1978 and 1994, the Wenzhou economy developed at the high annual rate of 16 per cent on average.[78] The economic development of Wenzhou during China's economic reform shows the very important role of the private sector in economic development. The method of development of the Wenzhou economy is also popularly called the Wenzhou model.

The Wenzhou model has the following characteristics:

1 *Active and specialized family enterprises.* By the end of 1984, more than 130,000 family enterprises with 330,000 entrepreneurs and labourers had produced 60 per cent of the gross industrial products in the rural areas of Wenzhou.[79] Most of the family enterprises were engaged in the production and marketing of light industrial products such as buttons, electronic products, shoes, textile products, etc.

2 *Well-developed specialized markets for light industrial goods.* By the end of 1984, there existed 135 specialized markets in Wenzhou.[80] Among these, ten specialized markets are well known in China. Examples include the specialized market in Yongjia county for the production and sale of buttons, the specialized market in Cang Nan for the production and sale of textile products, and the specialized market in Le Qing for the production and sale of hardware and electronic products.[81]

3 *A large number of sales persons.* These former farmers or residents of small towns started to adjust their jobs and played an important role in the acquisition of raw materials, signing contracts, promoting goods from their areas and the facilitation of the flow of information. When the transfer of information was not very smooth during the early stage of economic reform, large sales team became very important.

79

4 *Various market factors.* They included the labour market, the technology market, and the financial market.

Obviously, the informal financial market developed by the private sector made a significant contribution to the development of the Wenzhou economy. According to statistics, the demand of funds by individuals, family enterprises, and township and rural enterprises in 1985 was RMB 600–700 million.[82] Of that demand 30 per cent was met by loans from banks and credit cooperatives, 36 per cent was supplied by the informal financial market developed by the private sector, and the rest was retained earnings of the enterprises themselves.[83] In some more developed coastal areas, the supply of fund by the private sector was even more significant. A survey of 10 wholesalers, 26 retailers, and 9 manufacturing enterprises revealed that the demand of funds in 1985 by these enterprises was RMB 366 million.[84] Except for the retained earnings, loans from credit cooperatives only solved 38 per cent of the shortage of fund while 62 per cent of the gap was filled in by the informal financial market.[85] Similarly, 50 per cent of the demand of working capital from family enterprises, township and rural enterprises was from the informal financial market.[86] Moreover, the methods of financing were very innovative when the banking financing was rigid and the stock market in China was only linked to the reform of state-owned enterprises in the 1980s and 1990s.

Direct private borrowing

This is the most primitive borrowing method under which interest varies according to market conditions. Normally, borrowers and lenders between individuals and enterprises are very familiar with each other. The close relations between borrowers and lenders reduce the moral hazard problem under imperfect information at the time of borrowing. After the reform, private sector lending has changed in its role from personal use to financing production and marketing of various enterprises. According to statistics, direct private borrowing between individuals and enterprises in Dai Tou Village of Ruian County reached RMB 779,000, accounting for 86.2 per cent of total lendings.[87]

Borrowing through the intermediary of yinbei

This is an indirect borrowing method through an individual called *yinbei* or *qianzhong*. *Yinbeis* in the rural area of Wenzhou were already engaged in the facilitation of borrowing between borrowers and lenders before the economic reform. After the economic reform, the activities of *yinbeis* became more open and the number has increased significantly.[88] *Yinbeis* do not own large amounts of money themselves, but they know the potential lenders very well and have established good relations with lenders as well as borrowers. *Yinbeis* charge borrowers and lenders different types of fees such as brokerage fee, service fee, and guarantee fee. A survey in 1992 in Xincheng District of Ruian County showed that there existed on average one *yinbei* in each village among the 30 administrative villages.[89] Roughly each *yinbei* had the credit amount of RMB one million, with a total of RMB 30–40 million.[90]

Juhui

Juhui is organized by a promoter called *huitou* (leader of the organization). The promoter usually invites friends and/or relatives called *huijia* (member) to join the group. Members of the group hold meetings every month, quarter, or year depending on the availability of the members and the need of funds by the members. In meetings, each member contributes a specific amount of money for the use of a particular member. This goes on so that other members also get the opportunity of borrowing money – this method serves the *juhui's* purpose of mutual assistance.[91] The interest rate is normally higher than the official bank lending rate. The number of members of *juhuis* varies from group to group, ranging from two to hundreds. Investigation reveals that some *juhuis* only exist for a year while others have lasted for eight or nine years.[92] Participants of *juhuis* may include farmers, individual industrial and commercial households, city residents, workers, teachers, and cadres. In some cases, *juhuis* also include people from outside the region.[93] It has been estimated that the financial scale of the *juhuis* reached several hundred million yuan, with the number of members around several hundred thousands.[94] There are examples of collapse of *juhuis*, particularly when the monthly interest rate reached 4–5 per cent and a large number of members are from outside the region. The often cited case of collapse of a *juhui* happened in Leqing County within half a year of its establishment in 1986, involving hundreds of thousands of members from 14 counties.[95]

Direct fund raising by enterprises

According to incomplete statistics made by the Agricultural Bank of China in Wenzhou, 2,301 enterprises raised RMB 136 million in 1985, representing 79.45 per cent of the enterprises.[96] The amount of funds raised in this way accounted for 84.59 per cent of the total funds raised by township and rural enterprises.[97]

The main methods of raising capital by large enterprises on the informal financing market are[98] (1) cooperatives: investors use this method of financing to establish new enterprises. There are two different ways under this method. First, investors assume senior-level positions and hire non-investors to carry out the production work. Employees are normally paid a per hour rate or per piece rate.

81

Second, all investors are also employees of the enterprise. (2) Employee investment: this method is usually used when existing enterprises urgently need capital, but banks and credit cooperatives are not able to satisfy the need for capital of the enterprises. The enterprises generally pay interest according to the proportion of investment of employees.[99] Some enterprises also pay dividends from after tax profits. This type of raising capital is also very significant in Wenzhou. (3) Raising capital from outside the region: this method is used for newly established enterprises when lending from employees is not adequate.[100]

In some of the methods of financing described above the term of lending is normally short, varying between 1–3 years.[101] Most borrowers perform according to their contractual arrangements. For other temporary needs of equity capital the normal method of voluntary investment and free exit is adopted. Interest or dividends are normally very high, reaching a monthly rate of 2–3 per cent in most cases.[102]

The Wenzhou informal financial market emerged in the 1980s when the official financial system was very rigid and the official interest rate of banks and credit cooperatives was too low to reflect the risks of small family and rural enterprises. The informal market had an important role during Wenzhou's high rate of economic development in the 1980s and 1990s when the official financial institutions were not able to satisfy the capital requirement needs of private enterprises. Now some of these early small enterprises have developed into very large companies and play significant roles in national and international trade. The lack of efficiency of government involvement in venture capital investment and the vigorous development of private enterprises in Wenzhou have provided a good contrast. Lack of experience in venture capital investment and the efficiency of private firms led the government to turn its attention to foreign investment.

Introducing foreign venture capital

In 2001 the Ministry of Foreign Trade and Economic Cooperation, the Ministry of Science and Technology, and the State Administration of Industry and Commerce jointly issued the Tentative Provisions on the Establishment of Foreign-invested Venture Capital Investment Enterprises. The Provisions allow the formation of foreign-invested venture capital investment enterprises (FIVCIE) as a wholly foreign owned company, an equity joint venture, or a contractual joint venture.[103] Requirements for establishing FIVCIEs address issues of competence, qualifications, capitalization, legal establishment, and good standing.

As not many FIVCIEs had been established since 2001, in 2003 the Provisions on the Administration of Foreign-invested Venture Capital Investment Enterprises[104] were promulgated to replace the 2001 Tentative Provisions.

82

The 2003 Provisions have liberalized the regime on venture capital in several aspects. A significant change in the new rules is that it lowered the minimum capitalization requirement to US$10 million for a non-legal person FIVCIE and US$5 million for a legal person FIVCIE, thus expanding the pool of people eligible to establish FIVCIEs.[105] In contrast to the provisions in the Company Law, which require that the registered capital must be made up-front at the time of establishment, the Provisions permit investors to contribute their capital periodically up to a maximum period of five years.[106] Compared with the Regulations for the Establishment of Securities Companies with Foreign Capital,[107] which limit the capital contribution of foreign investors to no more than 33 per cent,[108] the new Provisions only require one essential investor, who can be either foreign or Chinese.[109] This change provides foreign investors greater freedom if they want to control how they want their fund managed. While the current Partnership Enterprises Law does not clearly allow limited partners, the new Provisions limits the liability of investors to their capital contribution even in partnership FIVCIEs although the essential investor has to bear unlimited liability.[110]

In addition to special regulations on venture capital investment companies, other changes and regulations have also made it easier to operate FIVCIEs. More liberal attitudes towards foreign involved mergers and acquisitions have been reflected in the Tentative Provisions on the Acquisition of Domestic Enterprises by Foreign Investors.[111] While the Company Law requires a minimum capital of RMB 50 million and a profit record of three consecutive years to be eligible for listing,[112] indirect listing abroad of an offshore parent company of a FIVCIE in China has already taken place. Further, direct listing of venture firms incorporated in China on overseas stock exchanges has also been permitted by the China Securities Regulatory Commission from time to time. All these changes have made it easier for foreign investors to exit from the venture firms that they have invested in and cycle the funds among other Chinese venture firms. Successful listings of venture firms overseas include Sina, Sohu, SMIC, Shanda, and CTrip.com. Despite the limited success of the venture capital regime in China, there are lessons that the Chinese government should learn and more effort should be made.

FURTHER STEPS IN DEVELOPING THE VENTURE CAPITAL MARKET

In any economic system, the outcome of economic activities is based on millions of contractual arrangements. No economic plans or policies can substitute the incentive arrangements made by parties through contracts. Obviously, human beings cannot directly control the exact outcome of the economic activities they

83

are engaged in. At most, people can only show their preference for the different outcomes of economic activities. To achieve the preferred outcome people need to change institutional arrangements.

With respect to the role of government, people have chosen many different models in history. China once adopted the planned economic model with public ownership of the means of production. History has proven that there are two major defects inherent in the planned economic model. First, the planned economic model allocates resources in society only in a very primitive way. The disadvantage of such a model is that the drafter of plans cannot efficiently co-ordinate all sorts of information in society.[113] Second, with public ownership of the means of production, it is difficult to develop better incentive and moni-toring systems. In the traditional planned economic model with the public ownership of the means of production, the use and disposition of the means of production are executed mainly by state-owned enterprises and partly by collective enterprises. Since state-owned enterprises cannot create better incen-tive and monitoring systems than privately managed enterprises because of the lack of options in choosing monitoring devices,[114] the government should not establish state-owned enterprises to produce general consumer goods.

Similarly, direct government involvement in financial arrangements in the production process is not efficient as proved by evidence in China. Even in mature market economies the government's direct intervention on the financial market of small enterprises or venture capital market cannot achieve efficient outcomes. The experience of the USA and Korea provide good examples.

In 1958 the USA established the small business investment company (SBIC) programme that allows qualified individuals, enterprises and banks to establish investment companies that provide long-term equity and debt to small enterprises.[115] Small business investment companies are able to get low interest loans guaranteed by the Small Business Administration (SBA). Every small business investment company may receive leverage from the SBA equal to four times its private capital. The maximum loan is US$90 million.[116] The small business investment company plan has accounted for 15 per cent of the total venture capital disbursements during recent years. In 1995, small business investment companies provided 1,168 small enterprises with US$1.1 billion among which the loan of US$122 million was given to 394 small enterprises, the other US$97.2 million was invested in 774 small enterprises in the forms of equity or debt-with-equity.[117]

Empirical research has shown that the performance of the small business investment companies was dismal. The Federal Reserve Bank of Chicago found that half of the 280 small business investment companies existing in 1986 failed by 1993; by 1995, 189 small business investment companies were put into liquidation, with over US$500 million guaranteed by the SBA outstanding.[118] More importantly this report discovered that the failure of the small business investment companies was positively related to the leverage of the SBA, while return-on-equity was negatively related to the leverage of the SBA. The findings explained that the small businesses that enjoyed the government's guarantee and subsidy were more likely to invest in excessively risky assets (moral hazard).[119] Also, riskier small business investment companies are more likely to make use of the government's guarantee and subsidy (adverse selection).

In the USA, the failure of Kansas State Government's direct involvement in venture capital investment also proved that government should not directly intervene on the venture capital market. The economy of Kansas State was to a great extent dependent on the agriculture, natural gas, petroleum and manu-facture.[120] Although the economy of Kansas was very prosperous during the 1970s and early 1980s, the revenue of the Kansas State considerably went down in 1986 because of the economic recession in the middle of the 1980s. In the same year, the state legislature appointed Redwood and Krider to study the problems and put forward a report. The Redwood–Krider report was submitted to the state legislature. Its main conclusion was that the traditional industries relied upon by Kansas would no longer provide the means for the state to compete effectively with other states or countries. They thought that the two major economic goals of Kansas should be: (1) 'the formation of innovative, technology-based, new businesses' and (2) 'the encouragement and leverage of private investment capital'.[121]

However, establishing a technological industry needed enormous investment capital. Redwood and Krider thought that there was not enough private invest-ment capital to establish these new industries. To solve the capital gap, they suggested that the Kansas State directly invest in high technology start-up companies in the form of seed and venture capital.[122] In 1986 the Kansas State's legislature approved most suggestions made in the report and agreed to establish the Kansas's Technology Enterprise Corporation. The principle mission of the company was to provide high technology start-up companies within the state with business support service, and seed and venture capital.[123] The Kansas Technology Enterprise Corporation did not receive any funds from general state revenue. Its funds[124] were mainly from the Economic Development Initiatives Fund which received its money from proceeds generated from the Kansas lottery and pari-mutuel racing.[125] In 1998 the Kansas Technology Enterprise Corporation received nearly US$80 million from the Economic Development Initiatives Fund. From the establishment of the Kansas Technology Enterprise Corporation to 1996 the distribution of the capital invested in all of its programmes was as follows:

State investment amount: US$76.5 million;
Industry investment amount: US$68.8 million;
Federal investment capital: US$76.2 million;
Venture capital investment: US$53.5 million;
Institutional investment amount: US$11.2 million.[126]

The amount the state invested in directly was the amount of funds provided to the Kansas Technology Enterprise Corporation for its programmes. Industry invested capital, federal invested capital and venture capital disbursements were made by these bodies to support the Kansas Technology Enterprise Corporation. But for the subsidy policy of the State, these bodies would not have invested to support the Kansas Technology Enterprise Corporation.[127]

Even though Kansas State had actually considered the matter thoroughly, the return of investment in high technology enterprises was very low. Over the past few decades in the USA, private venture capitalists had obtained an average of 40 per cent of annual investment return.[128] During the same period, the normal annual investment return of the stock market in the USA was 12 per cent.[129] However, from the time the Kansas State began to invest in high technology enterprises in 1984 to 1996 its annual investment return was only 0.94 per cent.[130]

The government of South Korea passed a law entitled 'Special Law to Promote Venture Capital Companies' in 1997.[131] Although the law adopted a series of indirect subsidy measures, it seemed that there was not much impact on improving the venture capital market in South Korea.

South Korea's venture capital market first appeared in the early 1970s. Venture capital companies gradually increased in the early 1980s. The institutional foundation of venture capital was established in 1986.[132] In that year, South Korea passed several laws including the 'Law to Promote Small and Medium Sized Companies' administered by the Ministry of Commerce, Industry and Energy and the 'Law to Assist the Financing of New Technology Ventures' administered by the Ministry of Finance and Economy. The number of venture capital firms had increased from 12 in 1986 to 49 by 1995.[133] From 1987 to 1997 these firms had a total investment of $1.5 trillion won in 1,891 projects.[134] At the end of 1995, 86.1 per cent of the total venture capital disbursements of these venture capital firms were in the form of company lending. But the rate of return of cumulative equity investment was only 6.5 per cent.[135] The enactment of the 'Special Law to Promote Venture Capital Companies' in 1997 was designed to promote venture capital companies in South Korea's high technology industry and raise South Korea's capacity against competition internationally.

The main aims of the Special Law to Promote Venture Capital Companies were to provide subsidies for venture firms invested in by venture capital funds and to safeguard the entrepreneurs to some extent. Here are two examples. First, Article 16 of the Law provided the entrepreneurs who left public institutions or universities to start a venture undertaking with a safeguard. Such personnel had the option of returning to the original institution within three years of their departure. The provision obviously reduced the risk of venture failure. Of course, such a provision also alleviated the market's punishment of relatively incompetent entrepreneurs. In countries with a relatively weak capacity of venture capitalists such an article could indirectly reduce the investment return of venture capital. Second, Article 18 of the Law granted the buildings occupied by venture companies preferential tax treatment. Under this article if at least 75 per cent of a building was occupied by venture firms or their related offices, the building is considered a venture capital building ('VCB'). VCBs were entitled to real estate tax cuts of 50 per cent.[136]

The venture capital market in Korea has not made marked progress since the enactment of the 'Special Law to Promote Venture Capital Companies.' The main reason is that there has not been a well-functioning stock market. Although the intention of establishing the Korea Security Dealers Association Automated Quotation (KOSDAQ) is to provide liquid capital for smaller companies, especially venture firms, KOSDAQ has not lived up to its expectations since its opening in April 1987. The amount of shares traded per year in KOSDAQ is equal to the amount of shares traded per day on the Korea Stock Exchange.[137] Furthermore, there are not enough well-trained venture capitalists with appropriate screening and monitoring ability in Korea. Some sorts of incentive and monitoring contractual devices have not been well developed. In addition, Korea's lifetime employment system is very unfavourable to the formation of venture capital entrepreneurs. The market of human capital with limited labour mobility also hinders the development of a venture capital market.[138]

The above examples illustrate that direct governmental intervention in the venture capital market or indirect involvement in the form of subsidies cannot achieve the intended purposes. A natural question is what role the Chinese government should play in developing the venture capital system.

First, the Chinese government can encourage private funds and foreign capital into high-risk and high-return venture capital investment firms rather than increase its direct investment in venture capital. In China, there are often no efficient monitoring systems during the operating process of governmental investment no matter which area the investment funds have invested in. At present the Chinese government is trying to attract private capital and expand the sources of funds.[139] China's insurance sector is looking to expand its investment scope beyond the low risk and low yield areas. While the 1995 Insurance Law prohibited investment in other firms by insurance companies,[140] the China Insurance Regulatory Commission (CIRC) published a list of insurance companies that were permitted to invest in securities funds and the legally limited amount of money they were able to invest in securities funds in 2000.[141] Ironically, the Insurance Law was amended in 2002 to remove this legal restriction.[142] While the removal of the restriction on insurance companies to invest funds in other companies is risky, as the stock market in China is replete with events of fraud and misrepresentation, the liberalization of the insurance companies is another effort of the Chinese government to attract investment funds into the high-tech sector.

Second, the governments should take great effort to provide laws and regulations – public goods. Such a role is essential during the transitional period from a planned economy to a market economy. To establish a mature and efficient stock market, there must be laws and regulations to prohibit fraud and misrepresentation occurring in the market. Such laws and regulations should be strictly enforced. While market discipline can punish repeating players who commit fraud and misrepresentation, they cannot penalize one-shot players on the market and final-period players. The law also can provide protection to private institutions for information production and information assessment. In stock markets the disclosure requirements of enterprises and the publication of financial reports are very crucial. The prohibition of insider trading and market manipulation is absolutely necessary. Implementation of such laws and regulations requires the government to allocate enough human capital and financial resources. The Chinese government should also make a systemic analysis of the current financial laws by utilizing the theories of modern financial economics to enact new laws, and to improve the not so perfect ones.

Third, the Chinese government is also able to play a very important role in nurturing and developing intermediary institutions. The Angel Capital Electronic Network (ACE-Net) in the USA is a good example.[143] ACE-Net is a nation-wide internet-based listing service that provides information about small and growing companies seeking equity capital from US$250,000 to US$5 million to qualified angel investors. This system is managed by a network of non-profit, mostly university-based operators. Under this system, a qualified angel investor gets a password through which he can receive information on the issuance of shares by small companies in the state where the investor lives. These angel investors are able to contact the issuers directly to purchase the shares. The Security Exchange Commission exempted the network to register as a national securities exchange. Those non-profit network operators do not have to register as broker dealers. This example and the developed over the counter (OTC) market illustrates that a developed OTC market is very important to the development of a venture capital market. National securities exchanges alone with very high listing requirements are not able to help the development of an efficient venture capital market.

Fourth, the lesson from the South Korean experience shows that South Korean law cannot efficiently promote the venture capital market, proving that it is important to know what the incentive and monitoring contractual arrangements are between venture capitalists and venture capital fund providers and also between venture capitalists and venture entrepreneurs. Typically, the documentation includes a shareholders' agreement that sets out the specific powers and rights that the private equity investors should have and the conditions that need to be satisfied. In many cases, the agreement is quite different from the usual joint venture/shareholders agreement between two commercial parties.[144]

The Chinese government can also promote standard contract terms in venture capital financing by making the forms available on the Internet.[145]

CONCLUSION

In this chapter an examination has been made of the current direction in which the Chinese government has tried to develop a stock market oriented venture capital market. New incentive schemes are being developed there. However, the task to remove artificial barriers for the establishment of an efficient capital market through legal means is still large. Deregulating the entrance restrictions of capital market players and establishing ex post monitoring devices to penalize misconduct are indispensable towards the development of an efficient capital market. Furthermore, a series of concomitant legal and social practices rather than direct government involvement in venture capital investment should be nurtured as well. The burden on the Chinese government is very large and the road before the government is also long to build an efficient venture capital market. The construction and operation of an efficient venture capital market requires the necessary institutions within which a venture capital market can operate. Some of the institutions are easy to build while others may require decades' worth of effort. The experience of other countries in the establishment and operation of venture capital markets holds lessons for China in the sense that some of the institutions can be transplanted. Other institutions such as the court system, civil remedies, procedural rules like discovery and class action, however, are very hard to replicate.[146]

Chapter 4

The case against uniformity in corporate governance

INTRODUCTION

The problem of separation of corporate control and residual claims has been documented by Berle and Means and has attracted considerable attention in the USA.[1] The early economic explanation for the cause of separation of corporate control and residual claims emphasizes the economics of scale and specialized knowledge of managerial experts. If the economic explanations were true, competitive economic forces would drive nations towards a single best model of corporate governance. Roe's pioneering works, however, find that similar matured economies have widely diversified corporate governance regimes.[2] Roe's research suggests that there are alternatives. Despite the differences in corporate governance regimes around the world, considerable research is still focused on whether there is a 'best' corporate governance model. I argue from a functional approach in section two that there might be no single best corporate governance model in the world. I examine in section three the transplantation of an English-style takeover law in China and the adjustment of the transplanted takeover law under a different social and political background. The analysis reveals that similar legal provisions at the beginning may still lead to different adaptation and outcomes. I conclude in section four that even a functional analysis shows one corporate governance model does not fit all, not to mention the inclusion of larger social and political considerations.

THE SEARCH FOR A BEST MODEL

The formation and growth of companies requires capital. Capital may be raised through equity financing or debt financing. Both methods of corporate finance create friction between users and suppliers of capital. Equity financing gives rise to the agency costs of equity financing while debt financing gives rise to the agency costs of debt financing.[3] As the methods of financing corporate projects through either debt or equity are not mutually exclusive,[4] most companies adopt both. Differences, however, do exist. Companies in the USA and the United Kingdom rely far more heavily on the securities market for raising capital than companies in Germany and France. For instance, while the United Kingdom has 36 listed firms per million citizens and the USA has 30, France and Germany have only eight and five respectively.[5] Similarly, the ratio of total stock market capitalization to GDP contrasts sharply between Germany on the one hand and the United Kingdom and the USA on the other. In Germany, stock market capitalization was 17 per cent of the GDP during the middle of 1990s as compared to 132 per cent of the GDP in Great Britain.[6] In the USA in 1995, the stock capitalization of the New York Stock Exchange and NASDAQ was around 87 per cent of the total GDP.[7]

Different corporate finance methods create different sets of conflict of interest problems. The solutions to these different problems call for different corporate governance regimes. Corporate governance is defined as ways designed to make the management work for the best interest of the company and to assure a reasonable return to the suppliers of capital. In the USA, the supply of capital is predominantly derived from the securities market. In such an economy, the growth of companies under competitive conditions is mainly determined by the economics of scale,[8] shareholder diversification,[9] reduction of transaction costs[10] and the special knowledge of managerial experts.[11] According to Demestz and Lehn, share ownership concentration levels are inversely related to the aggregate size of the company.[12] This relationship holds because as the value-maximizing size of firm increases, the cost of acquiring a control block will also rise, deterring control accumulation. In addition, when the benefits from control transactions are smaller than the benefits resulting from share diversification, people will choose the latter. Berle and Means documented the phenomenon of widely dispersed shares in the USA.[13] Within a regime where corporate finance is mainly from the securities market and shares are widely dispersed, the costs of equity financing would be higher if the corresponding corporate governance regime did not respond well to agency problems. As a matter of fact, the product market, the stock market and the takeover market play important roles in the USA in solving the problem of conflict of interest between management and shareholders.

In Germany, initial public offerings are rare – in total only ten throughout all of 1994.[14] The stock markets are famously illiquid[15] and volatile.[16] As a result, debt financing plays a much more prominent role than equity financing.[17] Debt financing creates the problem of conflict of interest between a borrowing company and the creditor. The corporate governance regime in Germany is very responsive to the agency costs of debt financing. German banks' historically significant roles in debt financing, without political and legal constraints, make it desirable for them to have the option of holding shares in the debtor companies.[18]

91

In debt financing, creditors normally can intervene in the debtors' business only after debtors default. As bankruptcy generally diminishes claims of general creditors, creditors prefer early exit if they do not have sufficient control of the debtor. If a creditor is also a major shareholder, it may deter wealth transfer transactions. Ex ante, the creditor–shareholder may prevent wealth transfer transactions being adopted by the management of the borrower. Such intervention is normally done by the creditor–shareholder's representative on the supervisory board. The supervisory board can always ask the management board for reports. The supervisory board may also ask the management board to obtain its approval prior to important transactions, such as credits above a certain amount.[19]

Ex post, the creditor–shareholder may penalize managers through the supervisory board. Significant shareholding in the debtor-company makes voice more important than exit; otherwise the creditor–shareholder will suffer both on equity investment and on credit investment. Thus, it is not surprising to see that German banks often take over the reorganization of companies in distress.[20] Empirical studies show that there is a significant involuntary 'fluctuation' of management board members not only in cases of serious problems within the company but also in less serious cases in which the supervisory board was displeased with the performance of individual managers or with the management board as a whole.[21] Hence, creditor–shareholders' active participation in corporate governance in Germany reduces both the agency costs of debt financing and the agency costs of equity financing.

Since the beginning of the 1990s there has been a search for a best corporate governance model. Porter has argued that the Anglo–US pattern of dispersed ownership was clearly inferior to the bank-centred capital markets of Germany and Japan because the latter systems enabled corporate executives to manage for the long term, while US managers were allegedly forced to maximize short-term earnings.[22] Grundfest argued that the US regulatory regime systematically subordinated the desire of investors to resolve agency problems to the desire of managers to be protected from capital market discipline.[23] He states:

> As a consequence of the harmony of interests created by joint equity and debt holding position, Japanese firms have to compensate lenders less to induce them to bear the risks associated with potential bondholder–stockholder conflict. Thus, all else being equal, Japanese capital structures reduce agency costs and allow investors to monitor management more effectively than in the USA. In particular, the amelioration of agency problems allows Japanese firms to invest more in research and development and to maintain more liquid and flexible asset structures than their comparably leveraged American counterparts.

Similar criticisms of the US corporate governance regime can be found in certain political theories. Political theories explain the dispersed share ownership in large US companies as the product of political forces and historical contingencies as well as economic efficiency.[24]

Doubts were soon raised concerning whether the corporate governance regime in the USA is inferior to its counterparts in Japan and Germany. Macey and Miller argue that the presence of powerful banks in corporate governance carries with it an entirely new set of conflicts between the risk-averse claimants who make loans and the residual claimants who invest risk capital, preventing the equity claimants from undertaking socially optimal risks.[25] However, this argument is not entirely satisfactory. The conclusion that powerful banks, as fixed claimants, care far less about maximizing their firm's potential upside performance than about minimizing potential downside performance ignores a major fact that German universal banks sometimes do hold substantial shares in the borrowing companies. For instance, in 1986 the Deutsche Bank held 41.8 per cent of the shares in Daimler-Benz, 30.82 per cent shares in Bayer and 17.64 per cent of the shares in Siemens.[26] Presumably, the Deutsche Bank would also be able to share a high proportion of benefits from the optimal risk-taking activities in these borrowing companies.

Neoclassical economists have long argued that efficiency considerations will ultimately prevail and determine corporate structure. Stigler and Friedland criticize the main theme of Berle and Means on the grounds that empirical evidence available at the time when Berle and Means wrote their book was not able to establish any effect of different types of control upon profits.[27] Demsetz views the ownership structure of the company as an endogenous outcome of a maximizing process.[28] Although agency costs may be higher in companies with a dispersed shareholding structure, such costs may be more than offset by the reduction in risk-associated capital cost, benefits from economic scales and the specialized knowledge of managers.[29]

More recently, the focus of studies has been on the relationship between a jurisdiction's ability to finance economic development and growth, and its legal system.[30] As previously discussed, the USA and United Kingdom have strong stock markets while Germany and France have relatively weak stock markets. Financial economists in this school of thought argue that only those legal systems which provide significant protection for minority shareholders can develop active equity markets.[31] Coffee raises the point that, if this explanation from financial economists is accepted, it amounts to a rejection of the political theory of US corporate finance offered by Roe and others.[32] This is because dispersed share ownership may be the product not of political constraints on financial institutions, but of strong legal protection, which encourages investors to become minority owners.[33] This point is not new. Demsetz once said that in a world in which self-interest plays a significant role in economic behaviour, it is foolish to believe that owners of valuable resources will systematically relinquish control to managers who are not driven by the need to serve the interests of owners.[34]

93

Regardless of whether the dispersed ownership structure in the USA is a function of legal restrictions on financial institutions, the explanation that concentrated ownership is the consequence of weak legal protection for public or minority investors[35] is not entirely satisfactory. It is true that the premium for control blocks in Italy is much higher than that in the USA,[36] but it is still difficult to come to the conclusion that the concentrated ownership structure is worse than the dispersed ownership structure. Shareholders with concentrated ownership have both the incentives and ability to monitor the management team. The higher share premium for control is a reward for their monitoring activities. It is very difficult to argue that a system linking monitoring efforts to reward is defective or inferior. Although the share premium for control is low in the USA, compensation to managers is much higher in the USA than in Germany and Japan.[37] For instance, in the year before its merger Chrysler's Chief Executive Officer (CEO) received cash compensation of US$6 million and stock options worth US$5 million while Daimler's CEO received approximately one-eighth of that amount.[38] A plausible explanation is that minority shareholders in countries with dispersed ownership have to provide the managers and CEOs with greater remuneration to motivate the managers to maximize shareholder wealth. These differences, however, do not indicate which system is better from a contractual perspective. The ability to survive in a large number of countries indicates that concentrated ownership is also consistent with efficiency given the relevant constraints in these economies. Concentrated ownership may also occur in a country with good legal protection to minority shareholders. For instance, entrepreneurs prefer to have control when venture capitalists exit from successful firms.[39] Leveraged buyouts (LBOs) provide another example that just as dispersed ownership in the USA is consistent with efficiency,[40] so too is concentrated ownership in the USA. Shleifer and Vishny point out that LBOs are efficient organizations because large investors reduce agency problems.[41]

So far there is no clear evidence to show whether the corporate governance system in the USA is better or worse than the corporate governance system in Japan or Germany. Claims that one corporate governance system is better than the other are influenced largely by the prosperity of the economy in that country compared to the economy in another country. For instance, when the Japanese economy was very successful, at least until the beginning of 1990s, many people expressed their preference for to the Japanese corporate governance system.[42] However, the economic performance in the USA during the 1990s reversed the tide in the corporate governance literature, with people stating their preference for the US corporate governance system.[43]

Since it is difficult to use the connection between corporate governance and economic performance to establish the claim that one particular corporate governance system is superior to another, which is best corporate governance model remains an open question. The major difficulty in connecting corporate governance systems with economic performance is that the approach fails to measure the substitution effects and the effects of complementarities of the different diversified subsystems in different corporate governance systems.

TRANSPLANTATION AND ADJUSTMENT OF AN ENGLISH-STYLE TAKEOVER LAW

In part one of this section, I try to explain that the transplantation of a foreign law may be quite accidental rather than based on careful cost and benefit analysis of the best law available. The adoption of an English-style takeover law at the beginning of 1990s in China can be explained by Chaos theory. In part two I use empirical evidence to analyse the theory of path-dependence and conclude that the adaptation of the transplanted law to a country with differing social and political backgrounds is in fact path-dependent. More, the case of the transplanted English-style takeover law in China provides good evidence that adaptation of the law in a different country is subject to local social and political forces. This also demonstrates that diversified corporate governance subsystems exist as a result of local adaptation and innovation.

Chaos theory and the importation of takeover law

China's company law and the stock market were designed primarily to improve the performance of the inefficient state-owned enterprises (SOEs).[44] As part of company law, the law of takeover had a similar purpose. Here I will discuss the poor performance of SOEs and banks until the beginning of the 1990s. The inefficiency of SOEs called for a major change of corporate finance from bank loans to issuing shares to the public through the stock exchanges both inside and outside of China, particularly in Hong Kong.

Although the reform of SOEs began in 1978, the performance of SOEs and banks remained poor throughout the 1980s into the beginning of the 1990s. In 1987 losses incurred by state-owned, economically independent industrial enterprises amounted to 6.1 billion yuan.[45] Losses increased to 34.8 billion yuan in 1990 and to 45.2 billion yuan in 1993.[46] During the first four months of 1994, 50.1 per cent of these enterprises were running at a loss.[47] Although things improved slightly in the later half of that year, 34.4 per cent of these SOEs were still running at a loss at the end of 1994.[48] Overstocking of products, mass defaulting of debts and poor management of funds has also taken an increasingly heavier toll on the economic performance of enterprises. For instance, stockpiled products were valued at 412.4 billion yuan at the end of 1994.[49] Most of these loans were to medium- to large-sized SOEs.

Despite the reform of the financial sector, the performance of banks remained poor at the beginning of the 1990s. Overdue payments and non-performing

95

loans were high. While official reports indicate that overdue payments and non-performing loans accounted for 15 per cent of all credit offered by banks in 1992,[50] unofficial estimates show that overdue payments and non-performing loans made up close to 40 per cent of all outstanding loans.[51] Continuation of the process of financing SOEs with loans from state banks heightened the risk of bank insolvency at a time when banks were unable to tighten the soft budget constraints among the various loan users.[52]

Soft budget constraints and the legal prohibition against banks owning shares in non-financial companies necessitated the use of alternative means to finance corporate activities. The stock market was a natural option. It is argued that if share prices reflect enterprise profitability, capital markets will channel investment funds to the most efficient enterprises as investors seek to maximize their returns.[53] It is further argued that capital markets create a market for corporate control. Reformers believe that market mechanisms are more efficient at rationalizing productive assets than are the powers given to banks.[54]

Under the support of reformers, two stock exchanges opened in China: Shanghai in 1990 and Shenzhen in 1991.[55] Raising capital domestically was not the only objective. The government also wanted to attract and utilize foreign capital, particularly via Hong Kong. This offered regulatory experts in Hong Kong the opportunity to persuade the relevant authorities in China to adopt certain necessary laws and regulations similar to those used there.

The regulations passed during that period provide some evidence that China was keen to use Hong Kong as a base for raising foreign capital. In 1992, before the Company Law was enacted in 1993, the State Economic Restructuring Commission issued Opinions on the Standardization of Joint Stock Companies (Standardization Opinions)[56] to facilitate the conversion of SOEs to joint stock companies. Soon after the issuance of the Standardization Opinions, the Commission issued Supplementary Measures Concerning the Implementation of the Opinions on the Standardization of Joint Stock Companies by Companies Seeking a Listing in Hong Kong (Supplementary Measures).[57] These Supplementary Measures were designed to adapt the listing in Hong Kong by companies incorporated in China and planning to list in Hong Kong.

As the Standardization Opinions and the Supplementary Measures do not contain detailed provisions for the protection of minority shareholders, concern over the extent of the protection of minority shareholders in Hong Kong needed to be addressed. For this purpose, the Mainland and Hong Kong Joint Working Committee on Securities Affairs was established with the approval of the State Council. Essential Clauses of the Articles of Association of Companies Seeking a Listing in Hong Kong proposed by this Committee was endorsed by the State Economic Restructuring Commission (Articles of Association).[58]

The Articles of Association list typical English company law provisions, including among other things the duty of directors[59] and what to do should a company be found guilty of a breach of duties.[60] The Standardization Opinions were replaced by the Company Law enacted in 1993 and the Articles of Association were replaced by the Prerequisite Clauses of the Articles of Association of Companies Seeking a Listing Outside the PRC (Prerequisite Clauses) in 1994.[61] In 1993 the State Council also promulgated the Tentative Regulation on the Administration of the Issuing and Trading of Shares (ITS).[62] These laws and regulations provided the legal infrastructure for the issuing and trading of shares both on the stock exchanges in China and the stock exchange in Hong Kong by companies incorporated in China. In the ITS, provisions on takeovers are very similar to those in the Hong Kong Code on Takeovers and Mergers,[63] which was itself based on the London City Code on Takeovers and Mergers.[64]

Chaos theory argues that some phenomena are extremely sensitive to historical events.[65] According to Chaos theory, accurate predictions about where a system is headed are hard, if not impossible, to make. The winding road described by Roe is a good example.[66] Today's winding road depends upon the choice by early fur traders to avoid a wolves' den close to a potentially straight road. Had the fur traders been better hunters of wolves, they might have chosen a straight road. The common law system in many different parts of the world is another example that historical events matter. The colonization of countries and regions such as Canada, Australia, New Zealand and Hong Kong led to the transplantation of the English-style common law system in these countries or regions. Similarly, China's utilization of capital overseas discussed previously played a critical role in the transplantation of the English-style takeover law.[67] The PRC maintained a rigid socialist economic planning system from 1949 until 1978. It was the Economic Reform Program initiated at the end of the 1970s that significantly changed the way of financing corporate activities. An important part of the policy change was the utilization of capital through the stock market to be established in China and existing stock markets outside China, particularly in Hong Kong. The inducement of capital in Hong Kong gave great leverage to the regulatory authorities there in persuading the Chinese regulatory authorities to adopt a takeover law familiar to Hong Kong and which was derived from the United Kingdom. Next I will discuss the adaptation of the transplanted English-style takeover law in China.

The law and adjustment

As discussed previously, China's early takeover transactions were regulated by the ITS.[68] While there are only seven articles on takeovers in the ITS, the key provision is based on the London City Code.[69] According to this provision, within 45 working days after any legal person's (other than a promoter's) direct or indirect holding of outstanding common shares in a listed company reaches 30 per cent of such company's total outstanding common shares, such legal person shall make an offer of takeover to all the shareholders of the target company, offering to purchase their shares through cash payment.[70] If a takeover is made, the higher of the following two prices should be adopted as the offer price: (1) the highest price paid by the offeror for the purchase of such shares during the 12 months preceding the issuance of the takeover offer; or (2) the average market price of such shares during the 30 working days preceding the issuance of the takeover offer.[71] I will call this provision the mandatory purchase provision and discuss the matter below.

A few other provisions are related to the fair treatment of minority shareholders and are much easier to justify. For instance, all the conditions contained in a takeover offer shall apply to all the holders of the same kind of shares.[72] If the total number of shares that the maker of a takeover offer prepares to buy is less than the total number of shares for which the offer is accepted, the offeror shall purchase shares from the offeree shareholders on a pro rata basis.[73] In the event of a change in any of the main conditions of offer after a takeover offer has been issued, the offeror shall promptly notify all offerees.[74] Such notice may be made in the form of a press conference or newspaper announcement or by another means of dissemination. During the term of a takeover offer and for a period of 30 working days thereafter, the offeror may not purchase the shares in question on any conditions other than those set forth in the offer.[75]

Still other provisions are related to disclosure and the facilitation of potential competing takeover offers. If a legal person holds, pursuant to the disclosure provision, directly or indirectly, more than 5 per cent of the common shares of another listed company, a public announcement shall be made and a written report disclosing the fact shall be sent to the listed target company, the relevant stock exchange and the China Securities Regulatory Commission (CSRC) within three working days from the date of acquisition.[76] In addition, any change of increase or decrease of the above acquired shares of such a legal person reaching 2 per cent will again trigger the reporting duty.[77] Such a legal person shall not directly or indirectly buy or sell shares of the target company two working days from the date when it makes the announcement and submits the report and before the submission of the report.[78] According to another provision for the purpose of facilitating takeover offers, the takeover offer period, calculated from the date of issuing the offer, shall not be less than 30 working days.[79] Offerors shall not withdraw their takeover offer during the offer period.[80] Furthermore, the offeree shareholders have the right to withdraw their acceptance during the offer period.[81] As will be discussed below, the political goal of maintaining control over large SOEs makes the disclosure provision and the provision for facilitating competing takeover offers irrelevant in the 1990s.

The mandatory purchase provision was adopted in the United Kingdom in 1968[82] and later spread to many other countries or regions including Australia,[83] Germany, Portugal, Italy and Switzerland.[84] The takeover law in the

USA does not have such a provision. The rationale behind the provision is the equality of treatment of minority shareholders. If an acquiring company pays a premium to the majority, block or some shareholder(s) of a target company when purchasing their shares, the acquiring company shall also be required to extend the same premium to minority shareholders. An introductory provision in the London City Code reflects that policy concern. The provision stipulates that the Code is designed principally to ensure fair and equal treatment of all shareholders in relation to takeovers.[85] This rationale, however, is based on an unrealistic assumption that, whatever the law, the number of takeovers will not be reduced. The provision takes the ex post view that the gains from the takeover, once it has taken place, should be shared equally by all the shareholders in the target.

Before proceeding to an evaluation of the mandatory purchase provision, it is necessary to discuss the motivations of acquiring companies in taking over target companies. The transfer of a controlling interest in a given company can take place in two types of situations. First, an acquiring company may believe that the target company in question can be managed in a more efficient manner and will thus generate more profit as the incumbent managers are indulging in excessive perquisites or are simply not working hard and/or are incompetent.[86] Second, the acquiring company may be able to employ synergistic practices to realize economies of scale or scope after the takeover to increase profits.[87] In both of the above cases, the transfer of control will be efficient at a price between the ceiling price of the present value of the future income stream generated by the acquiring company and the floor price of the present value of the future income stream of the firm as it is currently being operated by the target management. While abusing minority shareholders may occur in some takeovers, which can be safeguarded by the general corporate law on the protection of minority shareholders and on penalties being imposed on looters,[88] empirical evidence to a large extent supports the theories of disciplining inefficient managers and of synergy effects.[89]

The mandatory purchase provision can be evaluated by the autonomy value and the welfare value.[90] Neither criterion can justify this premium sharing provision. On a Nozickian rights-based approach, a distinction is made between threats and offer:[91] threats reduce the possibilities open to the recipient of an offer whereas offers expand them. From this perspective, takeovers would seem properly to be viewed as offers rather than as a threat. The possibility of having a new management team indicates that takeovers increase target shareholders' possibilities relative to their position prior to their interaction with the acquirer. Even the threat of takeovers disciplines managers in a potential target company.

Despite the conclusion that takeover transactions enlarge shareholders' contractual possibilities and despite the overwhelming empirical evidence that shareholders of target companies receive abnormally high returns resulting from

99

takeover transactions,[92] an enormous body of academic writing has focused on the problem of coercion in takeovers, particularly in partial bids.[93] Coffee notes that demonstrated examples of coercion remain as rare as confirmed sightings of the Loch Ness monster.[94] The ex ante Nozickian rights-based approach provides hardly any justification for the mandatory purchase provision. If takeovers enlarge the opportunities of the target shareholders as they are considered as offers rather than threats, then mandatory purchase provisions cannot be justified. Even from the perspective of the remaining target shareholders, mandatory purchase provisions may reduce their contractual opportunities as the heavy burden of the provision on the acquirer could result in few takeovers ex ante. Ex post, mandatory purchase provisions may be viewed as offers to particular offeree shareholders in the target as they can choose either to sell their shares to the acquirer with the premium or to remain in the target and expect the improvement of the target by the acquirer. Mandatory purchase provisions, however, are certainly threats to the acquiring company and the shareholders in the acquiring company. If takeovers do not create third party effects of coercion on the remaining shareholders in the target, it is not clear why the contractual freedom between the acquirer and part of the shareholders in the target should be restrained.

Autonomy value provides little support for such a provision. Welfare value would also rule against mandatory purchase provision as such provisions would increase the cost of acquiring the control of target companies. The harmful effects of the mandatory purchase provision are obvious. In the first place, they reduce the number of offers by making targets more expensive to acquire. According to the economic law of demand, the higher the price, the lower the demand from purchasers. Lower demand in the context of takeovers means fewer takeovers, hence, possibly, a smaller piece of pie for society. Second, the philosophy of sharing the gains from takeover transactions contained in the mandatory purchase provision reduces the return of investment on the part of the acquirer and this inability of acquirers to appropriate the full value of their investment will lead them to undertake too few takeovers. This is the classic public good problem.[95] The proper management of an inefficient target company is a public good to all the shareholders of the target. Grossman and Hart have pointed out that there are significant costs in ensuring that directors/managers act in the interest of shareholders.[96] If one shareholder (acquirer) devotes resources to improving management, then all shareholders benefit.[97] The mandatory purchase provision exacerbates the externality problem by allowing the remaining shareholders of the target company to share equal gains from takeovers. This severe externality problem indicates that it cannot be assumed that a company which is not being run in the interests of shareholders will always be vulnerable to a takeover bid. An antidote to this externality problem is to exclude the remaining shareholders in the target from sharing equal gains resulting from takeovers ex post. Hence, an argument for abolishing the mandatory purchase provision can be made at least at the low threshold of 30 per cent.

To understand how the imported takeover law adjusts to China's local conditions, it is necessary to understand the ownership structure of the listed companies on the two stock exchanges. As discussed previously, the development of China's corporate law and the establishment of the stock market at the beginning of the 1990s were closely related to the reform of SOEs. A survey in May 1999 revealed that among the 862 listed companies on the two stock exchanges, state shares existed in 541 listed companies, accounting for 62.76 per cent.[98] Among the 541 listed companies, state shares accounted for 45 per cent of the total issued shares in these companies.[99] In 473 listed companies, the state shareholder had either absolute or relative control[100] of the company, occupying 87.43 per cent of the 541 listed companies.[101] The state shares were mainly held by state asset administration bureaus, state investment companies or the parent companies of the state-owned listed companies.[102] To be sure, the percentage of state ownership is much higher as state ownership may be held by legal persons of state-owned companies.[103] In 70.79 per cent of the 541 listed companies, state shares ranged from 30 to 80 per cent.[104] These differ from the shares held by individuals, which are traded at the two stock exchanges, state shares and legal person shares of state-owned enterprises are not traded. Another statistic shows that traded shares owned by individual investors in most listed companies comprise only 25 to 40 per cent.[105]

The structure of shareholding in most listed companies makes it impossible for an acquiring company to accumulate control through buying shares on any stock exchange. So far, there has been no successful acquisition of control of a listed company by purchasing shares on the stock market. To acquire a sufficient percentage of shares in a target listed company requires the purchase of part of the non-traded shares owned by the state or other companies. This makes the negotiated takeover the preferred method of takeovers within China. Using this method, an acquiring company negotiates with a majority or block shareholder in the target listed company and enters into a share transfer agreement with that shareholder.

Negotiated takeovers in China, however, have to overcome some procedural and legal hurdles. On the procedural side, acquiring state shares or legal person shares of SOEs requires approval by the relevant authority. Article 29 of the Provisional Measures on the Administration of State-owned Shares of Joint Stock Companies provides that the transfer of state-owned shares need the approval of the State Asset Administration Commission and the provincial government.[106] Transferring more than 30 per cent of state-owned shares in a listed company requires the joint approval of the State Asset Administration Commission and the State Economic Restructuring Commission.[107] The approval procedure is consistent with the goal of the government to maintain control of the large SOEs on the stock market.

In addition to overcoming this procedural hurdle, negotiated takeovers have to comply with the requirement of the mandatory purchase provision, which is central to the London City Code. The cost of following such a mandatory purchase provision is well recognized by regulators in China.[108] The practice of dealing with negotiated takeovers and the adjustment of the English-style takeover law to the Chinese takeover market reflected concern that a strict following of the mandatory purchase provision would be inefficient.

The first negotiated takeover took place in 1994, under the early takeover regime. Hengtong Investment Ltd (Hengtong) was incorporated in Zuhai in 1981.[109] Focusing on property development, Hengtong expanded into shipping, communications, textile and electronic products. To market its electricity meters in Shanghai, Hengtong planned to acquire a property development company there. Search efforts revealed Shanghai Lingguang Ltd (Lingguang), which produces glass and electronic components, to be a suitable target. Lingguang issued 33.8 million shares in total. Among all the issued shares, Shanghai Construction Ltd held 55.26 per cent of the shares on behalf of the state while individual investors and legal person investors accounted for 32.55 per cent and 11.89 per cent of the shares respectively. Shortly before the transfer of control, Lingguang shares were trading at around 13 yuan per share on the secondary market. Hengtong's motivations for acquiring a controlling block of the shares of Lingguang were twofold: (1) to rely on Shanghai Construction Ltd's connection with the property market in Shanghai; and (2) to take advantage of Lingguang's technology. The deal was encouraging news to Lingguang and Shanghai Construction Ltd based on the information available then as Lingguang was short of funds to carry out ambitious development projects. An agreement was reached among Hengtong, Shanghai Construction Ltd and Lingguang to transfer 35.5 per cent of the shares held by Shanghai Construction Ltd to Hengtong at a price of 4.3 yuan on 28 April 28 1994. Transferring more than 30 per cent of the shares of a target, however, triggers the mandatory purchase provision. To avoid the high cost of mandatory purchase of the remaining shares, Hengtong applied to CSRC for an exemption. The CSRC granted permission mainly on the grounds that the transferred shares were non-trading state-owned shares.[110]

The Hengtong case raises a number of questions. Could the CSRC approve the transfer price of 4.3 yuan when the individual shares traded on the secondary market were priced at around 13 yuan? Is the significant discount of control shareholding able to ensure that the productive resources of the target move towards a more efficient purchaser? Are there legal grounds for the CSRC to give exemption from the mandatory purchase obligation when the ITS contains no legal provisions which confer such discretion upon the Commission. Finally, should China follow the US approach by exempting transfer of control through agreement under the need of protection test[111] if it is well recognized that the cost of following the English mandatory purchase provision is too high?

Later development of the takeover law partially addressed the issues arising from the Hengtong case. The Securities Law[112] modified the mandatory purchase provision and gave the CSRC discretion to exempt acquirers from following the mandatory purchase requirement if they acquire shares through any stock exchange.[113] The modified mandatory purchase provision now provides that if an investor holds 30 per cent of the issued shares of a listed company and continues to buy such shares through a stock exchange, the investor shall make a takeover offer to all the shareholders of the target listed company.[114] The Securities Law seems to make a difference with respect to negotiated takeovers. Article 89 of the Securities Law stipulates:

> In the case of takeover by agreement, the acquirer may execute the equity transfer by entering into an agreement with shareholders of the target company as prescribed in laws and administrative regulations.
>
> When a listed company is taken over by agreement, the acquirer must, within three days after the agreement is reached, submit a written report on the takeover agreement to the State Council's securities regulatory authority and the stock exchange, and make an announcement.

The above article seems to be based on the need of protection test in US securities regulation on the grounds that the selling of shares by sophisticated investors does not need the protection of law.[115] It is relatively clear that the article does not expressly compel the acquirer to make an offer to all the shareholders in a negotiated takeover. Nor does the article necessitate the acquirer to obtain approval from the CSRC for such a negotiated takeover, except for compliance with the reporting and announcement requirement. The article seems to recognize the high cost of the mandatory purchase provision and the need for a corporate control market to improve the inefficient state-owned listed companies. This article, however, has not been used in this way. The CSRC's position is that, whatever the method of acquiring control, the mandatory purchase provision must be complied with unless it grants the acquirer an exemption. This position is consistent with the practice of negotiated takeovers in China. By the end of 2000, all the 121 negotiated takeovers had followed the pattern of Hengtong in that an exemption was obtained from the CSRC.[116]

As discussed previously, most of China's SOEs on the stock market are not very efficient. A study has found that there is a negative correlation between firm performance and the percentage of state-owned shares.[117] Empirical evidence in another study also suggests that takeovers in China are, on the whole, efficient compared with the status of many companies before the takeover. However, the

103

market could be more efficient if ideological issues are properly dealt with.[118]

The inefficiency of the listed SOEs and the need for an active takeover market to facilitate the reallocation of productive resources requires China to modify the English-style takeover law in the Chinese takeover environment. This objective has led the CSRC to reconsider its position on negotiated takeovers. In 2002 the CSRC issued Procedures on the Administration of the Takeover of Listed Companies (Takeover Procedures).[119] While the Takeover Procedures reaffirm the position of the CSRC that, whatever the method of acquiring more than 30 per cent of the shares in a target listed company, the mandatory purchase requirement must be complied with unless exemption is obtained from the CSRC,[120] the Takeover Procedures have expanded the grounds upon which the CSRC is prepared to grant an exemption.

Among the exceptions, some are related to debt restructuring and insolvency reorganization. For instance, an exemption will be given if the transfer of shares is applied for on the basis of a court ruling and results in the percentage of shares held by the purchaser exceeding 30 per cent of the listed company's issued shares.[121] An exemption will also be provided if a bank engaging in normal business has acquired more than 30 per cent of the issued shares of a listed company but the bank has no intention or taken no action to actually control such a listed company and has made arrangements to transfer the excess shares to non-affiliated parties.[122] The exemption on insolvency pertains to an acquirer taking over a listed company in financial distress in order to rescue it and who has proposed a feasible restructuring plan.[123]

Other exceptions are based on the grounds that no shareholder in a target listed company has received any takeover premium. For example, when an acquirer has accumulated more than 30 per cent of the shares of a listed company resulting from the company issuing new shares.[124] Another exception is if the acquisition of more than 30 per cent of the issued shares of a listed company is caused by the reduction of the capital of the company.[125]

In the past the CSRC frequently gave exemptions if governmental transfer of state-owned shares had caused the transferee to hold more than 30 per cent of the issued shares of a listed company. This exemption is still in place.[126] Finally, the Takeover Procedures have added a catch-all provision, giving the CSRC the discretion to exempt the mandatory purchase provision if the CSRC considers it necessary to meet the needs of the development and changes within the securities market and the need to protect the legitimate rights and interests of investors.[127] The transfer of control through administrative means as practiced in the past has made the mandatory purchase provision largely irrelevant. If the catch-all provision is also used liberally, the mandatory purchase provision will also be made partly irrelevant.

The discussion of the adjustment of the English-style mandatory purchase provision clearly shows that application of the provision in China is path-dependent. The political goal of maintaining control of the state-owned listed companies has completely changed the rationale of using such a provision. The past socialist system of public ownership of the means of production created interested parties which controlled both the political and economic resources. These interested parties will try to protect their vested rights and interests. A very important way of maintaining control is to retain control of the large state-owned listed companies. However this driver requires a different way of using the law of takeovers: I echo the view of Art and Gu when stating that China's developing securities market can be properly understood only in the context of its underlying motivation, by carefully avoiding the mistake of assuming that the adoption of Western-style structures and laws implies movement toward Western goals.[128]

If we take the ex ante efficiency view discussed previously, the adjustment of the imported takeover law is very positive in the sense of achieving the primary goal of improving the efficiency of the large number of listed SOEs. Another positive use of the English-style takeover law is the adoption of the position of non-frustration on the part of the directors in a target listed company when facing a takeover offer.[129] Article 33 of the Takeover Procedures provides that the decisions made and measures taken by the directors, supervisors and senior management of the target company with respect to the takeover offer made by an acquirer may not prejudice the legitimate rights and interests of the company or its shareholders. More specifically, the said article prohibits the adoption of measures for the issuing new shares or convertible bonds, the re-purchase of its own shares, the amendment of Articles of Association and the signing of contracts, all of which could have a major effect on the company's assets, liabilities, rights, interests or business outcome, except in the ordinary course of business after an acquirer has announced its takeover intention.

In the USA a controversial issue is whether the board of directors or the shareholders should be given the ultimate power to decide whether the company should be sold to a bidder that offers to buy all the company's shares at a substantial premium above the current stock market price. Easterbrook and Fischel argue that the management should remain completely passive in the face of a takeover bid.[130] Their argument is based on the assumption that most takeovers are efficient in that they discipline bad managers in the target. When bad managers are facing a takeover bid which tends to remove them, it is unlikely that their action of defeating the takeover will be in the best interests of the company.[131] Bebchuk argues that, once mechanisms to ensure undistorted shareholder choice are in place, boards should not be permitted to block offers beyond the period necessary for putting together alternatives for shareholder consideration.[132] In contrast, Lipton argues against a regime of shareholders voting and no board veto.[133] According to Lipton, there are significant costs to companies in being managed as if they were constantly for sale.[134]

105

The Delaware General Corporation Law (DGCL) takes a middle ground. The DGCL gives the board of directors a central role in corporate decision-making,[135] but it also requires stockholder assent for many fundamental transactions.[136] The DGCL is, however, silent on the most contentious question in the debate: in what circumstances, and to what extent, are directors empowered to prevent shareholders from accepting a tender offer? The Delaware courts also follow a middle ground. While in principle Delaware case law holds that the purpose of the company is to maximize the wealth of its stockholders,[137] Delaware decisions also give directors substantial authority to deploy the powerful weapon of a poison pill[138] and to block takeover offers that appear to be in the best interests of the current array of stockholders.[139] The Delaware courts, however, have subjected defensive measures to a heightened form of judicial review under which directors must prove the reasonableness and good faith of their actions.[140] The result is a regime in which directors are given substantial authority to forge corporate strategies while leaving room for stockholders to vote down management-preferred directors and to use the election process to avail themselves of a tender offer.[141]

The adoption of the English-style mandatory purchase provision at the beginning of 1990s has educated regulators in China relatively well on other parts of the London City Code. When the CSRC issued the Takeover Procedures in 2002, it again chose the English position of non-frustration over the Delaware type of takeover law on the proper role of the target board when the target is facing a takeover offer. The choice is largely satisfactory in the context of China for at least two reasons. Delaware law is very complicated. At this stage, regulators and judges in China are still not sophisticated in takeover law. To expect them to administer the Delaware type of takeover law when even judges in other parts of the USA are not able to do so is likely to be counterproductive. Second, directors in the USA are subject to greater constraints because of very strict fiduciary duties, derivative suits and various market mechanisms, none of which are available in China.[142]

While the adoption of the English-style takeover law and the adjustment of the law in China are steps in the right direction, negotiated takeover transactions in China have a serious defect. As discussed previously, only shares held by individuals in listed companies are traded on the two stock exchanges. state shares and legal person shares of SOEs are not traded on the stock exchanges. This raises the issue of pricing the control block of state-owned shares. In the Hengtong case, the control block was priced at 4.3 yuan per share when the shares traded at the stock exchange were around 13 yuan per share.[143] The Opinions Concerning the Exercise of State-owned Shares in Joint Stock Companies[144] dictate that the lowest transfer price of state-owned shares is the net asset value per share.[145] In Hengtong and all other cases prior to 2004 when the control block of state-owned shares was transferred, the price of the shares of the block was several times lower than the price of the shares traded on the stock market. In a few cases, even the requirement of the lowest transfer price of net asset value per share was not followed.[146] The practice of negotiated take-overs in China also indicates why the mandatory purchase provision, which is central to the London City Code, is not followed in China. The mandatory purchase provision is based on the premise that the acquirer has to extend the same premium to all other shareholders in the target if they buys shares at a price higher than the market price from the majority, block or some shareholders, who are more likely to get the benefits because of their position. This ensures equality of treatment of all shareholders in the target. In China, when the control block is priced at a much lower price than the market price of other shares traded on the stock market, the mandatory purchase provision loses its rationale. This again leads to the conclusion that the political goal of maintaining the control of state-owned listed companies has made the imported law considerably irrelevant. While not following the mandatory purchase provision can be justified on efficiency grounds, cheap transfer of control block in China has left minority shareholders with no adequate protection.

In the USA and United Kingdom, the concern of takeover law is to ensure the minority shareholders obtain a premium over the market price if the acquirer gains control by offering the outgoing shareholder(s) in the target a price higher than the market price. Because of the benefits of control, the price of a control block is normally higher than the price of the shares of a target on the secondary market. The higher price of a control block is a basic market mechanism to protect the minority shareholders in that only those who are able to manage the target better are willing to obtain control given the constraints. There might be mistakes in prediction or judgement on the part of the acquirer and the effect of takeover may be disastrous. However, the market will correct the mistake in the long run. Nonetheless, the cheap transfer of control in China is not able to ensure that acquirers are necessarily better than the existing management in targets. Furthermore, the discount of share price of the control block creates serious risks of exploitation of minority shareholders. Recently, the State Asset Administration Bureau and the Ministry of Finance jointly issued Provisional Measures on the Administration of the Transfer of State-owned Shares in January 2004 (Provisional Measures).[147] The Provisional Measures now permit but do not compel the use of auctions or biddings in takeovers in addition to negotiated takeovers. Similar to other administrative rules, Provisional Measures is more interested in ensuring that the state-owned assets are not depleted in low price transfer of control to private-sector enterprises.

While auctions and biddings in takeovers will alleviate the problem of cheap transfer of control in listed companies in China, the move towards an efficient takeover market requires a radical reform of large scale exit of state-owned enterprises in many sectors of the economy. State-owned enterprises are

THE CASE AGAINST UNIFORMITY

unlikely to be efficient. As Trebilcock and Iacobucci have argued, there are not adequate means to motivate the agents in SOEs and there are not adequate means to discipline such agents in SOEs compared with the means available to private-sector firms.[148] To realize the goal of achieving efficiency through corporate law in general and takeover law in particular, the Chinese government must abandon the concept of controlling the state-owned listed companies for the purposes of political control. Only then can the law of takeover fully realize its efficiency goal.

The discussion on the transplantation and adjustment of an English style takeover law has been significantly affected by China's social and political factors. The adaptation of that law in China is not only path-dependent but also very local in nature, with legislative and administrative innovations. This again raises serious doubt as to whether a single corporate governance model can fit all countries.

CONCLUSION

Corporate governance has attracted enormous attention both in the area of law and in the area of financial economics. In comparative corporate governance studies, many people have devoted their research to find a best corporate governance model. I argue that a functional analysis does not support the view that there is a single best model in the world. I further use the transplantation of an English-style takeover law into China to explain that the importation of a foreign law is not always based on careful analysis on whether the imported foreign law is in fact the best model in the world. Furthermore, I discuss the subsequent adjustment of the transplanted English takeover law to the takeover market in China to show that the transplantation of foreign law is subject to local political and economic conditions. If there is no best corporate governance model and the transplantation of foreign law into other countries with different social and political backgrounds does not achieve similar objectives, the search for a best corporate governance model is misguided.

Chapter 5

The regulation of executive compensation

INTRODUCTION

From an agency perspective, directors and managers who do not own all the shares of the company for which they work do not bear all the consequences of their decisions. In order to better align the interests of shareholders and of directors and managers, agency theorists consider it necessary to establish market and contractual mechanisms that motivate and discipline directors and managers.[1] Among the various incentive and monitoring mechanisms, executive compensation has proven to be of great importance. This is owing to the fact that the bankruptcy and takeover markets are inefficient and have very little effect in China. In fact, reform of SOEs in China began with the contract responsibility system, which emphasized the effect of incentives upon senior managers.

Although the executive compensation system is very important, the establishment of an efficient system is challenging. Not only are the contributions and efforts of managers difficult to quantify, their decisions affecting the performance of the firm cannot always be accurately assessed. Under these circumstances, the executive compensation system must rely upon proxies such as corporate profit or share prices to assess performance. It goes without saying that these proxies are influenced by factors not under the control of senior managers. As a result, comments on the amount or level of executive compensation differ considerably. Magazines such as *Forbes*,[2] *Economist*,[3] and The *Globe and Mail*[4] all contain articles suggesting that senior managers receive too much. On the other hand, some economists believe that these executives deserve everything they receive.[5] In the USA and Canada, popular opinion, the demand of shareholders and the relevant special interest groups have more or less influenced the regulation of executive compensation. Section two briefly describes the historical development of executive compensation and the restrictions imposed upon executive pay in China. Section three analyses tax restrictions and their effects upon executive compensation in the USA. Section four discusses the disclosure of executive compensation and the impact of such a disclosure system, and further analyses the correlation between executive pay and firm performance. Section five discusses policy implications of the regulation of executive compensation for China. Conclusions follow in section six.

THE DEVELOPMENT OF, AND RESTRICTIONS UPON, EXECUTIVE COMPENSATION

Prior to the initiation of the economic reform programme in 1978, employee remuneration in Chinese enterprises was frequently influenced by leftist ideologies. For instance, during the 'Great Leap Forward' period from 1958 to1961, income distribution based upon employee performance and bonus systems was seriously affected.[6] Although income distribution based upon employee performance and incentives was gradually reaffirmed after 1961,[7] the Cultural Revolution from 1966 to 1976 once again negatively affected the incentive pay system.[8] In general, the difference between the remuneration of executives and the wages of other employees was not significant from 1950 to 1978.

After the economic reform programme in 1978, bonus and other incentive plans for employees were gradually re-adopted.[9] Previously bonuses and other incentives were not closely related to the economic performance of the enterprises, but in 1979 the incentive policy was changed. Starting from that year, the amount of bonus had to be allocated from retained profits, thus increasing the correlation between bonuses and the economic performance of the enterprise.[10] In 1981, the State Council stipulated that only those enterprises which were able to comply with economic criteria on quality, quantity, profit and supply specified by the state could allocate and distribute bonuses.[11] Furthermore, the total annual amount of the bonus for employees could not be greater than the equivalent of an employee's three-month standard wage.[12] Later, in 1984, the ceiling on bonuses was removed. However, bonuses exceeding a specified amount were subject to a bonus tax.[13] Enterprises were also allowed to carry out wage reforms as a motivation for employees. The method of linking wages and bonuses with the economic performance of enterprises considerably enhanced morale. The successful outcome of incentive remuneration led to the decision by the State Council in 1985 to provide greater freedom to enterprises so that the wages of enterprises might float within a proportional range according to its economic performance.[14] In the same year, the State Council also decided to de-link the wage system of enterprise employees from that of public servants in governmental institutions, universities and hospitals.[15] These two significant changes not only reduced the importance of governmental control with regard to the wages of employees in enterprises but also increased the role played by the labour market. During that period, however, the difference between the remuneration of executives and employees was not very great.

There were no separate legal provisions regarding the remuneration of executives and thus the directions were neither specific nor clear.

In 1986, the State Council promulgated Several Provisions Concerning the Deepening of Enterprise Reform and Strengthening of Enterprise Vitality (Several Provisions).[16] The Several Provisions permitted enterprises owned by all the people to provide the factory director or the general manager with remuneration one to three times the average wage of employees, or even higher.[17] In 1988 the State Council issued Provisional Regulation on the Leasing Operation of Small Enterprises Owned by all the People (Provisional Regulation).[18] This Provisional Regulation allowed for the remuneration of the operator of a local enterprise to be up to five times the average wage (including bonus) of the employees of the enterprise.[19] While these administrative measures provided enterprises with greater room to increase the difference in remuneration between executives and ordinary employees, restrictions on executive compensation remained in place.

In 1994 an experiment was carried out in Shenzhen which allowed the system of annual remuneration to be applied to the chairperson of the board of directors and/or the general manager.[20] In 1996 the annual remuneration system for general managers in SOEs was standardized there. According to Article 22 of the Provisional Measures on the Work of Company Managers in the City of Shenzhen (Provisional Measures),[21] the annual remuneration of the general manager shall consist of basic annual remuneration, performance annual remuneration and bonus annual remuneration.[22] The basic annual remuneration depends upon factors including the amount of assets of the company, the realized amount of profit, the amount of tax paid, the sales volume and/or the foreign exchange earned. Specific classification was to be made by the State Asset Administration Office of that city. The performance annual remuneration comprises two components: 40 per cent of the performance annual remuneration is based upon the growth rate of the net asset; the other 60 per cent is based upon the growth rate of the realized profit. The annual bonus remuneration is linked with the requirement that the growth rate of the company based upon the above factors exceeds that of the industrial average. Bonuses can be in the form of cash, in kind or in share dividend.[23]

The Ministry of Labour and Social Security extended the annual remuneration system to other parts of the country in 1997.[24] The main purposes of adopting the annual remuneration system in China include the separation of executive compensation from the remuneration of other employees; linking executive compensation with the level of difficulty inherent in enterprise management and firm performance; and the enhancement of transparency of executive compensation.[25] Although one of the purposes of the annual remuneration system was to increase the correlation between executive compensation and the performance of the firm, the current basic annual remuneration of

111

corporate executives was still constrained to a few times the average annual wages of ordinary employees. In addition, the annual performance remuneration of corporate executives was not allowed to exceed the basic annual remuneration. With China moving further towards a market economy, it is necessary to examine whether such restrictions on corporate executives are conducive to firm performance. I will discuss below the experience and lessons drawn from the regulation of executive compensation through tax law or, alternatively, through the law on disclosure of executive compensation in other countries.

TAX RESTRICTIONS ON EXECUTIVE COMPENSATION

In the USA and United Kingdom, the high growth rate of the amount of executive compensation is an undisputed fact. An investigation in the United Kingdom showed that the actual average salary and bonuses of executives in the surveyed companies increased 149 per cent over 13 years during the period from the 1980s until the 1990s.[26] A survey in the USA in 1990 also revealed that the average compensation of CEOs was 35 times of that of manufacturing employees; in Japan this ratio was 15 times and in Europe 20 times.[27] Although the increase of remuneration of manufacturing employees between 1980 and 1989 was less than 15 per cent, the growth rate of compensation of CEOs was more than 150 per cent.[28] For example, in 1993 total compensation to the CEO of Walt Disney Company reached US$200 million.[29]

Both populists and shareholders in the USA have strong reactions to the high levels of executive compensation. Most populist criticisms of executive compensation focus on the level of pay rather than on the relationship between CEO pay and firm performance, while shareholder criticisms of CEO pay have centred on the lack of meaningful rewards for superior performance and the strict penalties for failure.[30] Opinions of populists and shareholders with regard to higher levels of executive pay received responses of a political nature in the Congress. It is obvious that simultaneously satisfying the concerns both of popular groups and shareholders is impossible. As will be discussed further, satisfying shareholders by increasing pay-performance sensitivities implies higher levels of pay, while yielding to populist pressure to restrict pay levels results in lower incentives and firm value. The tax regulation of executive compensation in the USA in 1994 clearly reflects this dilemma.

The Omnibus Budget Reconciliation Act of 1993 (OBRA) added section 162(m) to the Internal Revenue Code. Section 162(m) limits corporate tax deductions for compensation paid to the CEO and the next four highest-paid executive officers to US$1 million each.[31] Performance-based pay, however, may be exempted. Qualification for exemption requires, inter alia, approval by shareholders in advance to link executive compensation to specific and objective performance targets formulated by a compensation committee composed solely of outside directors and ex post certification of performance by the compensation committee.[32]

After section 162(m) became effective, people carried out follow-up studies to examine the effects of this provision. Murphy's study discussed previously reveals that it is impossible to deal with both the concerns of populists and of shareholders adequately through legislation. Section 162(m) not only fails to restrict the amount of executive compensation but also accelerates an increase in the amount of such compensation. There are two explanations. First, some companies ignore the legislative restrictions in tax law and continue to pay more than US$1 million as annual salary to executives. A survey of 91 firms showed that one-third of the companies are not concerned with the negative impact of section 162(m) and continue to provide executives with an annual compensation beyond the US$1 million limitation.[33] Second, section 162(m) and the exemptions led some firms near the US$1 million cap to restrain their salary increases, and perhaps to increase the performance components of their pay packages.[34] An investigation in 1996 revealed that while the salaries and bonuses to corporate executives only increased by 7 per cent, the value of the options they received increased by 27.9 per cent.[35] According to figures supplied by the Internal Revenue Service, section 162(m) did not result in a decrease in executive compensation. Quite the contrary: executive pay actually rose 29 per cent faster in the first year after the law took effect.[36]

Although the tax reform has led firms using more stock options and has, to a certain degree, increased the correlation between executive pay and firm performance, it is very difficult to satisfy both the demands of shareholders and populists. Responding to the demand of shareholders means an enhancement of the correlation between executive compensation and firm performance. Whether to use incentive bonuses or to use stock options to strengthen the correlation will result in increased payments. First, the process of moving from fixed salary to performance-based pay means managers require a higher amount of compensation for the greater risks involved[37] – compared with stock options, salaries are relatively stable. Also, the welfare effects resulting from the exercise of stock options may be affected by external factors unrelated to the efforts of managers. To overcome this potential problem, companies normally have to provide a greater value in stock options; it is generally not acceptable for managers to receive an expected US$100 in stock options in exchange for a reduction of US$100 in their salary.

Second, the reason why the greater use of performance-based stock options increases the amount of executive compensation is because companies routinely but erroneously perceive options as a relatively low-cost way to deliver compensation.[38] From the perspective of senior managers, the standard option pricing models are not appropriate for valuing options held by undiversified, risk-averse employees who cannot freely sell the options or hedge their risks.[39] From the perspective of companies, options are perceived as inexpensive because they can be granted without any cash outlay and without incurring an accounting charge.[40] Further, when options are exercised, the accounting income is left unchanged, but the taxable income is reduced under US accounting and tax rules.[41]

Third, the reason why stock options will result in an increase in the amount of executive compensation is because of the endowment effect.[42] Economic theories normally assume that there is no fundamental difference between a foregone gain (opportunity cost) and an out-of-pocket loss. Experimental economists have, however, demonstrated that people view opportunity costs as less important than out-of-pocket costs. This bias towards retaining what one possesses is called the 'endowment effect'.[43] Applying the endowment effect to executive compensation, Iacobucci reached the conclusion that the endowment effect may result in a bargain whereby the executive retains their salary but is granted an additional variable pay package.[44]

The above discussion shows that satisfying the demands of shareholders requires performance-based variable pay. The result of using variable pay, the perceived cost of stock options and the endowment effect all tend to increase the amount of executive compensation. This is not a desired outcome for the populists. On the other hand, yielding to the pressure of populists to reduce the amount of executive compensation requires restrictions on the amount of executive compensation. However, restrictions on the amount of executive compensation are likely to result in a welfare loss on the part of shareholders. The discussion also reveals that the legislative endeavour to use tax laws to restrict the amount of executive pay is likely to fail. In a market economy, what constitutes a reasonable amount of executive pay is determined by market conditions. There does not exist any ideal legislative, administrative or judicial criterion on how much executives should be paid.

LEGISLATIVE REQUIREMENT OF DISCLOSURE OF EXECUTIVE PAY

Populist criticisms of executive pay and shareholder concerns over the method of executive pay that occurred during the 1990s also led to an expansion of the scope of, or the adoption of, disclosure of executive pay in North America. Despite the fact that US regulators have required disclosure of executive compensation for over 50 years, the USA has by far the world's highest-paid executives.[45] Obviously people need to reconsider the role of disclosure of executive pay. Two questions naturally arise. The first is whether the disclosure of executive pay improves the method of executive remuneration in relation to shareholder demands for greater returns. The second is whether the disclosure of executive pay serves the purpose of controlling the amount of executive compensation demanded by the populists. After discussing the content of disclosure of executive pay, the following two parts of this section will deal with each of the two questions given above.

In 1992, the Securities Exchange Commission (SEC) further enlarged the scope of disclosure of information on corporate executive compensation.[46] Among other things, the new rules require companies to produce the following: (1) a table summarizing the major components of compensation received by the CEO and other highly paid executives over the past three years; (2) tables describing option grants, option holdings and option exercises in greater detail; (3) a chart showing the company's stock-price performance relative to the performance of the market and the company's 'peer group' over the prior five fiscal years; and (4) a report by the compensation committee describing the company's compensation philosophy.

The function of pay disclosure on the relation between pay and firm performance

The system of disclosing executive compensation has played an active role in increasing the correlation between executive pay and firm performance. In the first place, disclosure has a desirable effect in lowering the costs of shareholders monitoring executive compensation.[47] In companies where shares are widely dispersed, small investors do not have incentives to monitor the activities of management. This passive participation of small investors in corporate governance is understandable. Participation in corporate governance requires time and information, and the cost of time and acquiring the necessary information is borne by the active monitoring shareholders. Any benefits derived from active monitoring by these active shareholders must be shared with other shareholders. Being unable to fully capture all the benefits of monitoring management results in reduced incentives for small investors and leads to a problem of free riders. Although the disclosure of executive compensation does not affect the positive externalities, it may significantly reduce the private costs of monitoring compensation. This is true because it may have been very difficult for an investor to find out the composition of executive pay packages prior to mandatory disclosure: mandatory disclosure makes it much easier to uncover such details. Under such systems, both in the USA and in Canada, the information disclosed by companies must reveal the performance of the company and the strategy and reasons for adopting different compensation methods. Other things being equal, the lower the monitoring cost, the greater the benefits from monitoring for shareholders. Another reason why disclosure of executive compensation increases the benefits of monitoring is the lower cost of evaluating pay packages, because disclosure

115

rules require companies to explain their compensation strategy and to provide comparative tables showing the firm's financial performance.[48]

Also, mandatory disclosure rules facilitate shareholder activism and increase monitoring reputation. In the USA, in 1992, the SEC revised proposals on executive compensation.[49] Disclosure has not only lowered the cost of monitoring executive pay but also made it easier for activist shareholders to publicize their monitoring activities. Both aspects have had a positive effect upon institutional investors. Institutional investors accounted for more than two-thirds of investment in Canada during the 1990s.[50] As relatively large shareholders, institutional investors are able to obtain a higher proportion of monitoring gains. Diversification of investment by institutional investors through portfolios will also result in positive externalities of their monitoring activities. Proposals on compensation packages by institutional investors will deter unjustifiable executive pay packages for the same company in the future. Furthermore, the good reputation and credible threat of active monitoring of executive pay by institutional investors may deter the adoption of executive pay packages by other companies which do not have the shareholder's best interests in mind.[51] Examples of active monitoring of executive pay by institutional investors include the California Pension Fund, CalPERS (California Public Employees' Retirement System). CalPERS has scrutinized and demanded changes to compensation schemes in a number of firms.[52]

Finally, disclosure of executive pay policies may be important in requiring the compensation committee to explicitly formulate a compensation strategy. Under a disclosure regime, the compensation committee is forced to justify its choice of a particular pay package.[53] Viewed from the standpoint of shareholders, only those compensation packages that will bring more wealth to the company will receive support. Empirical studies in Canada have shown that mandatory disclosure of executive pay strengthens the correlation between executive compensation and firm performance.[54]

Kevin Murphy, a renowned scholar in financial economics, summarizes the 1992 reform on the disclosure of executive pay as follows:[55]

> Overall, the new SEC rules make it much easier for shareholders to quantify and distinguish between the level of pay and the pay-performance relation and have helped to focus attention on stock-price appreciation as the preeminent measure of corporate performance. These changes facilitate better monitoring of compensation committees and boards of directors in general, which in turn leads to the design of more effective compensation policies. Perhaps more importantly, the compensation committee report requirement and the other SEC initiatives have dramatically increased the visibility and the accountability of compensation committees as the architects of top-management compensation plans. Because the scrutiny on compen-

sation committees emanates from political sectors as well as shareholders, it is not a foregone conclusion that the increased scrutiny will lead to more effective compensation policies.

The impact of disclosure upon the amount of compensation

There are four reasons to explain why the disclosure of executive pay will lead to higher amounts of executive compensation. First, under the disclosure regime on corporate executive compensation post reform, more companies have adopted performance-based pay. As discussed in section three, performance-based variable pay is more likely to lead to an increase in the total amount of executive compensation. Where there is a divergence of interest between management and shareholders and where managers have greater discretion, the company needs to give executives more performance-based variable pay in order to provide incentives for them to produce more wealth for the company. Compared with the old pay regime, in which executive remuneration is not based upon firm performance, performance-based variable pay allows managers to receive part of the wealth they help to create, resulting in higher rates of pay for successful management of the company. Under the old regime, there is no close relationship between executive remuneration and firm performance. Executive remuneration under the former regime is a zero-sum game.[56] Higher pay for managers means less profit for shareholders. Performance based compensation, however, is more likely a positive-sum game. Under the regime where executive remuneration is closely linked with firm performance, performance-based variable pay to executives is proportionally related to the growth of total wealth of the company. Thus, from an efficiency perspective, the negative reaction from the public towards an increase in the amount of executive compensation is not reasonable.

Second, under the performance-based pay regime, executive pay is positively connected with firm performance. The firm's performance, however, is not necessarily linked only to the performance of managers as it is difficult to separate the contribution of managers from external factors. In these circumstances, managers bear the risk of external factors negatively influencing the firm's performance.[57] Other things being equal, risk-averse managers prefer a fixed salary to receiving the same amount in expected variable pay. For risk-averse managers, an increase in the expected amount of the variable pay must be higher than the reduction in the amount of fixed salary for managers to accept performance-based variable pay.[58] To the extent that disclosure increases the positive correlation between executive remuneration and firm performance, managerial risk aversion and bargaining will result in higher levels of pay.[59] Moreover, the human capital of managers is normally firm-specific and cannot be

117

perfectly diversified. Performance-based pay generally requires that managers take on more risky projects in the expectation of higher expected pay-offs. The risk a higher probability of bankruptcy for the firm in undertaking riskier projects also requires a higher payment to managers.

Third, mandatory disclosure of executive compensation necessarily requires the adoption of variable executive pay by companies; this indicates the close link between executive compensation and firm performance. Performance-based pay for executives is practiced widely through the adoption of stock options.[60] The discussion in section three reveals that both companies and employee managers tend to undervalue the cost of such options.[61] This undervaluation results in the award of a greater value of stock options compared to the actual economic cost of the options. The result is a higher amount of total executive compensation.

Fourth, the endowment effect discussed above is also likely to have an indirect effect upon the amount of executive compensation. Mandatory disclosure of executive pay reduces the cost of shareholder monitoring and generates pressure on the compensation committee or the board of directors to adopt performance-based variable pay. The endowment effect suggests, however, that the change in executive compensation from fixed salary to performance-based variable pay may not mean the replacement of a proportion of salary with the same expected amount in terms of variable pay. From a distributive perspective, this may sound slightly negative. On the other hand, judged by the efficiency criterion, a higher amount of executive compensation under a regime of pay sensitive to performance is not negative, the higher amount of executive compensation resulting in greater net corporate wealth. In this sense there is no need to worry about higher amounts of executive compensation.

THE REGULATION OF EXECUTIVE COMPENSATION

Although China has moved more towards a market economy, the transition is not yet complete. During the transitional phase of the economy, the method of executive compensation continued to be adversely affected by the mentality of the old economic planning regime. Currently, there is significant tension between the market-oriented efficiency perspective and egalitarian values. In this sense the intellectual debate as well as the reforms on executive compensation is highly political. This section will discuss the empirical evidence related to executive compensation in Chinese listed companies followed by the regulation of executive compensation.

A survey of 78 listed companies in China in 1997 revealed that there was virtually no correlation between the annual compensation of corporate executives and firm performance.[62] Another empirical study carried out in 2000 confirmed that there was no connection between executive compensation and firm performance amongst listed companies.[63] Although the reforms taken by state-owned enterprises are slow, the trend of reforming the methods of corporate executive compensation is promising: several studies indicate a positive correlation between executive compensation and firm performance. Another study conducted in 2002 revealed that there was in fact a positive relationship between executive compensation and firm performance in Chinese listed companies.[64] Another survey of executive compensation in 381 listed companies reveals a positive link between the proportion of shareholding by of the most influential director and firm performance.[65] The same study also discovered that there is a further negative impact upon firm performance if the most influential director (the general manager or the chairperson of the board of directors) does not receive pay from the listed company.[66]

Considering the issue from the perspective of total executive compensation, opinions of economists are largely rational although populist criticisms of executive compensation occasionally appear in the media.[67] The following survey results also affirm the above point. A survey of 89 listed companies, which disclosed executive compensation in 1997, reveals that the average annual compensation of the general managers in listed companies was only RMB 38,650.[68] The average annual compensation of senior managers in listed companies in 2002 increased to RMB 157,400. There are, of course, some extreme cases where the executives received RMB 6 to 7 million in 2002.[69]

The regulation of executive compensation in other countries shows that restrictions on the amount or level of executive compensation, either through tax law or by disclosure rules, are unlikely to have any positive effect. The discussion above demonstrates that laws which try to restrict the amount of executive pay are counterproductive. What constitutes a reasonable amount of executive pay should be determined by the managerial market. Any attempt to find an ideal legislative, administrative or judicial criterion for the purpose of regulating executive pay in a market economy is doomed to failure. If the amount of executive compensation in a company is suspiciously high, and there is no correlation between executive compensation and firm performance of a particular company in a market economy, this is a good indication that there are weaknesses in the corporate governance of that company. A study in the United Kingdom found that there was a negative correlation between the amount of executive pay and the absence of a compensation committee in the surveyed companies.[70] However, it must be pointed out that demanding a reduction of executive compensation is not necessarily in the interests of shareholders. A study in the USA revealed that proposals by institutional investors that impose restrictions upon executive pay might in fact have a negative effect upon the share prices of these companies.[71]

On the other hand, regulation of executive pay emphasizing the increasing correlation between executive pay and firm performance will normally have

119

better results. As discussed in above, regulation in the USA on executive pay either through tax law or disclosure rules both promote the positive correlation between executive pay and firm performance. Nevertheless, regulation by using disclosure rules is more conducive to corporate management in a market economy. Disclosure rules have a clear advantage with respect to the promotion of transparency and the efficiency of the stock market. Discussion in section four has shown that disclosure of executive pay reduces the costs of the monitoring the management by shareholders. In addition, disclosure rules enhance the reputation of active shareholder monitoring and create a deterrent effect in the same company as well as in the other companies in which institutional investors may have invested. Finally, disclosure rules promote the accountability of the compensation committee, as a heightened policy of transparency means that directors on the committee have to explain their reasons for the executive pay package.

A mandatory disclosure regime plays a significant role in strengthening the positive correlation between executive pay and firm performance. As long as there are no externalities, the higher the correlation between executive pay and firm performance, the greater the net wealth created by the company. The lessons to be learned from the regulation of executive pay in other countries have clear policy implications for China, which is in transition from a planned economy to a market-oriented economy. However, the benefits from mandatory disclosure of executive pay would require institutional changes in China.

The requirement of disclosing executive pay in China's listed companies began in 1996. The CSRC issued the Notice Concerning the Implementation of Regulating the Disclosure of Information in Listed Companies in 1995 (Notice).[72] The Notice requires listed companies to disclose in their annual report information regarding the shareholdings of directors, supervisors and senior managers both at the beginning and the end of the year, any changes regarding shareholding and annual compensation paid by the company, including salary, bonuses, benefits, special treatments in the form of cash, in kind or other form, and securities.[73] Subsequently, the CSRC issued the Code on Corporate Governance for Listed Companies (Governance Code).[74] Although Article 77 of the Governance Code emphasizes the establishment of incentive schemes to link executive compensation with firm and personal performance, the provisions on the disclosure of compensation to directors and senior managers in listed companies are very brief. Article 72 of the Governance Code stipulates that directors and supervisors shall report to the shareholders at shareholder meetings about the performance of their duties, firm performance and their remuneration and shall disclose the same to the public. Article 79 of the Governance Code provides that the pay package for senior managers shall be approved by the board of directors, explained to the shareholders and disclosed to the public. After promulgation of the Governance Code, the CSRC revised its disclosure requirements for information in the annual report by listed companies. The provisions require, among other things: the disclosure of the decision-making process concerning the compensation of directors, supervisors and senior managers; the basis of determining such compensation; the total annual pay of directors, supervisors and senior managers, including basic salary; all bonuses, welfare benefits, housing and other allowances; and the total compensation awarded to the three highest paid directors and the three highest paid senior managers.[75]

An examination of the disclosure requirements of executive compensation in China shows some inadequacies. Future reforms will require amendment of the Governance Code on both disclosure and the annual report, meaning that listed companies will need to disclose detailed information on the composition of executive pay packages – particularly the disclosure of performance-based remuneration in the form of stock options or restricted stocks and their quantities. In addition, the price of shares at the date of the granting of stock options, the exercise price of stock options by senior executives and restrictions on the holding period after the exercise of the stock options will need to be disclosed. Moreover, any information necessary for a comparison with other similarly situated companies associated with the appreciation of stock prices and the distribution of dividends must also be disclosed. Finally, the compensation committee or the board of directors must disclose in detail, to the shareholders, the basis or reasonableness of adopting different pay methods or the composition of pay packages and the correlation between executive pay and firm performance. It can be said with reasonable certainty that improvement of the mandatory disclosure regime on executive compensation in China will enhance the efficiency and effectiveness of shareholder monitoring of executive compensation. With the external monitoring mechanisms of bankruptcy and takeover very weak, the mechanism of executive compensation is of vital importance.

Although the mechanism of disclosing executive compensation is very important, to strengthen the positive correlation between executive compensation and firm performance requires a move towards the liberalization of corporate finance in order that companies can issue shares and options, repurchase shares and allow the strict enforcement of law against violations of corporate law and securities regulations. While the use of such instruments will help companies enhance the relationship between executive compensation and firm performance, the implementation of such methods requires a liberalized and open stock market. If China wishes to carry out reforms to strengthen the correlation between executive compensation and firm performance, it must improve its corporate law and securities regulation regimes and strictly enforce any such laws. On the other hand, the use of stock options does not fully enable the separation of external factors from the efforts of executives.[76] Viewed from this perspective,

121

the compensation method of using stock options is not perfect. In the real world, we can only compare this performance-based method with other methods that have little or no correlation between executive pay and firm performance. Furthermore, with the legal system in China not yet fully mature, the stock option compensation method is more likely to be abused. Prevention of abuses of the stock market requires heavy penalties against insider trading, market manipulation of share prices and misrepresentation by corporate executives. With corporate scandals erupting in the USA, which boasts a far more established and mature legal system than China, it is highly unrealistic to expect that there will be no such abuse or manipulation by executives in China. The crucial point is that despite the existence of some fraud against small investors, the adoption of performance-based pay methods such as stock options will result in a faster growth of shareholder wealth and wealth in society when compared with the use of compensation methods that are not sensitive to firm performance. With respect to any resulting distributional issues, other regimes, including the tax system, are in a much better position than corporate law to address the problem of income disparity.

CONCLUSION

This chapter has dealt with the issue of executive compensation and applied it to the case of China. Given that China's market economy is still is in its early stages, it is necessary to compare and learn from the experiences of more mature economies regarding executive compensation. However, it is also necessary to avoid comparison with performance-based executive pay methods in an ideal system. With this in mind, here I have discussed the regulation of the differing levels and methods of executive pay. In terms of efficiency, regulation of the level of executive compensation is meaningless – any attempt to formulate an ideal legislative, administrative or judicial criterion on the level of executive compensation is likely to be counterproductive. Instead the emphasis of regulation of executive compensation should be placed upon the correlation between executive compensation and firm performance. Comparatively speaking, the mechanism of disclosure in executive compensation is more conducive to a market economy and beneficial to the further development of the stock market in China. The reform of executive compensation emphasizing the correlation between executive compensation and firm performance makes it necessary for China to liberalize the use of performance-based executive pay in corporate law and securities regulation. The flexible use of stock options and other performance-based pay methods require heavier penalties on insider trading, market manipulation and misrepresentation by executives. With the insolvency market and the takeover market too weak to penalize incumbent managers, reform on executive compensation becomes very important in motivating corporate executives. While there are still distributional concerns in China during its transitional phase, the fact that performance-based methods of executive compensation enhance not only the net growth of corporate wealth but of social wealth as a whole, makes this the only viable option at present.

Chapter 6

Towards a functional approach to comparative corporate governance studies[1]

INTRODUCTION

The problem of separation of corporate control and residual claims documented by Berle and Means has attracted considerable attention in the USA.[2] The early economic explanation of the cause of the problem of separation of corporate control and residual claims is the emphasis on the scale of economics and specialized knowledge of managerial experts. If the economic explanations were true, competitive economic forces would drive nations towards a single best model of corporate governance. Roe's pioneering works, however, find that similar matured economies have widely diversified corporate governance regimes.[3] Roe's research suggests that there are alternatives. Despite the differences in corporate governance regimes around the world, considerable research is still focused on the issue of whether there is a best corporate governance model in the world. Some scholars boldly link corporate governance regimes to the performance of the economy. I argue from a functional approach in section two that there might be no single optimal corporate governance model in the world. If this is correct, the search for a single best model is largely misguided. I examine in section three whether it is feasible to link directly corporate governance regimes with performance of the economy in comparative corporate governance studies. In section four, I develop an institutional competition model in comparative corporate governance studies and discuss its implications for emerging economies such as China.

THE SEARCH FOR AN OPTIMAL MODEL

The formation and growth of corporations require capital. Capital may be raised through equity financing or debt financing. Both methods of corporate finance result in friction between users and suppliers of capital. Equity financing gives rise to the agency costs of equity financing while debt financing gives rise to the agency costs of debt financing.[4] As the methods of financing corporate projects through either debt or equity are not mutually exclusive,[5] most companies adopt both debt financing and equity financing. Differences, however, do exist. Corporations in the USA and the United Kingdom rely far more heavily on the securities market than corporations in Germany and France. For instance, while the United Kingdom has 36 listed firms per million citizens and the USA has 30, France and Germany have only eight and five respectively.[6] Similarly, the ratio of total stock market capitalization to GDP contracts sharply between Germany on the one hand and the United Kingdom and the USA on the other. In Germany, stock market capitalization was 17 per cent of GDP compared to 132 per cent in Great Britain.[7] In the USA in 1995, the stock capitalization of the New York Stock Exchange and NASDAQ was around 87 per cent of the total GDP.[8]

Different corporate finance methods create different sets of conflict of interest problems. The solutions to these different problems call for different corporate governance regimes. Corporate governance is defined as ways designed to make management work in the best interests of the corporation and to assure a reasonable return to the suppliers of capital. In the USA the supply of capital is predominantly from the securities market. In such an economy, the growth of corporations under competitive conditions is mainly determined by the scale of economics,[9] shareholder diversification,[10] reduction of transaction costs[11] and the special knowledge of managerial experts.[12] According to Demestz and Lehn, share ownership concentration levels are inversely related to the aggregate size of the corporation.[13] This relationship holds because as the value-maximizing size of firm increases, the cost of acquiring a control block also rises, deterring control accumulation. In addition, when the benefits from control transactions are smaller than the benefits resulting from share diversification, people will choose the latter. Berle and Means documented the phenomenon of widely dispersed shares in the USA.[14] Within a regime where corporate finance is mainly from the securities market and shares are widely dispersed, the costs of equity financing would be higher if the corresponding corporate governance mechanisms were not available. In fact, the product market, the stock market and the takeover market play important roles in the USA in solving the problem of conflict of interest between management and shareholders.

In Germany, initial public offerings historically have been rare; only 10 occurred in 1994.[15] The German stock markets are famously illiquid[16] and volatile.[17] Generally speaking, debt financing plays a much more significant role than equity financing.[18] Debt financing creates the problem of conflict of interest between a borrowing corporation and the creditor. The corporate governance regime in Germany was very responsive to the agency costs of debt financing.

125

German banks' historical and significant roles in debt financing, without political and legal constraints, make it desirable for them to have the option of holding shares in the debtor corporations.[19]

In debt financing, creditors can normally intervene in the debtors' business only after the debtors default. As bankruptcy generally diminishes the claims of general creditors, creditors prefer an early exit if they do not have sufficient control of the debtor. If a creditor is also a major shareholder, it may deter wealth transfer transactions. Ex ante, the creditor–shareholder may prevent wealth transfer transactions being adopted by the management of the borrower. Such intervention is normally done by the creditor–shareholder's representative on the supervisory board. The supervisory board can always ask the management board for reports. The supervisory board may also ask the management board to obtain its approval before important transactions, such as credits above a certain amount.[20]

Ex post, the creditor–shareholder may penalize managers through the supervisory board. Significant shareholding in the debtor corporation makes voice more important than exit; otherwise the creditor–shareholder will suffer both on equity investment and on credit investment. Thus, it is not surprising to see that German banks often take over the reorganization of corporations in distress.[21] Empirical studies show that there is a significant involuntary 'fluctuation' of management board members not only where there are serious problems within the corporation but also in less serious cases in which the supervisory board is displeased with the performance of individual managers or with the management board as a whole.[22] Hence, creditor–shareholders' active participation in corporate governance in Germany reduces both the agency costs of debt financing and the agency costs of equity financing.

The search for the best corporate governance model has been underway since the beginning of the 1990s. Porter argued that the Anglo–US pattern of dispersed ownership was clearly inferior to the bank-centred capital markets of Germany and Japan because the latter enabled corporate executives to manage for the long term, while US managers were allegedly forced to maximize short-term earnings.[23] Grundfest argued that the US regulatory regime systematically subordinated the desire of investors to resolve agency problems to the desire of managers to be protected from capital market discipline.[24] He states:

> As a consequence of the harmony of interests created by joint equity and debt holding position, Japanese firms have to compensate lenders less to induce them to bear the risks associated with potential bondholder - stockholder conflict. Thus, all else being equal, Japanese capital structures reduce agency costs and allow investors to monitor management more effectively than the US capital structures do. In particular, the amelioration of agency problems allows Japanese firms to invest more in research and development and to

maintain more liquid and flexible asset structures than their comparably leveraged American counterparts.

Similar criticisms of the US corporate governance regime can be found in political theories, which explain dispersed share ownership in large US corporations as the product of political forces and historical contingencies as well as the product of economic efficiency.[25]

Doubts were soon raised concerning whether the corporate governance regime in the USA is inferior to their counterparts in Japan and Germany. Macey and Miller argue that the existence of powerful banks in corporate governance carries with it an entirely new set of conflicts between the risk-averse claimants who make loans and the residual claimants who invest risk capital, preventing the equity claimants from undertaking socially optimal risks.[26] The argument of Macey and Miller is not entirely satisfactory, however. The conclusion that powerful banks as fixed claimants care far less about maximizing borrowing firms' potential upside performance than about minimizing potential downside performance ignores the major fact that German universal banks sometimes do hold substantial shares in the borrowing corporations. For instance, in 1986 the Deutsche Bank held 41.8 per cent of the shares in Daimler-Benz, 30.82 per cent shares in Bayer and 17.64 per cent of the shares in Siemens.[27] Presumably, Deutsche Bank would also be able to share in the high proportion of benefits from the optimal risk-taking activities in these borrowing corporations.

Neoclassical economists have long argued that efficiency considerations ultimately prevail and determine corporate structure. Stigler and Friedland criticize the main theme of Berle and Means on the grounds that the empirical evidence available at the time when Berle and Means wrote their book was not able to establish any effect of the different types of control on profits.[28] Demsetz views the ownership structure of the corporation as an endogenous outcome of a maximizing process.[29] While agency costs may be higher in corporations with a dispersed shareholding structure, their higher costs may be more than offset by the reduction in risk-associated capital cost, benefits from economies of scale and the specialized knowledge of managers.[30]

Recent studies also raise doubts as to whether institutional investors would play useful roles in corporate governance even if legal barriers were removed. Romano has shown that public pension funds face political constraints that are likely to prevent them from serving effectively as monitors of corporate management.[31] Coffee has argued that long-term relational investing by institutional investors may be too costly to such investors because it will require them to sacrifice liquidity.[32] Macey has explained that the public goods nature of institutional investors, 'particularly mutual funds', makes it difficult for institutional investors to actively participate in corporate governance in the corporations in which they have invested.[33] An institution that invests a great deal in efforts to increase the performance of one firm has to share the benefits with other passive institutional investors who own the same stock whereas the cost of monitoring has to be borne entirely by such an active institutional investor. Furthermore, it is not clear that the human capital skills needed to be a successful institutional investor are the same as the skills necessary to provide management advice to the corporations in which the fund is invested.[34] Empirical evidence in the USA also seems to suggest that institutional investors do not have a skilled pool of employees capable of offering suggestions and advice that would improve corporate performance.[35] In addition, active roles played by institutional investors may not create net wealth. Smith has argued that institutional investors cannot acquire large shares in fewer corporations without significantly compromising diversification and thus increasing the risk of their portfolio.[36] He has also observed that, under the condition of imperfect information, large-scale activities in corporate governance inevitably entails a great deal of risk and puts activist institutions at a disadvantage compared to their more passive competitors.[37] Empirical evidence has partially supported Smith's position. After assessing the finance literature on institutional investors' activism in corporate governance, Romano has found that it has had an insignificant effect on targeted firms' performance.[38] Proposals by institutional investors calling for limits on executive compensation produce negative price effects in the target corporations.[39] Similarly, proposals by institutional investors to increase the number of independent directors in target corporations result in a negative price impact.[40]

More recently, the focus of studies has been on the relationship between a jurisdiction's ability to finance economic development and growth and its legal system.[41] As previously discussed, the USA and United Kingdom have a strong stock market while Germany and France have a relatively weak stock market. Financial economists of this school argue that only those legal systems that provide significant protection for minority shareholders can develop active equity markets.[42] Coffee raises the point that, if this explanation from financial economists is accepted, it amounts to a rejection of the political theory of US corporate finance offered by Roe and others.[43] This is so because dispersed share ownership may be the product not of political constraints on financial institutions, but instead of strong legal protection that encourages investors to become minority owners.[44] This point is not new: Demsetz once said that in a world in which self-interest plays a significant role in economic behaviour, it is foolish to believe that owners of valuable resources systematically relinquish control to managers who are not driven by the need to serve the interests of owners.[45]

Regardless of whether the dispersed ownership structure in the USA is a function of legal restrictions upon financial institutions, the explanation that concentrated ownership becomes the consequence of weak legal protections for public or minority investors[46] is not entirely satisfactory. It is true that the premium for control blocks in Italy is much higher than that in the USA,[47] but it is still difficult to come to the conclusion that the concentrated ownership structure is worse than the dispersed ownership structure. Shareholders with concentrated ownership have both the incentives and ability to monitor the management team. The higher share premium for control is a reward for their monitoring activities. It is very difficult to argue that a system linking monitoring efforts with reward is defective. Although the share premium for control is low in the USA, compensation to managers is much higher in the USA than in Germany and Japan.[48] For instance, in the year before the merger the Chrysler CEO received cash compensation of US$6 million and stock options worth US$5 million while the Daimler CEO received approximately one-eighth of that amount.[49] A plausible explanation is that minority shareholders in countries with dispersed ownership have to provide the managers and CEOs with greater remuneration to motivate the managers to maximize the shareholders' wealth. These differences, however, do not indicate which system is better from a contractual perspective. The ability to survive in a large number of countries indicates that concentrated ownership is also consistent with efficiency given the relevant constraints in these economies. Concentrated ownership, however, may also occur in a country with good legal protection for minority shareholders. For instance, entrepreneurs prefer to have control when venture capitalists exit from successful firms.[50] Leveraged buyouts provide another example that in the USA, just as dispersed ownership is consistent with efficiency,[51] so too is concentrated ownership. Shleifer and Vishny point out that LBOs are efficient organizations as large investors reduce agency problems.[52]

So far, there is no clear evidence to show whether the corporate governance system in the USA is better or worse than the corporate governance system in Japan or Germany. Claims that one corporate governance system is better than the other are largely influenced by the prosperity of the economy in that country at that time compared with the economy in another country. For instance, when the Japanese economy was very successful until at least the beginning of 1990s many people expressed their preference for the Japanese corporate governance system.[53] The economic performance in the USA during the 1990s, however, changed the tide in corporate governance literature. Soon people voiced their views that the corporate governance system in the USA may be actually better than that in Japan and Germany.[54] Linking the performance of a particular corporate governance system with the success of the economy can further be found from persons who were once quite cautious with comparative corporate governance studies. For example, Romano has stated:

> While we cannot predict whether the United Stated will be surpassed as the economic leader, the key factors that economists believe affect absolute productivity performance are the national savings rate (investment), the labor

129

force's education, and the magnitude of efforts devoted to basic and applied research. There is no theory or evidence relating any of these factors to corporate governance arrangements. It is telling that commentators who are concerned about the effect of corporate governance on comparative economic performance do not mention these key factors; the probable explanation is that it is extremely difficult to relate such fundamental factors to corporate governance patterns.[55]

Recently, Romano also stated:[56]

Commentators have, in general, commended institutional shareholder activism, at least in part from a belief that it would replicate the block holding-backed governance systems of Germany and Japan and thereby fill the void in managerial monitoring which occurred at the end of the 1980s with the decline in hostile takeovers in the USA (although the bloom now is off Germany and Japan's corporate governance systems given far superior US economic performance for more than a decade and the increase in hostile takeover activity in recent years).

Since it is difficult to use the connection between corporate governance and economic performance to establish the claim that one particular corporate governance system is superior to another, we are still further away from discovering the best corporate governance model. The major difficulty with connecting corporate governance systems with economic performance is that the approach fails to measure the substitution effects and the effects of complementarities of the different diversified subsystems in different corporate governance systems.

A CAUTIOUS APPROACH TO USING ECONOMIC PERFORMANCE AS A JUDGEMENT CRITERION

Fox and Heller define corporate governance by looking to the economic functions of the firm.[57] Based on this definition, they develop a typology that comprehensively shows all the channels through which bad corporate governance can inflict damage on a country's real economy.[58] According to their definition, two things are required: (1) managers must maximize their firm's residuals; and (2) they must distribute those residuals on a pro rata basis to shareholders.[59]

Obviously, their requirement of good corporate governance is very strict. Even in countries with relatively good corporate governance systems, managers pursue their own interest under constraints. Stigler and Friedland point out in their comment on Berle and Means' *The Modern Corporation and Private Property* that Berle and Means' contribution to economic theory was that the maximizing of the present value of a firm should be modified to take account of the separate interests of the management.[60] In reality, managers maximize the residuals of corporations under both pressure and incentives. The second requirement of pro rata distribution of a firm's residual is neither normatively necessary nor entirely feasible in practice. There is no reason why some shareholders cannot receive better treatment as long as they make greater contributions to the corporation. If it is acceptable for managers to receive a much higher remuneration in the USA where shareholders are not active in monitoring managers, then there is nothing wrong with block shareholders in Germany or Italy receiving a greater proportion of the residual as a result of their active role in monitoring managers. Both systems reward those who make greater contributions to corporations. There is no a prior criterion to determine which system is better. Zingales found that voting stock generally have a premium of 10 per cent to 20 per cent above non-voting shares.[61] Zingales' finding indicates that pro rata distribution of residuals is not the universally accepted rule. Even in the USA, where corporate finance depends to a greater extent upon equity, voting shares enjoy a premium of 5.4 per cent.[62]

Other scholars would relax this second requirement. Shleifer and Vishny define corporate governance as ways in which suppliers of capital to corporations assure themselves of getting a return on their investment.[63] When defining two essential prerequisites for strong public securities markets, Black provides that a country's laws and related institutions must give minority shareholders the following: (1) good information about the value of a company's business; and (2) confidence that the corporation's insiders (its managers and controlling shareholders) will not cheat investors out of most or all of the value of their investment through self-dealing transactions or even outright theft.[64]

What is more problematic is Fox and Heller's approach, which links their two requirements with the poor economy in Russia. In their article, no systematic empirical evidence is provided detailing the percentage of companies with a different pathology. At most, they provide some anecdotal evidence and try to link bad corporate governance with the poor performance of the economy in Russia. Most of the pathologies found in Russia equally exist in China. Below I will provide a few examples in the context of China and then discuss the approach of linking corporate governance to the performance of an economy.

Chengdu Hong Guang Industrial Ltd (Hong Guang)

In 1996, Hong Guang applied to the CSRC for the listing of its shares.[65] Despite the fact that the corporation suffered a loss of RMB 103 million, the corporation claimed that it had a profit of RMB 54 million. Falsification of its profit record also occurred in 1997 and 1998 after its shares were listed. In addition to covering the huge losses it suffered, Hong Guang used 34.3 per cent of the capital raised (RMB 140 million) to buy and sell shares on the stock market by itself and through a securities company. As speculative trading by state-owned enterprises and listed companies was prohibited,[66] the speculative trading of shares was carried out through the opening of 228 individual trading accounts. In fact, Hong Gunag only used 16.5 per cent of the capital for the projects described in the prospectus. Most of the capital raised was actually used by the company to pay its debts to banks both at home and abroad. After investigation, CSRC confiscated illegal trading profits of RMB 4.5 million derived from speculative trading, imposed an administrative fine of RMB 1 million and permanently prohibited the chairman of the board of directors, the general manager and the deputy financial officer from assuming senior officer positions in listed companies or securities institutions. Subsequently, the Intermediate People's Court of Chengdu sentenced these three people for a jail term of three years or less.[67] While this was the first case where criminal liability was imposed upon responsible persons in listed companies, the court refused to hold a trial for the claim of civil liability. Even though the fraud would be a clear case of tort of deceit in well-developed common law juris-dictions and civil liability can also be grounded on Article 77 of the Provisional Regulation on the Administration of Issuing and Trading of Shares[68] and Article 63 of the Securities Law,[69] the Court justified its decision on the grounds that the loss suffered by investors was not necessarily caused by the fraud.[70]

Energy 28

Energy 28[71] falsely claimed to have a profit of RMB 16 million at the time of its application for share listing and a total profit of RMB 211 million during the three years thereafter. Furthermore, the company changed the use of funds as specified in the prospectus in 1996 and in documents for the additional issue of shares in 1997. CSRC imposed an administrative fine of RMB 1 million on the company; RMB 50,000 upon the chairman of the board of directors and RMB 30,000 upon three other directors. There were neither criminal proceedings nor civil lawsuits instituted in this case.

Sanjiu Medical and Pharmaceutical Co. Ltd (Sanjiu)

During an investigation conducted by the CSRC in June 2001, the CSRC discovered that the controlling shareholder of Sanjiu improperly used RMB 2.5 billion of the funds of Sanjiu, accounting for 96 per cent of the net assets of Sanjiu.[72] The board of directors and the supervisory board of Sanjiu did not support the use of such a large amount of the listing company's funds by the controlling shareholder for a connected transaction. Except for public criticism by the CSRC, no shareholder action was taken against the controlling shareholder in this case. Lack of clear provisions on derivative actions by shareholders makes it very difficult for individual shareholders to sue the wrongdoers, who violate provisions in either the Company Law or in the Articles of Association of Listed Companies.[73] Improper use of funds by listed companies also occurred in Hubei Meierya Co Ltd (Meierya).[74] In this case, the controlling shareholder improperly used RMB 368 million belonging to Meierya, accounting for 41 per cent of the net assets of the company. It does not appear from the report that either the board of directors of Meierya or the shareholders of Meierya authorized the use of the fund.

Shanghai Jiabao Industrial (Group) Co. Ltd (Jiabao)

The CSRC investigated Jiabao in August 2000. Among other violations of law uncovered by the CSRC, Jiabao engaged in illegal speculative trading of shares in other companies.[75] The investigation results reveal that Jiabao injected RMB 228 million into both the primary market and the secondary market in Shanghai. As listed companies are prohibited from speculative trading,[76] Jiabao utilized more than 300 individual accounts to circumvent the ban during the period 1996 to 1998.[77] The illegal gain from the trading of shares in other companies amounted to RMB 840,000. Besides illegal trading of shares in other companies, Jiabao also traded the shares of its own company by using three different individuals' accounts. The investigation did not discover any illegal gain from the trading of its own shares. The CSRC imposed an administrative fine of RMB 50,000 upon the chairman of the board of directors, confiscated the illegal trading gain of RMB 840,000 and publicly criticized the directors of Jiabao.

Shandong Bohai Holding Ltd (Bohai)

This was a case concerning manipulation of the company's own shares. Senior officers of Bohai engaged in repeated trading and false purchases and sales without actual transfer of title of the shares of its own company on 1 August

133

1994.[78] Like the previous cases, the senior officers used the accounts in the name of four individuals. As a result of the market manipulation, the share price of Bohai rose 102 per cent. Bohai spent RMB 19.9 million of its own funds purchasing 3,981,200 of its own shares on the Shanghai stock exchange.[79] Eventually selling all these shares, together with 845,600 shares held before 1 August, Bohai made a profit of RMB 5.9 million.[80] The CSRC discovered numerous violations of securities regulations by Bohai and made the following decisions – it issued an official reprimand, confiscated the illegal profits of RMB 5.9 million made by Bohai, imposed a fine of RMB 1 million on the company and a fine of RMB 50,000 on Mr Li Gang, the officer responsible.[81]

These cases in China provide strong evidence that managers are not working in the best interests of the residual claimants. They cheated the investors of money at the time of listing by falsifying profit records (the case of Hong Guang). The strategy of using a false profit record was also adopted for the purpose of subsequent distribution of shares after the company has become a listed company (the case of Energy 28). The controlling shareholders' abuse of the fund of the listed company in the case of Sanjiu and Meierya shows the lack of consideration on the part of controlling shareholders for the interests of the minority shareholders. A Chinese way of vividly describing the cheating of capital suppliers by the insiders (managers and controlling shareholders) is 'quanqian' (circling money). Using the funds raised for improper purposes on the stock market, as in the case of Jiabao, provides evidence that managers disregard the interest of minority shareholders as they do not have good projects before deciding to raise funds from the public. Such a case is far worse than the wasting of ANY free cash flow generated by the company itself; defrauding investors does not require any management skill whereas the free cash flow is earned by the management. Manipulating the shares of their own company as in the cases of Jiabao and Bohai is an indication that managers in these companies did not use all their skills and efforts to discover net present value projects or use the existing assets effectively. Such straightforward cases of cheating their own company's shareholders are very unlikely to occur in jurisdictions where minority shareholders are well protected.

While the corporate governance system in China is as bad as the Russian system, the economic performance in China during the 1990s was surprisingly good. Statistics show that the average economic growth rate of China during the first nine years of the 1990s was 11.2 per cent, ranking the country first in the world.[82] This does not mean that there is no correlation between corporate governance and the performance of an economy. Corporate governance does matter. The point is that it is not possible to link corporate governance with the economy. The difficulty is that there are too many variables in addition to the variables of the corporate governance system to examine the effects of a corporate governance system upon the entire economy.

Precisely because of the difficulty of measuring the effects of a corporate governance system, Macey proposed three ways to measure empirically the performance of corporate governance systems.[83] The first way to examine the performance of corporate governance systems is to place emphasis upon how effective they are in limiting a manager's ability to divert firm resources for their private use. Recognizing the difficulty of collecting systematic empirical data, Macey, following Zingales,[84] proposes that the size of the premium at which voting shares trade in relation to non-voting shares can test the performance of different corporate governance systems. There are several problems with this method. First, this method does not examine the effect of different corporate governance systems on an equal footing. It is very unlikely to pinpoint the advantages of corporate governance systems adapted to debt financing. For instance, under this method, the corporate governance system in the USA will significantly outrank the corporate governance system in Germany or Italy. Further, this method is unlikely to pinpoint the different effects of costs–rewards of corporate governance systems impinging on the shareholder managers and professional managers. In the USA, shares in very large corporations are widely dispersed. In these manager-controlled corporations, higher remuneration to managers is essential to make sure that they will be well rewarded if they work in the best interests of residual claimants. In Italian corporations, in contrast, where the control rests with the majority shareholders, there is nothing wrong with providing better rewards to the majority shareholders who are constantly monitoring the management. Whether the higher rewards go to the majority shareholders in Italy or to managers in the USA does not provide a normative or empirical basis to suggest which system is superior. Higher rewards for owner-managers also occur on the venture capital market in the USA when venture capital exits.[85]

Macey's second way to compare different corporate governance systems is empirically to examine the willingness of entrepreneurs to make initial public offerings of stock.[86] A similar problem with this method is the potential failure to include the advantages of corporate governance systems adjusted to heavy reliance upon debt financing. The other side of the coin is that this second method favours corporate governance systems well adjusted to equity financing. Judged by this method, the corporate governance system in Germany would be far worse than the corporate governance system in the USA. So far, there is no clear evidence to show whether the German corporate governance system is necessarily worse.[87]

The third way to measure the performance of different corporate governance systems suggested by Macey is to examine the function of internal and external markets for corporate control.[88] Among the three ways proposed by Macey, this third method is relatively neutral. A comparison of the replacement of managers in the USA and Germany is helpful. In the USA, replacement of managers is the function of both the board of directors and the market of takeover. In contrast, replacing managers in Germany is dominantly the function of the supervisory board. Empirical studies in Germany show that there is a significant involuntary 'fluctuation' of management board members not only in cases of serious problems within the corporation but also in less serious cases in which the supervisory board was displeased with the performance of individual managers or with the performance of the management board as a whole.[89]

In large competitive economies such as the USA, shares are more likely to be dispersed when financial institutions such as banks are not permitted or not willing to play active roles in corporate governance. Without the involvement of banks, other non-financial corporations are unlikely to be active as knowledge of managers in these corporations is quite firm-specific. Widely dispersed shareholding in non-financial corporations requires alternative monitoring devices. Although the USA restricts the role of financial institutions in corporate governance, it encourages a relatively active corporate control market. The takeover market imposes a potential threat on managers in inefficient corporations.[90] If the bad performance of corporations is actually the result of poor management skills, takeovers provide the acquiring company with the chance to replace bad managers. While the takeover market in the USA is relatively active, this market is at low ebb. Public choice theories can explain this change. Populist sentiment has captured legislatures and managers are the happy beneficiaries of a public opinion that helps insulate them from takeovers.[91]

The demise of the takeover market as a disciplinary device in the USA has directed people's attention to internal monitoring devices. Recently, reforms have been carried out to strengthen the role of the board of directors. This is achieved mainly by appointing more outside directors. While many have observed that internal forces in corporations whose shares are widely dispersed are too weak to force timely and efficient responses to excess capacity,[92] the board does play some role in corporate governance. Rosenstein and Wyatt's study[93] of the wealth effects surrounding outside director appointments finds significantly positive share-price increases. Their study indicates that the board of directors has its role to play in checking managers' opportunistic behaviours. Moreover, there are also examples of board initiated ousters of senior corporate executives of widely held corporations such as IBM, General Motors, American Express and Manufacturers Life.[94]

While this third method is useful in measuring the effects of corporate governance systems, it is not able to quantify the effects, not to mention the effects on the economy. I will explain why it is difficult to measure the performance of different corporate governance systems below. I will then propose a new way of carrying out comparative corporate governance studies.

136

INCREASED OPTIONS AND INSTITUTIONAL COMPETITION WITHIN A COUNTRY

Corporate governance systems is a system evolved to encourage or constrain managers to work in the best interests of their corporations and to ensure that company insiders (managers and controlling shareholders) do not cheat capital suppliers out of most or all of the value of their investment. There are subsystems under any corporate governance system, [95] some of which have substitution effects and some of which complement each other. The substitution theory suggests that one subsystem can serve as a substitute for another subsystem.[96] The theory of complementarities suggests that various components or subsystems of a given system complement one another in certain situations. In this case, the value of each component may vary, depending on the degree to which the component, as a whole or in part, is complementary to another component.[97]

The different effects of the subsystems can also be examined from the standpoint of the roles these subsystems play in solving the conflict of interest problems related to different methods of financing. Some of the subsystems are adjusted to equity financing and serve the purpose of reducing the agency costs of equity financing. Other subsystems are adapted to debt financing and play the role of curbing the agency costs of debt financing. Both types of subsystems include contractual mechanisms and market forces. Examples of subsystems associated with equity financing include capital market, takeover market, product market, shareholder control, board of directors, managerial market and compensation systems. Subsystems relevant to debt financing mainly consist of the lending market, creditors' intervention in cases of default, convertible bonds, the institution of secured debt, insolvency law, creditors' holding of shares in the debtor company, product market, board of directors, managerial market and compensation schemes.[98]

As previously discussed, some countries such as the USA and the United Kingdom rely heavily on equity financing whereas other countries such as Germany favour debt financing. Virtually all corporations in the world, however, utilize both equity and debt for the purpose of financing the activities of their corporations. Modigliani and Miller once demonstrated that in the absence of bankruptcy costs and tax subsidies on the payment of interest, the value of the firm is independent of the financial structure.[99] They later demonstrated that the existence of tax subsidies on interest payments would cause the value of the firm to rise with the amount of debt financing by the amount of the capitalized value of the tax subsidy.[100] The existence of tax subsidies indicates that a corporation should be financed entirely by debt. The positive costs of bankruptcy and other limitations imposed by creditors, however, suggest that corporations are not able to use the maximum amount of debt in their capital structures.

137

Jensen and Meckling argue that the existence of agency costs provides reasons for arguing that the probability distribution of future cash flows is not independent of the capital or ownership structure.[101] Their argument would suggest that countries with better corporate governance subsystems are more likely to have lower agency costs in corporations. Other things being equal, lower agency costs mean higher firm value. Recent financial literature provides support of the argument of Jensen and Meckling. Levine and others develop evidence of a causal connection running from investor protection to strong capital market to future growth. They find that: (1) legal protection of creditors and general contract enforcement predicts strong banks and the portion of banking development attributable to stronger creditor protection predicts future economic growth; and (2) legal protection of shareholder rights and strong accounting rules predict strong stock markets and the portion of stock market development attributable to shareholder rights and accounting rules predicts future economic growth.[102] La Porta *et al.*, also demonstrated that countries with poor investor protections, measured by both the character of legal rules and the quality of law enforcement, have smaller and narrower capital markets.[103]

Although the recent finance literature is able to link corporate governance to future economic growth in a crude but more scientific way, it is still difficult to provide more specific law reform suggestions based on such literature. As corporations may use debt and equity, a more scientific way of comparing different corporate governance systems is to quantify the reduction of agency costs of both debt financing and equity financing by examining all the subsystems of corporate governance. Such a task will be enormously difficult if not impossible. So far, knowledge has been limited as to which subsystems may substitute others and which subsystems complement each other. Even if two countries rely on both debt and equity to the same extent, they may rely upon different subsystems to curb agency costs of both debt financing and equity financing. As long as these two countries are able to use their own subsystems to effectively alleviate agency costs, both systems are functionally the same. No empirical research is able to collect the necessary data to compare the overall reduction of agency costs in the two countries. If two countries use both debt and equity to a different extent, the difficulty in collecting data to compare the total reduction of agency costs significantly increases. An alternative way of comparing two different corporate governance systems is to examine the effect of corporate governance on economic performance. Even if it is possible to quantify the total reduction of agency costs of both debt financing and equity financing by measuring the effects of all the subsystems, linking corporate governance to economic performance is still problematic. The key factors affecting absolute productivity performance are the national savings rate (investment), the workforce's education and the magnitude of efforts devoted to basic and applied research.[104] North would add institutional change as a factor that would determine economic performance.[105] Despite the fact that corporate governance is a contributing factor in economic performance, it is only one of the many variables determining economic performance. Naturally, even if country A may have a much better corporate governance system than country B, the economic performance in country A may still be much worse than that in country B since other variables are all in favour of country B. This suggests that quantitative studies on comparative corporate governance systems must control all other contributing factors of economic growth in order to determine which corporate governance system is better. This type of empirical study in comparative corporate governance is extremely difficult, if not impossible.

Finding it difficult or unnecessary to search for the best corporate governance system, this author argues for an institutional competition model of comparative corporate governance studies. As virtually all corporations use both debt and equity, it is important to develop corporate governance subsystems to alleviate the agency costs of both debt financing and equity financing in any given country. Using this model, a country should keep as many options open as possible so that different subsystems of corporate governance may develop under the environment of competition and adaptation. Competition and adaptation under this institutional competition model focuses mainly upon the subsystems within a country. The institutional competition model, however, allows international borrowing of healthy subsystems of corporate governance. Once a particular subsystem of corporate governance is introduced into a country, experimentation, learning and adaptation can be very local in nature. Recognizing that initial path[106] and politics[107] may make some subsystems of corporate governance less effective in a country, this institutional competition model also favours incremental change or improvement of the subsystems whether they are domestically evolved or internationally borrowed.

This author advocates the removal of restrictions on domestic and international trading and investments. Domestic and global competition in the product market and the capital market and increasing an understanding of the role of corporate governance will shape and reshape people's views of corporate governance subsystems in a particular country. Such a result in turn will make it possible to enlarge the options regarding subsystems in a country. This institutional competition model does not require that all subsystems be equally effective. One country may rely heavily upon some subsystems of corporate governance whereas another country may utilize some other subsystems depending on the method of financing. As long as a country does not deliberately prohibit the development of some essential corporate governance subsystems and the option of institutional change and competition remain available, the corporate governance system will achieve the goals of making the managers of corporations work in the best interests of corporations and ensure a reasonable return for the suppliers of capital.

This institutional competition model can provide policy guidance for emerging countries. I will discuss the case of China below.

Although banks traditionally did not play important roles in screening loan applications and monitoring the activities of borrowers in the history of the PRC,[108] the experience in Germany and Japan after the Second World War indicates that banks can play an important role in financing corporate projects. As relatively sophisticated players in the economy, banks may become good monitors in corporate governance in China. However, no serious efforts have been made to allow banks to actively participate in corporate governance of their debtor corporations. Weak protection of creditors and legal constraints both impact upon banks in regard to this issue. First, the rights of banks as secured creditors in state-owned enterprises in 18 cities including Shanghai, Tianjin and Chengdu are badly eroded. The Notice[109] of the State Council on Some Questions Concerning the Experiment of Bankruptcy by State Owned Enterprises in Certain Cities (Notice) has modified the priority of distribution of bankruptcy property in cases of liquidation. Pursuant to the Enterprise Bankruptcy Law,[110] bankruptcy property in liquidation should be used in the sequence of satisfying: (1) liquidation costs; (2) wages and employment insurance owed to employees; (3) tax; and (4) money owed to creditors.[111] The Enterprise Bankruptcy Law clearly states, however, that secured assets are not treated as bankruptcy property.[112] According to Article 89(2) of the General Principles of the Civil Law (GPCL)[113] and Article 116 of the Supreme People's Court's Opinion on Certain Issues Concerning the Implementation of the GPCL,[114] secured creditors are entitled to priority when a debtor has inadequate assets to satisfy all the secured and unsecured creditors. Despite the fact that the State Council has less law-making power compared to the National People's Congress and the Standing Committee of the National People's Congress,[115] the Notice has modified the priority in the distribution of bankruptcy priority. While the Enterprise Bankruptcy Law does not remove any assets of the bankrupt enterprise from the bankrupt property, the Notice excludes the proceeds received from assigning the land-use right for the purpose of settling (laying off) employees.[116] Only the remaining part of the proceeds from the assignment is to be treated as bankruptcy property. The settlement fee for each employee is three times the average wage of the previous year.[117] If the proceeds from the assignment of the land-use right are not adequate to allocate settlement fees for all employees, other assets of the enterprise must be considered.[118] Thus, if employees cannot be properly settled, it is required by law that other assets are used to achieve this purpose.[119] While the Notice still does not affect the priority of secured creditors,[120] the Supplemental Notice from the State Council (Supplemental Notice) subjected secured creditors to employees at least as far as the layoff payment is concerned.[121] Pursuant to the Supplemental Notice, even if the land-use right has been mortgaged, employees remain entitled to priority with respect to the settlement fee.[122] Further, the Supplemental Notice raises the priority of employees with regard to retirement benefits and medical benefits for those employees whose employers do not participate in pension schemes or medical insurance schemes.[123]

The status and powers of banks in China leaves much to be desired. When banks, either as secured creditors or unsecured creditors, are not well protected, it is unlikely that they will be active in taking debtor companies to the bankruptcy courts. Statistics show that there were 11,627 bankruptcy cases between 1988 and 1996,[124] but of all bankruptcy cases in 1996, only 1.2 per cent were instituted by banks themselves.[125] Also, creditors are not well protected in China because of the bad bankruptcy regime and the difficulty in enforcing the bankruptcy law. More, currently, there is no comprehensive bankruptcy law that applies to all types of enterprises. Above all, there is the difficulty of using the law to protect creditors' rights.[126] Finally, banks in China are not allowed to hold shares in commercial corporations.[127] Given this, one concludes that as banks in China are not able to hold shares in debt corporations, it is difficult to solve the moral hazard problem in debtor corporations, monitoring by Chinese banks being much weaker compared to German and Japanese banks.

As China has established a stock market, the weak protection of creditors may be offset by a strong market that can be used as a chief source of capital supply to corporations. Thus there are high expectations of the stock market in China. It is argued that if share prices reflect the enterprise's profit record relatively accurately, then the capital market will channel investment funds to the most efficient enterprises as investors seek to maximize their returns.[128] It is further argued that capital markets create a market for corporate control. Reformers believe that capital market mechanisms are more effective at rationalizing productive assets than the powers given to banks.[129] Furthermore, the creation of a stock market gives enterprises more financial autonomy (since they no longer have to rely on the governments for funds), which also gives them more freedom to respond quickly to market opportunities, cutting through the regional, departmental and bureaucratic ties that continue to bind banks.[130]

Since the establishment of the Shanghai stock exchange in 1990 and the Shenzhen stock exchange in 1991,[131] the stock market in China has developed relatively quickly. By the end of 2000, there were 1211 corporations listed domestically and internationally.[132] In December 2000, 30 per cent of capital was raised by corporations on the stock market as compared with 10 per cent in 1993.[133] The capitalization of the stock market is 57 per cent of China's GDP.[134] This is very puzzling considering the weak protection of minority shareholders. The high savings rate and lack of alternative investment channels explain why the stock market in China can develop quickly when investors are frequently

141

cheated. Measured by the criterion of whether corporations assure a reasonable return to suppliers of capital, the corporate governance system in China requires considerable improvements.

The weak protection of minority shareholders is a consequence of several factors. Fisrt, criminal prosecution is rarely instituted. Although the Company Law[135] and the Provisional Regulation on the Issuance and Trading of Shares (ITS)[136] do not contain clear provisions on criminal liability for misstatements in disclosure documents, the Decision on the Punishment of Crimes in Violation of the Company Law (Decision)[137] provides that if a company issues shares or corporate bonds with a falsified prospectus, subscription forms or corporate bond distribution documents, thereby raising huge amounts of capital and resulting in serious consequences, the persons directly responsible shall be sentenced for a term of less than five years and/or subject to a criminal penalty of 5 per cent of the amount raised.[138] A similar provision was subsequently incorporated into the 1997 Criminal Law.[139] However, despite such a clear provision and numerous cases of misrepresentation, the first case where criminal liability was imposed on three directors occurred only in 2000.[140]

Second, the civil liability regime is not only poorly framed but also weak in enforcement. Compared with relatively clear provisions on criminal liability, there are only a few major provisions on civil liability. Article 77 of the ITS stipulates that anyone who violates the ITS and causes losses to others shall bear civil liability according to law.[141] Since four types of misconduct – misrepresentation, insider trading, market manipulation and fraud committed by securities intermediaries against customers – are regulated by the ITS, it is very difficult for judges who are not experienced in the field and do not have the law-making power to apply such a vague provision to deal with civil liabilities when capital raisers or intermediaries deliberately or negligently mislead investors through disclosure documents. Because of this, Article 77 of the ITS has not been used to hold any defendant civilly liable for misrepresentation. The Securities Law[142] provides in Article 63 that if the prospectus, documents of offer of corporate bonds, financial or accounting reports, listing documents, annual reports, mid-term reports or ad hoc reports distributed by the issuer or distributing securities company contain a falsehood, misleading statement or major omission and thereby causes investors to sustain losses in the course of buying and selling of securities, the issuer or distributing securities company shall be liable for damages and the responsible directors, supervisors and/or the managers of the issuer or distributing securities company shall be jointly and severely liable for damages. While Article 63 catches issuing companies and underwriters both for negligent statements and fraudulent statements made in these relevant disclosure documents, Article 202 provides the ground for civil liabilities in connection with fraudulent misstatements produced by intermediaries. Article 202 provides, among other things, that if a professional organization that issues documents such as audit reports, asset valuation reports or legal opinions for the issuance of, or listing of, securities or securities trading activities provides false certification and causes losses to investors, the professional organization shall bear liability.[143] The article further stipulates that if the fraud results in losses to investors, the intermediary shall bear joint liability. However, there are at least two problems with Article 202. First, fraudulent misrepresentation is difficult to prove in practice. A better approach is to add negligent misrepresentation as a ground for holding the intermediaries civilly liable. Second, there is no need to always hold the intermediaries jointly liable. They can be independently liable for their own negligence, particularly when the issuer has no fault. Leaving aside the problems in Article 202, civil liabilities for negligent misrepresentation provided in Article 63 are relatively clear. So far, however, there has not been a single case where an issuer has borne civil liability to hundreds and thousands of investors despite the large number of cases of negligent or fraudulent misrepresentation.

In the Hong Guang case discussed above, the First Intermediate People's Court of Chengdu in the Province of Sichuan sentenced several directors to three years' imprisonment or other criminal penalties.[144] Investors in that case also instituted civil actions, claiming for damages on the grounds of misrepresentation. The first person to bring a lawsuit was a small investor in Shanghai.[145] Unfortunately the District People's Court of Pudong did not accept his case, explaining that it did not fall within the scope of acceptance.[146] Civil lawsuits were also instituted in several cities in the similar case of Yin Guang Xia.[147] Many courts refused to accept cases of misrepresentation, but a court in Wuxi planned to allow a similar lawsuit.[148] However, shortly after the acceptance of the case by the court, the Supreme People's Court instructed all courts not to accept civil cases relating to securities fraud, insider trading and market manipulation.[149] Upon receiving the Notice, the Wuxi Court suspended the treatment of the case. The Notice of the Supreme People's Court invited a great deal of criticism.[150] Four months later, the Supreme People's Court circulated another notice to the lower courts, this time instructing them to accept civil suits related to misrepresentation in disclosure documents.[151] In this subsequent Notice, the Supreme People's Court conditioned the acceptance of civil lawsuits upon investigation and punishment of the wrongdoer by the CSRC.[152] Further, the Supreme People's Court stated that no class action, which exists under Chinese law although it is rarely used in practice, should be allowed.[153]

In addition to the weak enforcement of criminal and civil provisions, lack of remedies for the shareholder is another factor, contributing to the weak corporate governance system in China. Neither the Company Law nor the Securities Law contains any provision giving shareholders the right to bring actions derivatively against corporate directors or managers for their wrongful activities. Evidence in the USA shows that lawsuits are more common in firms more likely to need monitoring and that the probability of CEO turnover increases after a lawsuit is filed.[154]

Japan's experience is also helpful. In October 1993 Japan's Commercial Code was revised to reduce the fees required to file a derivative lawsuit.[155] Since then derivative lawsuits have increased fivefold.[156] Japanese managers have also heightened their awareness of their duties to corporations and their shareholders.[157] Law reform in China is also necessary in order to facilitate shareholders' derivative actions. This is particularly so as most of the listed companies in China are under majority control. Of the 1124 listed companies in April 2001, 79 per cent were controlled by a shareholder who owned more than 50 per cent of the total shares.[158] More, for 65 per cent of the listed corporations, the state shareholding dominated.[159] This is a further indication that insiders control most of these listed corporations. Without the threat of derivative actions, the interests of minority shareholders are unlikely to be well protected.

Still another factor contributing to the weak protection of minority shareholders is the low quality of certification by intermediaries. Wher companies that raise capital cannot be trusted, third-party certification plays an important role in solving the adverse selection problem.[160] Third parties here include investment banks, accounting firms and securities counsel. The principal role of securities intermediaries is to vouch for disclosure quality to the public and thereby to reduce information asymmetry between corporate insiders and public investors.[161] The system of third-party certification works well, however, only when the securities intermediaries are subject to constraints. Some of the constraints include self-regulation, licensing systems, civil liability to investors and criminal liability.

The role of self-regulatory organizations in China is currently too weak to curb serious securities fraud. The licensing system works better. Administered by the licensing system, for securities companies (investment banks) a license from the CSRC is a requirement. Qualified accounting firms still need a license jointly issued by the CSRC and the Ministry of Finance in order to carry out securities-related accounting. During the last several years, the CSRC has suspended the licenses of and penalized many securities companies and accounting firms. Due to its limited resources, however, many wrongdoers are unlikely to be caught. Under these circumstances, criminal liability and civil liability are needed to deter false certification. By the end of June 2002, there had not been a single case where an accounting firm or underwriter has been subject to criminal liability. As far as civil liability is concerned, holding accounting firms liable requires fraudulent misrepresentation.[162] Since it is difficult to prove the intention of cheating, imposing civil liability on accounting firms will be far more difficult. Although it is relatively easy to catch securities underwriters, as negligent misrepresentation or important omission gives rise to civil liability, there is not a single case where a securities underwriter has been sued. The logic is simple. If issuers have not been held liable for investors' losses, how can securities underwriters be held civilly liable for the losses suffered by investors? When securities intermediaries are not subject to adequate constraints, the role of third-party certification is considerably weakened.

CONCLUSION

Corporate governance has attracted enormous attention both in the area of law and in the area of financial economics. In comparative corporate governance studies, many people have devoted their energy either to finding the best corporate governance model or to linking corporate governance systems to the performance of the economy in different countries. Here I argue against this view. As it is impossible to measure the reduction of agency costs of both debt financing and equity financing resulting from different corporate governance subsystems, I argue for an institutional competition model in comparative corporate governance studies. Under this institutional competition model, people would focus their attention on alternative methods of financing corporate activities. Such an approach would facilitate competition between debt financing and equity financing. The facilitation of competition between debt financing and equity financing would further result in the adaptation, experimentation and competition of different corporate governance subsystems. Globalization of trade and investment and increasing the understanding of comparative corporate governance systems would make it easier for different countries to establish and improve such subsystems. By focusing on the process of institutional change, this institutional competition model would be useful in evaluating the effectiveness of corporate governance subsystems in developing countries and able to provide direction for institutional change.

Notes

Chapter 1 The relevance of comparative corporate governance studies

1 A. Smith, *The Wealth of Nations*, E. Cannan ed., (New York: The Modern Library, 1937).
2 Agency cost problem is a modern term invented by agency theorists.
3 A. Berle and G. Means, *The Modern Corporation and Private Property* (New York: Harcourt, Brace & World, 1932).
4 G. Stigler and C. Friedland, 'The Literature of Economics: The Case of Berle and Means', (1983) 26 *J. L. & Econ.* 237 at p. 259.
5 Ibid., pp. 248–49.
6 See R. Daniels and P. Halpern, 'Too Close for Comfort: The Role of the Closely Held Public Corporation in the Canadian Economy and the Implications for Public Policy', (1995–96) 26 *Canadian Bus. L. J.* 11; E. Furubotn, 'Towards a Dynamic Model of the Yugoslav Firm', (1971) 4 *Canadian J. Econ.* 182–97; M. O'Hara, 'Property Rights and Financial Firm', (1981) 24 *J. L. & Econ.* 317.
7 See Stigler and Friedland, op. cit., note 4, p. 258.
8 H. Demsetz and K. Lehn, 'The Structure of Corporate Ownership: Causes and Consequences', (1985) 93 (6) *J. Pol. Econ.* 1155.
9 Ibid., p. 1174.
10 Ibid., pp. 1174–76.
11 Ibid., p. 1174.
12 Ibid., p. 1158.
13 M. Roe, 'Some Differences in Corporate Structure in Germany, Japan, and the United States', (1993) 102 *Yale L. J.* 1927.
14 R. Coase, 'The Nature of the Firm', (1937) 4 *Economica* 386.
15 K. Arrow, 'The Role of Securities in the Optimal Allocation of Risk Bearing', (1964) 31 *Rev. Econ. Stud.* 91.
16 A. Alchian and H. Demesetz, 'Production, Information Costs, and Economic Organization', (1972) 62 *Am. Econ. Rev.* 777.
17 M. Jensen and W. Meckling, 'Theory of the Firm: Managerial Behaviour, Agency Costs and Ownership Structure', (1976) 3 *J. Fin. Econ.* 305.

18 E. Fama and M. Jensen, 'Agency Problems and Residual Claims', (1983) 26 *J. L. & Econ*. 327.

19 G. Stigler, 'The Economics of Scale', (1958) 1 *J. L. & Econ*. 54 at p. 55.

20 See Jensen and Meckling, op. cit., note 17, p. 308.

21 See Berle and Means, op. cit., note 3.

22 See Jensen and Meckling, op. cit., note 17, p. 308.

23 Ibid.

24 For more information on adverse selection, see K. Arrow, *The Limits of Organization*, (New York: Norton, 1974) pp. 36–37.

25 See Jensen and Meckling, op. cit., note 17, pp. 334–42.

26 Ibid., p. 334.

27 C. Smoth and J. Warner, 'On Financial Contracting: An Analysis of Bond Convenants', (1979) 7 *J. Fin. Econ*. 117 at pp. 118–19; also see Jensen and Meckling, op. cit., note 17, pp. 333–37.

28 For more information on this point, see A. Schwartz, 'A Theory of Loan Priorities', (1989) 18 *J. Legal Stud*. 209, 228–34; G. Triantis, 'Secured Debt Under Conditions of Imperfect Information', (1992) 21 *J. Legal Stud*. 225 at pp. 235–36.

29 S. Myers, 'Determinants of Corporate Borrowing', (1977) 5 *J. Fin. Econ*. 147 at pp. 149–54.

30 See Jensen and Meckling, op. cit., note 17, p. 338.

31 L. Weiss, 'Bankruptcy Resolution: Direct Costs and Violation of Priority of Claims', (1990) 27 *J. Fin. Econ*. 285.

32 See R. Coase, op. cit. note 14; S. Cheung, 'The Structure of Contract and the Theory of Non-Exclusive Resources', (1970) 13 *J. L. & Econ*. 49; Alchian and Demsetz, op. cit., note 16, p. 16.

33 O. Hart, 'The Theory of the Firm', (1989) 89 *Colum. L Rev*. 1757 at pp. 1758 (describes that neoclassical theory views the firm as a set of feasible production plans; a manager prescribes over this production set, buying and selling inputs and outputs in a spot market and choosing the plan that maximizes the owner's welfare).

34 M. Jensen and C. Smith Jr., 'Stockholder, Manager, and Creditor Interests, Applications of Agency Theory', in E. Altman and M. Subrahmanyam, (eds), *Recent Advances in Corporate Finance* (Homewood, IL: Irwin, 1985) p. 95.

35 Ibid., p. 96.

36 See Jensen and Meckling, op. cit., note 17, p. 342.

37 See Jensen and Smith Jr., op. cit., note 34, pp. 111–12.

38 G. Akerlof, 'The Market for 'Lemon': Quality Uncertainty and the Market Mechanism', (1970) 84 (3) *Q. J. Econ*. 488.

39 M. Pauly, 'The Economics of Moral Hazard: Comment', (1968) *Am. Econ. Rev*. 531.

40 F. Knight, *Risk, Uncertainty and Profit* (Boston, MA: Houghton Mifflin, 1921).

41 F. Weston, 'Some Economic Fundamentals for an Analysis of Bankruptcy', (1977) 41 (4) *Law and Contemp. Probs*. 47 at pp. 48–51.

42 For more information on this point, see H. Manne, 'Our Two Corporation

Systems: Law and Economics', (1967) 53 *Va. L. Rev.* 259; F. Easterbrook and D. Fischel, 'The Proper Role of a Target's Management in Responding to a Tender Offer', (1981) 94 *Harv. L. Rev.* 1161 at pp. 1168–74; E. Furubotn and S. Pejovich, 'Property Rights and Economic Theory: A Survey of Recent Literature', (1972) 10 *J. Econ. Lit.* 1137 at p. 1150.

43 G. Triantis and R. Daniels, 'The Role of Debt in Interactive Corporate Governance', (1995) 83 *Cal. L. Rev.* 1073 at p. 1085.

44 H. Manne, 'Mergers and the Market for Corporate Control', (1965) 73 *J. Pol. Econ.* 110.

45 For more information on corporate control transactions, see F. Easterbrook and D. Fischel, 'Corporate Control Transactions', (1982) 91 *Yale L. J.* 698 at pp. 705–08.

46 G. Jarrel and P. Polsen, 'The Returns to Acquiring Firms in Tender Offers: Evidence from Three Decades', (1989) 18 (3) *Fin. Magmt.* 12 ; P. Asquith *et al.*, 'The Gains to Bidding Firms from Mergers', (1983) 11 *J. Fin. Econ.* 121; M. Jensen and R. Ruback, 'The Market for Corporate Control: The Scentific Evidence', (1983) 11 *J. Fin. Econ.* 5.

47 F. Easterbrook and G. Jarrel, 'Do Targets Gain from Defeating Tender Offers', (1984) 59 *N.Y.U. L. Rev.* 227.

48 For more information on product markets, see J. Ziegel *et al.*, (eds), *Cases and Materials on Partnerships and Canadian Business Corporations* (Toronto: Carswell, 1989) pp. 374–75.

49 A. Hirschman divided reaction into two types of action: exit and voice. See A. Hirschman, *Exit, Voice and Loyalty: Responses to Decline in Firms, Organizations, and States* (Cambridge, MA: Harvard University Press, 1970) pp. 10–15; the point that exit activates voice is made by Triantis and Daniels, See Triantis and Daniels, op. cit., note 43, pp. 1085–86.

50 For more information on collective action problems, see M. Olson, *The Logic of Collective Action: Public Goods and the Theory of Groups* (New York: Schocken, 1968).

51 See Furubotn and Pejovich, op. cit., note 42, pp. 1150–52.

52 See E. Fama, 'Agency Problems and the Theory of the Firm', (1980) 88 *J. Pol. Econ.* 288.

53 Ibid.

54 See Jensen and Meckling, op. cit., note 17; R. Green, 'Investment Incentives, Debt and Warrants', (1984) 13 *J. Fin. Econ.* 115.

55 Another function of secured debt is its role in solving the problem of adverse selection between the creditor and debtor. See G. Triantis, op. cit., note 28.

56 C. Smith and J. Warner, 'On Financial Contracting: An Analysis of Bond Covenants', (1979) 7 *J. Fin. Econ.* 117.

57 Firm-specific assets are those whose worth to the firm greatly exceeds their market value.

58 On this point, see O. Williamson, 'Credible Commitments: Using Hostages to Support Exchange', (1983) 73 *Am. Econ. Rev.* 519.

59 R. Stulz and H. Johnson, 'An Analysis of Secured Debt', (1985) 14 *J. Fin. Econ.* 501.

60 E. Berglof and E. Perotti, 'The Governance Structure of the Japanese Financing Keiretsu', (1994) 36 *J. Fin. Econ.* 259.

61 R. Gilson and M. Roe, 'Understanding the Japanese Keiretsu: Overlaps Between Corporate Governance and Industrial Organization', (1993) 102 *Yale L. J.* 871.

62 See Berglof and Perotti, op. cit., note 60, p. 275.

63 E. Fama and M. Jensen, 'Separation of Ownership and Control', (1983) 26 *J. L. & Econ.* 301 at p. 313.

64 Ibid., p. 313. The position described here mainly suits the US model.

65 M. Jensen, 'The Modern Industrail Revolution, Exit, and Failure of Internal Control System', (1993) 48 *J. Fin. Econ.* 831 at pp. 835–47.

66 A. Berle, 'Modern Functions of the Corporate System', (1962) 62 *Colum. L. Rev.* 433.

67 P. Dodd and J. Warner, 'On Corporate Governance', (1983) 11 *J. Fin. Econ.* 401.

68 S. Rosenstein and J. Wyatt, 'Outsider Director, Board Independence, and Shareholder Wealth', (1990) 26 *J. Fin. Econ.* 175.

69 See Daniels and Halpern, op. cit., note 6, p. 17.

70 Even the ascertainment of the market price of products requires considerable costs, see G. Stigler, 'The Economics of Information', (1961) 69 *J. Pol. Econ.* 213.

71 Monitoring activities on the agents in corporations are a public good. For a discussion on the theory of public goods, see P. Samuelson, 'The Pure Theory of Public Expenditure', (1954) 36 *Rev. Econ. Statistics* 386.

72 For a full exposition of the prisoner's dilemma, see D. Mueller, *Public Choice*, (Cambridge: Cambridge University Press, 1979), Chapter 2.

73 D. Fischel, 'Organized Exchanges and the Regulation of Dual Common Stock', (1987) 54 *U. Chi. L. Rev.* 119 at p. 136.

74 For more information, see A. Alchian, 'Corporate Management and Property Rights', in H. Manne (ed.), *Economic Policy and the Regulation of Corporate Securities* (Washington, DC: American Enterprise Institute for Public Policy Research, 1969) pp. 337–60.

75 See Jensen and Smith, op. cit., note 34, pp. 103–04.

76 Ibid., pp. 103–05.

77 See T. Baums, 'Corporate Governance in Germany: The Role of the Banks', (1992) 40 *Am. J. Comp. L.* 503 at p. 508. There are only caps or limits with respect to a bank's capital to protect the depositors and creditors of the bank. A single participation in one firm may not exceed 50 per cent of the capital of the bank. Furthermore, investments of a bank in stockholdings and other illiquid assets may not exceed its own capital. The Second Banking directive of the EC lowers these limits: in the future no single holding may exceed 15 per cent, no all holdings together may be greater than 60 per cent of the capital of the bank.

78 D. Neuberger and M. Neumann, 'Banking and Antitrust: Limiting Industrial Ownership by Banks', (1991) 147 *J. Institutional and Theoretical Econ.* 188–89 (reporting an average of 40 per cent as compared to about 9 per cent in the United Kingdom and USA).; see also A. Gerschenkron, *Economic*

Backwardness in Historical Perspective (Cambridge, MA: Belknap Press, 1962); C. Mayer, 'Financial Systems, Corporate Finance and Economic Development' in G. Hubbard ed., *Asymmetric Information, Corporate Finance and Investment* (Chicago: University of Chicago Press, 1990). (Mayer claims that there is no empirical support for the commonly held view that German banks contribute a substantial amount of financing to industry.)

79 See Baums, op. cit., note 77, p. 513.
80 Ibid., p. 512.
81 See Roe, op. cit., note 13, p. 1937.
82 Ibid.
83 See Baums, op. cit., note 77, pp. 505–06.
84 Ibid., pp. 505–07.
85 Ibid., p. 505.
86 Ibid., pp. 515–16.
87 Ibid., p. 510.
88 Ibid.
89 Ibid.
90 P. Windolf, 'Codetermination and the Market for Corporate Control in the European Community', (1993) 22 *Econ. & Soc'y* 137, 143.
91 See Baums, op. cit., note 77, p. 511.
92 Ibid., p. 518.
93 Ibid., p. 508.
94 See Berglof and Perotti, op. cit., note 60, p. 277.
95 See Roe, op. cit., note 13, 1939.
96 Ibid.
97 These keiretsu include Sumitomo, Mitsubishi, Mitsui, Sanwa, Fuyo and DKB.
98 Fair Trade Commission, *The Outline Report on the Actual Conditions of the Six Major Groups* (Government of Japan, 1992).
99 M. Gerlach, *Alliance Capitalism: The Social Organization of the Japanese Business* (Berkeley: University of California Press, 1992).
100 I. Nakatani, 'The Economic Role of the Financial Corporate Grouping' in M. Aoki ed., *Economic Analysis of the Japanese Firm* (Amsterdam: North-Holland, 1984).
101 See Fair Trade Commission, op. cit., note 98.
102 Ibid.
103 See Gerlach, op. cit., note 99.
104 See Berglof and Perotti, op. cit., note 60, p. 268.
105 See Roe, op. cit., note 13.
106 See R. Romano, 'A Cautionary Note on Drawing Lessons from Comparative Corporate Law', (1993) 102 *Yale L. J.* 2021 at p. 2037.
107 T. Hoshi and T. Ito, 'Measuring Cohesion in Japanese Enterprise Groups', Working Paper (University of California at San Diego, CA, 1991).
108 See Berglof and Perotti, op. cit., note 60, p. 267.
109 Ibid.
110 S. Kaplan, 'Top Executive Rewards and Firm Performance: A Comparison of Japan and the United States', Working Paper (University of Chicago, Chicago, IL, 1992).

111 S. Kaplan and B. Minton, 'Appointments of Outsiders to Japanese Boards: Determinants and Implications for Managers', (1994) 36 *J. Fin. Econ.* 225.
112 See Berglof and Perotti, op. cit., note 60, p. 277.
113 Ibid.
114 Gilson and Roe, op. cit., note 61, p. 871.
115 T. Hoshi *et al.*, 'The Role of Banks', (1990) 27 *J. Fin. Econ.* 67.
116 Ibid.
117 R. Zielinski and N. Holloway, *Unequal Equities: Power and Ricks in Japan's Stock Market* (Tokyo: Kodansha International, 1990) p. 156.
118 R. Shearer *et al., The Economics of the Canadian Financial System* (Scarborough, Ontario: Prentice-Hall, 1984) p. 225.
119 'The Global Service 500: The 100 Largest Commercial Banking Companies', Fortune, 26 August 1991, pp. 174–75.
120 R. Roe, 'Political and Legal Restraints on Ownership and Control of Public Companies', (1990) 27 *J. Fin. Econ.* 7.
121 See, Roe, op. cit., note 13, p. 1948.
122 Ibid.
123 Ibid.
124 See Roe, op. cit., note 120, p. 11.
125 See Roe, op. cit., note 13, p. 1949.
126 See Roe, op. cit., note 120, p. 12.
127 Ibid.
128 Ibid.
129 Ibid., p. 20.
130 Ibid., p. 16.
131 G. Benson, 'The Effectiveness and Effects of the SEC's Accounting Disclosure Requirements', in H. Manne (ed.), *Economic Policy and the Regulation of Corporate Securities* (Washington, DC: American Enterprise Institute for Public Policy Research, 1969) pp. 23–79.
132 See Roe, op. cit., note 120, p. 17.
133 B. Black, 'Shareholder Passivity Reexamined', (1990) 89 *Mich. L. Rev.* 520 at pp. 527–28.
134 See Roe, op. cit., note 120, p. 17.
135 R. Romano, 'The Future of Hostile Takeovers: Legislation and Public Opinion', (1988) 57 *U. Cin. L. Rev.* 457; M. Ryngaert and J. Netter, 'Shareholder Wealth Effects of the Ohio Antitakeover Law', (1988) 4 *J. L. Econ. & Org.* 373.
136 For example, see Jensen, op. cit., note 65, pp. 835–47.
137 P. Lawton, 'Directors Remuneration, Benefits and Extractions: An Analysis of Their Uses, Abuses and Controls in the Corporate Governance Context of Hong Kong', (1995) 4 *Australian J. Corp. L.* 430, 434.
138 M. Garlord and C. Armitage, 'All in the Family: Corporate Structure, Business Culture and Inside Dealing in Hong Kong', (1993) 3 (1) *Asia Pacific L. Rev.* 26 at p. 28.
139 Ibid., p. 30
140 Ibid., p. 27.
141 For the concern of minority shareholder protection, see Lawton, op. cit., note

137; Gaylord and Armitage, op. cit., note 138; A. Eu, 'Hong Kong Code on Takeovers and Mergers: Toothless Watchdog or Handmaiden of Equality', (1987) 17 *Hong Kong L. J.* 24.

142 The shares of these state-owned enterprises are called H shares, which are traded on the Stock Exchange of Hong Kong.

143 During the last decade, some Chinese state-owned enterprises acquired a number of Hong Kong listed corporations. The motivations include the acquisition of available export markets and know-how, circumvention of the restrictions for listing shares in Hong Kong by Chinese corporations, better access to financial institutions, and flexible means of doing business which are not available to enterprises within China.

144 For a similar view on family controlled corporations in Canada, see Daniels and Halpern, op. cit., note 6.

145 See, M. Roe, 'Chaos and Evolution in Law and Economics', (1996) 109 *Harv. L. Rev.* 641.

146 Ibid., p. 656.

147 Ibid., p. 658.

148 C. Milhaupt, 'A Relational Theory of Japanese Corporate Governance: Contract Culture, and the Rule of Law', (1996) 37 *Harv. Int'l L. J.* 48–49

149 Ibid., pp. 50–52, 61.

150 Ibid., pp. 55–57.

151 Also see D. Eu, 'Comment, Financial Reforms and Corporate Governance in China', (1996) 34 *Colum. J. Trans. L.* 449, 486–90 (arguing that adopting German and Japanese corporate governance models by relying on bank monitors is more appropriate for China).

152 The soft budget constraint is a concept developed in J. Kornai, *Economics of Shortage* (Amsterdam: North-Holland Publ. Co., 1980).

153 F. Hayek, 'The Use of Knowledge in Society', (1945) 35 *Am. Econ. Rev.* 519.

154 Also see World Bank, *China: Finance and Investment* (1988) p. 72.

155 Jiang Qiangui, 'Like Wading Across a Stream: Law, Reform and the State Enterprise', in B. Bachner and H. Fu (eds), *Commercial Laws in the People's Republic of China* (Singapore: Butterworths Asia, 1995) p. 3.

156 This Law was adopted at the Fourth Session of the Sixth National People's Congress of China on 12 April 1986, and became effective as of 1 January 1987.

157 Ibid., Article 41.

158 Ibid., Article 48.

159 This Law was enacted by the Standing Committee of the National People's Congress on 2 December 1986 and became effective on 1 November 1988.

160 This Law was adopted at the First Session of the Seventh National People's Congress and promulgated by Order No. 3 of the President of the People's Republic of China on 13 April 1988.

161 Ibid., Article 2.

162 Ibid.

163 Jiang Qiangui, op. cit. note 155, p. 3.

164 Ibid.

165 Bin Ma and Zhunyan Hong, 'Enlivening Large State Enterprises: Where is the Motive Force?' (1987) 11 *J. Comp. Econ.* 503 at pp. 503–04.

166 Articles 6 to 21 of the Regulations.

167 This Commission has been given enormous power to initiate economic reform policies. Some of these policies were normally experimented in some cities or regions first before they were finally implemented nationwide.

168 This Law was enacted at the Fifth Session of the Standing Committee of the Eighth National People's Congress of China and became effective on 1 July 1994.

169 The Construction Bank, originally established in 1954, was absorbed by the Ministry of Finance in 1958. Established in 1955, the Agricultural Bank was dissolved in 1957 and its business was taken over by the People's Bank. These two banks reemerged in the 1960s and continued only for a very short period.

170 These Decisions were issued on 17 September 1983.

171 This bank came into existence on 1 January 1980.

172 Zhou Zhengqing, 'Explanations Concerning the Commercial Banking Law of the People's Republic of China', a speech delivered at the Thirteenth Session of the Eighth Standing Committee of the National People's Congress.

173 See, Eu, op. cit., note 151, p. 489.

174 Ibid.

175 This Law was adopted at the Third Session of the Eighth National People's Congress on 18 March 1995 and became effective on the date of adoption and promulgation.

176 This Law was adopted at the Thirteenth Session of the Eighth National People's Congress on 10 May 1995 and became effective on 1 July 1995.

177 Ibid., Articles 41 and 85.

178 Project Group of the China Academic of Social Sciences, 'Several Problems Related to the Establishment of a Modern Enterprise System', (1996) 17 (4) *Social Sciences in China* 19 at p. 20.

179 Ibid.

180 Ibid.

181 Ibid.

182 Ibid.

183 See Zhou Zhengqing, op. cit., note 172, pp. 20–21.

184 Rowena Tsang, 'Bad Debts Expected to Hit One Trillion Yuan', *South China Morning Post*, 15 December 1994, at Business 1.

185 Income Tax Law of the People's Republic of China for Enterprises with Foreign Investment and Foreign Enterprises, Articles 8–10, *China Laws for Foreign Business*, 32–505.

186 Wang Wuyi, 'An Analysis of the Factors Affecting Bankruptcy of State-owned Enterprises', (1994) 6 *Jingji Yanjiu* (Economic Research Journal) 41 at p. 42.

187 The Constitution was enacted at the Fifth Session of the Fifth National People's Congress and promulgated on 4 December 1982. This article was amended in 1993.

188 See Wong Wuyi, op. cit., note 186, p. 41.

189 Ibid.

190 Ibid.

191 See Zhou Zhengqing, op. cit., note 172, p. 21.

192 See Wong Wuyi, op. cit., note 186, p. 42.

193 Ibid., p. 41.

194 See Guanghua Yu, 'China's Intellectual Property Regime and Direct Foreign Investment', (1996) 5 (1) *Tilburg Foreign L. Rev.* 5.

195 See this Law, op. cit., note 176.

196 See Roe, op. cit., note 13 and 120; J. Grundfest, 'Subordination of American Capital', (1991) 27 *J. Fin. Econ.* 89.

197 See Eu, op. cit., note 151, p. 497.

198 Ibid.

199 Since the financial reform, a few localized commercial banks have come into existence. These small but flexible commercial banks were established by local governments such as the Shenzhen Development Bank and the Pudong Development Bank of Shanghai or by large corporations such as the Merchant Bank and the Guangda Bank of China.

200 Xie Ping, 'Reform of the State-owned Specialized Banks', (1994) 2 *Jingji Yanjiu* (Economic Research Journal) 22.

201 Zhou Tien Youn, 'Solutions for the Debts to Banks Owned by State-owned Enterprises', (1995) 8 *Jingji Yanjiu* (Economic Research Journal) 22 at pp. 22–23.

202 The three new policy banks are: the State Development Bank, responsible for channelling long-term development credit to infrastructure and key industrial projects, the Agricultural Policy Bank, responsible for channelling funds to the agricultural sector, and the Export–Import Bank, responsible for providing funds to trade projects guided by and compatible to trade policy.

203 T. Walker, 'Survey of China', *Fin. Times,* 7 November 1994, at VII.

204 Hui Xiao Bing, 'Alternative Models for the Banking Sector During China's Move Towards a Market Economy', (1994) 1 *Jingji Yanjiu* (Economic Research Journal) 17 at p. 22.

205 See Xie Ping, op. cit., note 200, p. 23.

206 Ibid.

207 Ibid.

208 See Dong Pu Reng, 'Reform of China's Banking System', (1994) 1 *Jingji Yanjiu* (Economic Research Journal) 12 at p. 14.

209 See Xie Ping, op. cit., note 200, p. 24.

210 This Law was adopted at the Fifth Session of the Standing Committee of the Eighth National People's Congress of China on 29 December 1993 and became effective on 1 July 1994; Article 152(2).

211 See Xu Jingan, 'The Stock-share System: A New Avenue for China's Economic Reform', (1987) 11 *J. Comp. Econ.* 509 at p. 514.

212 Ibid.

213 Ibid.

214 I obtained this information during an interview with an official of the Legislative Affairs Commission of the Standing Committee of the National People's Congress.

215 An English translation of this Regulation appears at *China Law and Practice* (Hong Kong: Asia Law and Practice, August 1993) p. 23.
216 Ibid., ITS, Article 47(1).
217 Ibid., ITS, Article 47(2); the current position is 5 per cent under the Securities Act of 1998 instead of 2 per cent.
218 Ibid., ITS, Article 48.
219 Ibid., ITS, Article 48; the current price provision in the Procedures on the Administration of Takeover of Listed Companies issued by the China Securities Regulatory Commission on 28 September 2002 follows the higher of the following two: (1) the highest price the acquirer paid during the six months prior to the date of public announcement; or (2) 90 per cent of the arithmetic mean of the daily weighted average prices of the target company's listed shares of that class during the 30 days prior to the date of public announcement.

Chapter 2 The problem with the transplantation of Western law

1 Gang Fan and Wing Thye Woo, 'State Enterprise Reform as a Source of Macroeconomic Instability: The Case of China', (1996) 10 *Asian Econ. J.* 207 (arguing that SOEs were an important contributing factor of macroeconomic instability); *The Chinese Economy: Fighting Inflation, Deepening Reforms 15–17* (Washington, DC: World Bank, 1996); *China's Management of Enterprise Assets: The State as Shareholder* (Washington, DC: World Bank, 1997).
2 S. Peltzman, 'Pricing in Public and Private Enterprises: Electric Utilities in the United States', (1971) 14 *J. L. & Econ.* 110.
3 S. Atkinson and R. Halvorsen, 'The Relative Efficiency of Public and Private Firms in a Regulated Environment: The Case of U.S. Electric Utilities', (1986) 29 *J. Pol. Econ.* 281.
4 A. Alchian and H. Demestz, 'Production, Information, and Economic Organization', (1972) 62 *Am. Econ. Rev.* 777.
5 M. Jensen and W. Meckling, 'Theory of the Firm: Managerial Behavior, Agency Costs and Ownership Structure', (1976) 3 *J. Fin. Econ.* 305.
6 A. Alchian, *Economic Forces at Work* (Indianapolis, IN: Liberty Press, 1977) pp. 127–49.
7 S. Kole and J. Mulherin, 'The Government As a Shareholder: A Case From the United States', (1997) 30 *J. L. & Econ.* 1.
8 M. Trebilcock and E. Iacobucci, Commentary, 'Privatization and Accountability', (2003) 116 *Harv. L. Rev.* 1422.
9 Although production of most goods or services was planned by the state, these goods or services were not directly allocated to individuals. Instead, these goods or services were exchanged through the medium of money on the market.
10 Also see D. Eu, 'Comment, Financial Reforms and Corporate Governance in China', (1996) 34 *Colum. J. Trans. L..* 449 at pp. 486–90.
11 The soft budget constraint is a concept developed in J. Kornai, *Economics of Shortage* (Amsterdam: North-Holland Publ. Co., 1980).
12 The Report is available online at <http://www.people.com.cn/GB/shizheng/252/5089/5106/5278/20010430/456648.html>.

13 The Speech is available online at <http://www.people.com.cn/GB/shizheng/252/5089/5106/5278/20010430/456627.html>.
14 Available online at <http://www.people.com.cn/GB/shizheng/16/20021117/868418.html>.
15 Article 6 of the 1999 Constitution in the *Collection of the Laws of the PRC* (Jilin: Jilin People's Press, 1993) pp. 3–4.
16 Project Group of the Chinese Academy of Social Sciences, 'Several Problems Related to the Establishment of a Modern Enterprise System', (1996) 17 (4) *Social Sciences in China* 19 at p. 20. One US dollar is equal to approximately 8.2 Chinese yuan.
17 Ibid.
18 Ibid.
19 Ibid.
20 Ibid.
21 Zhou Zhengqing, 'Explanations Concerning the Commercial Banking Law of the PRC', a speech delivered at the Ninth Session of the Eighth Standing Committee of the National People's Congress on 24 August 1994, *Gazette of the Standing Committee of the National People's Congress* (30 May 1995) 19 at pp. 20–21.
22 Interview with Mr Cai, a middle-level manager with the Bank of China in Hangzhou on 25 May 1993.
23 See generally J. Kornai, op. cit., note 11, for a discussion about soft budget constraints; for a discussion on the difficulty of enforcing the Bankruptcy Law in China in the 1990s, see Guanghua Yu, 'The Relevance of Comparative Corporate Governance Studies for China', (1997) 8 (1) *Australian J. Corp. L.* 49 at pp. 79–80.
24 See Xu Jingan, 'The State-share System: A New Avenue for China's Economic Reform', (1987) 11 *J. Comp. Econ.* 509 at p. 510.
25 Ibid., p. 513.
26 Ibid.
27 R. Art and Minkang Gu, 'China Incorporated: the First Corporation Law of the People's Republic of China', (1995) 20 *Yale J. Int'l L.* 273 at p. 307.
28 Zhang Zongxin and Sun Yewei, 'The Optimization of Shareholding Structure and the Improvement of Corporate Governance in Listed Companies', (2001) 1 *Econ. Rev.* 36.
29 Ibid.
30 Absolute control means that the state controls more than 50 per cent of the issued shares and relative control means that the state controls more than 30 per cent of the issued shares.
31 Zhang and Sun, op. cit., note 28.
32 Ibid.
33 Ibid.
34 Ibid.
35 Zhang Rui, 'A Legal Analysis of Negotiated Takeovers of Listed Companies', (July 2003) *Jilin University Journal (Social Sciences)* 108 at p. 109.
36 An English translation of this Regulation appears at *China Law and Practice* (Hong Kong: Asia Law & Practice, August 1993) p. 23.

37 The Code is available online at <http://www.hksfc.org.hk>.

38 London City Code on Takeovers and Mergers (7th edn 2002), available online at <http://www.thetakeoverpanel.org.uk>.

39 Ibid., Section 9.1.

40 ITS, Article 48. An English translation of this Regulation appears at *China Law and Practice* (Hong Kong: Asia Law and Practice, August 1993) p. 23.

41 This Law was enacted by the Standing Committee of the National People's Congress on 29 December 1998 and appears in the *Collection of the Laws of the PRC* (Jilin: Jilin People's Press, 1998) p. 671; an English translation appears at *China Law and Practice* (Hong Kong: Asia Law & Practice, February 1999) p. 25; Securities Law, Article 81.

42 ITS, op. cit., note 40. The current price provision in the Procedures on the Administration of the Takeover of Listed Companies issued by the China Securities Regulatory Commission on 28 September 2002 follows the higher of the following two: (1) the highest price the acquirer paid during the six months prior to the date of public announcement; and (2) 90 per cent of the arithmetic mean of the daily weighted average prices of the target company's listed shares of that class during the 30 days prior to the date of public announcement. An English translation of the Takeover Procedures can be found in *China Law and Practice* (Hong Kong: Asia Law & Practice, November 2002) p. 43.

43 Ibid., ITS, Article 50; currently, there are no preference shares in China's listed companies.

44 Ibid., ITS, Article 51(3).

45 Ibid., ITS, Article 52(1).

46 Ibid., ITS, Article 52(2).

47 Ibid., ITS, Article 47(1).

48 Ibid., ITS, Article 47(2).

49 Securities Law, Article 79(2).

50 ITS, Article 47(3).

51 ITS, Article 49(2).

52 Ibid.

53 ITS, Article 52(3).

54 P. Lee, 'Takeovers – The United Kingdom Experience' in J. Farrar (ed.) *Takeovers: Institutional Investors and the Modernization of Corporate Law* (Oxford: Oxford University Press, 1993) p. 192.

55 R. Austin, 'Takeovers – The Australian Experience' in J. Farrar (ed.) *Takeovers: Institutional Investors and the Modernization of Corporate Law* (Oxford: Oxford University Press, 1993).

56 P. Davies and K. Hopt, 'Control Transactions' in Reinier Kraakman *et al.* (eds), *The Anatomy of Corporate Law* (Oxford: Oxford University Press, 2004) pp. 179–80.

57 London City Code, op. cit., note 38, section 1(a)

58 Davies and Hopt, op. cit., note 56, p 180; P. Davies, 'The Notion of Equality in European Takeover Regulation' in J. Payne (ed.), *Takeovers in English and German Law* (Oxford: Hart Publishing, 2002) pp. 14 and 26.

59 Davies and Hopt, op. cit., note 56, p. 190.

60 For a discussion on interest group politics of the anti-takeover legislation, see R. Romano, 'A Guide to Takeovers: Theory, Evidence, and Regulation', (1992) *Yale J. on Reg.* 119.

61 M. Jensen, 'Takeovers: Their Causes and Consequences', (1988) 2 *J. Econ. Perspectives* 21; R. Morck *et al.*, 'Alternative Mechanisms for Corporate Control', (1989) 79 *Am. Econ. Rev.* 545.

62 See Romano, op. cit., note 60.

63 See Inshuranshares Corp. v. Northern Fiscal Corp., 35 F. Supp. 22 (E.D. Pa. 1940).

64 G. Jarrell *et al.*, 'The Market for Corporate Control: The Empirical Evidence Since 1982', (1988) 2 *J. Econ. Perspectives* 49; M. Jensen and R. Ruback, 'The Market for Corporate Control: The Scientific Evidence', (1983) 11 *J. Fin. Econ.* 5.

65 For empirical evidence that takeovers are more likely to produce social gains, see Jarrell *et al.* 'The Market for Corporate Control: The Empirical Evidence Since 1982', (1988) 2 *J. Econ. Perspectives* 49; Jensen and Ruback, 'The Market for Corporate Control: The Scientific Evidence', (1983) 11 *J. Fin. Econ.* 5.

66 R. Nozick, 'Coercion' in S. Morgenbesser *et al.* (eds), *Philosophy, Science, and Method* (New York: St Martin's Press, 1969) pp. 447–53.

67 L. Lowenstein, 'Pruning Deadwood in Hostile Takeovers: A Proposal for Legislation', (1983) 83 *Colum. L. Rev.* 249; M. Bradley and M. Rosenzweig, 'Defensive Stock Repurchases', (1986) 99 *Harv. L. Rev.* 1377.

68 J. Coffee, 'The Uncertain Case For Takeover Reform: An Essay on Stockholders, Stateholders and Bust-ups', (1988) *Wiscon. L. Rev.* 435 at p. 459.

69 Davies and Hopt, op. cit., note 56, p. 178.

70 Ibid.

71 Ibid., p.179.

72 For a discussion of the nature of public goods, see P. Samuelson, 'The Pure Theory of Public Expenditure', (1954) 36 *Rev. Econ. Statistics* 386.

73 S. Grossman and O. Hart, 'Takeover Bids, the Free-Rider Problem, and the Theory of the Corporation', (1980) 11 (1) *Bell J. Econ.* 42 at p. 59.

74 For a similar discussion of the problem of free-rider and externality in the context of freeze-out, see F. Easterbrook and D. Fischel, 'Corporate Control Transactions', (1982) 91 *Yale L. J.* 698 at pp. 705–06.

75 Although minority shareholders are not entitled to equal gains, they will still receive gains from the improvement of the target by a more efficient management team appointed by the acquiring company.

76 Paul Davies, op. cit., note 58, p. 28.

77 Ibid.

78 Ibid.

79 Ibid.

80 These administrative rules were jointly issued by the State Asset Administration Bureau and the State Economic Restructuring Commission on 3 November 1994. The document can be found in the legal database available online at <http://www.chinainfobank.com>.

81 Ibid.

82 Zhang Xin, 'Legislation and Regulation of Takeovers of Listed Companies', (August 2003) *Securities Market Herald,* p. 12.

83 Chen Gong *et al.,* (eds), *Principles and Cases of Corporate Mergers and Takeovers* (Beijing: Renmin University Press, 1996) pp. 421–25.

84 Ibid., p. 422.

85 Hanson Trust v SCM, 774 F. 2d 27 (2d Cir. 1985).

86 Securities Law, op. cit., note 41.

87 Securities Law, Article 81.

88 Ibid.

89 Kennecott Copper Corp. v Curtiss-Wright Corp., 584 F. 2d 1195 (2d Cir. 1978); Hanson Trust v SCM, 774 F. 2d 27 (2d Cir. 1985).

90 Li Bingan, 'A Discussion of the Exemption from the Mandatory Purchase Provision', (November 2003) 18 (6) *Legal Forum* 50.

91 He Xiaogang, 'Management Buyouts: the Status Abroad, Research, and Development in China', (2003) 4 *Reform* 54.

92 Fei Yiwen and Cai Mingchao, 'An Analysis of the Takeover Effects of Listed Companies on the Shanghai Stock Exchange', (2003) 5 *World Economy* 64.

93 An English translation of the Takeover Procedures can be found in *China Law and Practice* (Hong Kong: Asia Law & Practice, November 2002) p. 43.

94 Ibid., Articles, 13, 14 and 23.

95 Ibid., Article 49(4).

96 Ibid., Article 51(4).

97 Ibid., Article 49(2).

98 Ibid., Article 49(3).

99 Ibid., Article 51(2).

100 Ibid., Article 51(5).

101 Ibid., Article 49(5) and Article 51(7).

102 Art and Gu, op. cit., note 27, p. 139.

103 General Principle 7 of the London City Code, op. cit., note 38.

104 See F. Easterbrook and D. Fischel, 'The Proper Role of a Target's Management in Responding to a Tender Offer', (1981) 94 *Harv. L. Rev.* 1161.

105 For a similar view, see A. Schwartz, 'The Fairness of Tender Offer Prices in Utilitarian Theory', (1988) 17 *J. Legal Stud.* 165.

106 L. Bebchuk, 'The Case Against Board Veto in Corporate Takeovers', (2002) 69 *U. Chi. L. Rev.* 973.

107 M. Lipton, 'Pills, Polls, and Professors Redux', (2002) 69 *U. Chi. L. Rev.* 1037.

108 Ibid., p. 1078.

109 See, for example, 8 Del. Code Ann. § 141 (2001).

110 See, for example, 8 Del. Code Ann. § 251 (2001) (mergers), § 271 (2001) (sale of substantially all the assets of the firm).

111 See, for example, Cede & Co v Technicolor, Inc, 634 A2d 345, 360 (Del. 1993).

112 See, for example, Unitrin, Inc v American General Corp., 651 A 2d 1361, 1390 (Del. 1995).

113 Paramount Communications, Inc v Time Inc., 571 A 2d 1140, 1150.

114 Moran v Household International, Inc, 500 A 2d 1346, 1356 (Del. 1985).

115 For a discussion of the theoretical debate on takeovers in the USA and the current status of the Delaware law on takeovers, see W. Allen *et al.*, 'The Great Takeover Debate: A Meditation on Bridging the Conceptual Divide', (2002) 69 *U. Chi. L. Rev.* 1067.

116 For a regulator's view, see Zhang Xin, op. cit., note 82, pp. 15–17.

117 Hengtong, op. cit., note 83.

118 The Opinions were jointly issued by the State Asset Administration Bureau and the State Economic Restructuring Commission on 29 August 1997 and are available online at <http://www.chinainfobank.com>.

119 Ibid., Article 17.

120 Wang Huacheng and Tong Yan, 'Management Buyouts in China: The Case of Media', (2002) 10 *Economic Theory and Management* 66; An Chunmei and Dou Zhanguo, 'An Analysis of Benefits and Risks of Management Buyouts in Listed Companies', (2002) 7 *Finance and Accounting Research* 52.

121 These Provisional Measures are available online at <http://www.chinainfo bank.com>.

122 See Trebilcock and Iacobucci, op. cit., note 8.

123 *The Economist*, 5–11 June 2004, p. 56.

124 See generally J. Kornai, op. cit., note 11.

125 See Trebilcock and Iacobucci, op. cit., note 8, p. 1429.

126 W. Megginson and J. Netter, 'From State to Market: A Survey of Empirical Studies on Privatization', (2001) 39 *J. Econ. Lit.* 321 at p. 331.

127 See notes 28–35 and the accompanying text.

128 'Penalty Decision Regarding the Violation of Securities Regulation by Chengdo Hong Guang Industrial Ltd', *China Securities Regulatory Commission Gazette*, 8 December 1998, available online at <http://www.chinainfobank.com>.

129 Measures Concerning the Prohibition of Speculative Trading of Shares by State Owned Enterprises and Listing Companies. The State Council Securities Commission, the People's Bank of China and the State Economic and Trade Commission jointly issued these Measures on 27 May 1997. The Measures appear in the *Collection of the Laws of the PRC* (Jilin: Jilin People's Press, 1997) p. 498.

130 Yao Bei, 'Hong Guang: the First Case of Criminal Punishment', 15 December 2000, available online at <http://www.people.com.cn>.

131 This Regulation was promulgated by the State Council on 22 April 1993 and appears in the *Collection of the Laws of the PRC* (Jilin: Jilin People's Press, 1993) p. 480, see also ITS, op. cit., note 36.

132 Securities Law, op. cit., note 41.

133 Yao Bei, op. cit., note 130.

134 Luo Xiaoming, 'CSRC Investigated and Punished Energy 28', *People Net*, 20 December 2000, available online at <http://www.people.com.cn>.

135 Public Criticisms by the CSRC on Three and Nine Medical and Pharmaceutical Co Ltd and the Relevant Persons, 27 August 2001, available online at <http://www.chinainfobank.com>.

136 The Guidelines of Articles of Association of Listed Companies was issued by the China Securities Regulatory Commission on 16 December 1997 and appear

in the *Collections of the Laws of the PRC* (Jilin: Jilin People's Press, 1998) p. 779.

137 Public Criticisms by China Securities Regulatory commission on Hubei Meierya Co Ltd and the relevant persons of the company, 20 September 2001, available online at <http://www.chinainfobank.com>.

138 Han Zhiguo, 'The Development and Innovation of Shareholding Economy in China', *People Net*, 26 May 2001, available at http://www.peopledaily.com.cn.

139 Wu Feng, 'Ten Questions Required Quick Solutions', *People Net*, 22 September 2001, available online at <http://www.people.com.cn>.

140 Fang Yuan, 'Zhou Xiaochuan: the Securities Market Has A Big Opera Next Year', *People Net*, 29 December 2000, available online at <http://www.people.com.cn>.

141 See Wu, op. cit., note 139.

142 This law was enacted on 29 December 1993 and became effective on 1 July 1994. The official Chinese version appears in the *Collection of the Laws of the PRC* (Jilin: Jilin People's Press, 1993) p. 456.

143 The ITS was issued by the State Council on 22 April 1993 and appears in the *Collection of the Laws of the PRC* (Jilin: Jilin People's Press, 1993) p. 480; also see note 36.

144 This Decision was promulgated by the Standing Committee of the National People's Congress on 28 February 1995 and appears in the *Collection of the Laws of the PRC* (Jilin: Jilin People's Press, 1994) p. 51.

145 The Decision, Article 3(1).

146 See 1997 Criminal Act, Article 160.

147 See Hong Guang, op. cit., note 128.

148 See ITS, op. cit., note 36.

149 See Securities Law, op. cit., note 41.

150 Securities Law, Article 202.

151 See Hong Guang, op. cit., note 128.

152 Huang Xiangyuan, 'Hong guang Qizha An Mei Namo Rongyi Wanjie' (The Case of Fraud of Hong Guang Could Not Easily be Ended), *Securities Newspaper*, 28 December 2000.

153 Ibid.

154 Xue Li, 'Cong Hong Guang Dao Yin guang Xia, Minishi Peichange De Lu You Duochang' (From Hong Guang Dao Yin guang Xia, How Far We Still Have to Go For Civil Compensation), *Shanghai Securities Newspaper*, 6 September 2001, available online at <http://finance-sina.com.cn>.

155 Tao Feng, 'Cong Hong Guang Dao Yin Guang Xia Kan Gumin Weiquan' (Look at the Protection for Investors from Hong Guang to Yin Guang Xia), available online at <http://www.informationtimes.dayoo.com/content/2001-09/28/content_232281/htm>.

156 Notice of the Supre People's Court Concerning the Temporary Non-acceptance of Securities Cases for Civil Compensation, 21 September 2001, available online at <http://www.chinainfobank.com>.

157 Ji Wenhai, 'Zhongguo Remmin Daxue Sanwei Jiaoshou Tan Zhengquan Weifa Ji Chengzhi' (Three Professors Talked about Violation of and Punishment for

Illegal Acts on the Securities Markets), *Chinese Economics Times*, 17 October 2001, available online at <http://www.chinainfobank.com>.

158 Notice of the Supreme People's Court on Certain Issues Concerning the Acceptance of Tort Cases Involving Misrepresentation on the Securities Market, 15 January 2002, available at http://www.chinainfobank.com.

159 Ibid.

160 Civil Procedure Law, Article 55. This law appears in the *Collection of the Laws of the PRC* (Jilin: Jilin People's Press, 1993) pp. 303–06.

161 Ibid.

162 'Several Provisions Concerning the Trial of Civil Damages Cases Arising from Misrepresentation in the Securities Market', issued by the Supreme People's Court on 9 January 2003 and became effective as of 1 February 2003. The Provisions appear at *China Law and Practice* (Hong Kong: Asia Law & Practice Publishing Ltd, March 2003) p.53.

163 P. Straham, 'Securities Class Actions, Corporate Governance and Managerial Agency Problems', Working Paper, Federal Reserve of New York (1998), quoted from M. Gilson, 'Big Bank Deregulation and Japanese Corporate Governance: A Survey of the Issue' in T. Hoshi and H. Patrick (eds), *Crisis and Change in the Japanese Financial System* (Boston, MA: Kluwer Academic Publishers, 2000) 291 at p. 305.

164 M. Gilson, 'Big Bank Deregulation and Japanese Corporate Governance: A Survey of the Issue', in Hoshi and Patrick, op. cit.

165 See C. Milhaupt, 'Property Rights in Firms', (1998) 84 *Va. L. Rev.* 1145 at p. 1188.

166 Ibid.

167 See Wu Feng, op. cit., note 139.

168 Ibid.

169 See G. Akerlof, 'The Market for 'Lemon': Quality Uncertainty and the Market Mechanism', (1970) 84 *Q. J. Econ.* 488.

170 B. Black, 'The Legal and Institutional Preconditions for Strong Securities Markets', (2001) 48 *UCLA L. Rev.* 781 at p. 788.

171 Securities Law, Article 202.

172 Securities Law, Articles 24 and 63.

173 M. Minow, 'Public and Private Partnerships: Accounting for the New Religion', (2003) 116 *Harv. L. Rev.* 1129 at pp. 1249–55.

174 Ibid., p. 1247.

175 Ibid., pp. 1259–60.

176 See Trebilcock and Iacobucci, op. cit., note 8, p. 1422.

177 Ibid.

178 See Minow, op. cit., note 173, p. 1260.

179 Ibid., p. 1267.

180 Securities Act, Article 24.

181 Ibid.

182 Securities Act, Article 45; ITS, Article 12.

183 Securities Act, Articles 45 and 47.

184 Minow, op. cit., note 173, pp. 1267–68.

185 Ibid.

186 Zhong Guo Gong Chun Tong Zhang Cheng (Articles of Association of the Chinese Communist Party), Article 2, available online at <http://www.people.com.cn>.
187 Ibid., Article 39.
188 1997 Criminal Act, Article 163 in *Collection of the Laws of the PRC* (Jilin: Jilin Peoples' Press, 1996) p. 29.
189 1997 Criminal Act, Article 165.
190 1997 Criminal Act. Articles 166 and 168.
191 Company Law, Articles 59 and 61. An English translation of this law appears at *China Law and Practice* (Hong Kong: Asia Law & Practice Publishing Ltd, March 1994) p 7.
192 Zhu Baoxian and Miu Haiying, 'A Preliminary Discussion of Connected Transactions in Chinese Listed Companies', (2001) 18 *Economic Management*, available online at <http://www.e521.com>.
193 For examples, see K. Ong and C. Baxter, 'A Comparative Study of the Fundamental Elements of Chinese and English Company Law', (1999) 48 *Int'l & Comp. L. Quarterly* 88 at p. 121.
194 Minow, op. cit., note 173, p. 1268.
195 Ibid.
196 For brief information on the quota system, see 'The CSRC Notice of Opinions on the Administration of Certain Issues Concerning the Issuing of Shares'. This notice was issued by the CSRC on 24 October 1995 and appears online at <http://www.chinainfobank.com>.
197 'Checking and Approval Procedure of the China Securities Regulatory Commission on the Issuing of Shares', Section 1. This Procedure was issued by the CSRC on 16 March 2000 and appears in the *Collection of Securities Laws and Regulations* (Shanghai: Shanghai University of Finance and Economics, 2002) p. 177.
198 Ibid., Section 2.
199 Minow, op. cit., note 173, pp. 1268–69.
200 Ibid.
201 Ibid.
202 Trebilcock and Iacobucci, op. cit., note 8, pp. 1448–49.
203 Ibid., pp. 1436–37.
204 Ibid., p. 1451.

Chapter 3 The proper role of government in building a venture capital market

1 R. Coase, 'The Problem of Social Cost', (1960) 3 *J. L. & Econ.* 1.
2 D. North, *Institutions, Institutional Change and Economic Performance* (New York: Cambridge University Press, 1990) pp. 2–6.
3 B. Black and R. Gilson, 'Venture Capital and the Structure of Capital Markets: Banks Versus Stock Market', (1998) 47 *J. Fin. Econ.* 243 at p. 245.
4 See 'Establishing a Venture Investment Mechanism Several Opinions', 16 November 1999, issued by the Ministry of Science and Technology, the

163

State Development Planning Commission, the State Economic and Trade Commission, the Ministry of Finance, the People's Bank of China, the State Administration of Taxation and the China Securities Regulatory Commission. An English translation appears in *China Law and Practice* (Hong Kong: Asia Law and Practice, April 2000) pp. 22–29.

5　W. Sahlman, 'The Structure and Governance of Venture-Capital Organizations', (1990) 27 *J. Fin. Econ.* 473; P. Gompers and J. Lerner, 'The Use of Covenants: An Empirical Analysis of Venture Partnership Agreements', (1996) 39 *J. L. & Econ.* 463; and D. Smith, 'The Venture Capital Company: A Contractarian Rebuttal to the Political Theory of American Corporate Finance?' (1997) 65 *Tenn. L. Rev.* 79.

6　North, op. cit., note 2, pp. 80–82.

7　C. Milhaupt, 'The Market for Innovation in the United States and Japan: Venture Capital and the Comparative Corporate Governance Debate', (1997) 91 *Nw. U. L. Rev.* 865 at p. 874.

8　Ibid.

9　Ibid.

10　See note 4; see also Tong Guoshun, *Venture Capital* (Dalian: Northeastern University Press, 1993) p. 306.

11　'Several Rules of the State Council on Further Improving the Reform of Scientific Research Mechanism' (1987), available online at <http://www.china infobank.com> in the database of China Laws and Regulations.

12　See note 4.

13　G. Lock, 'PRC Strengthens the Regulation of Investment Funds', (February 1998) *Asia Law* 25; see also Li Kang *et al.*, *Principles and Practices of Venture Investment Funds in China* (Beijing: Economy and Science Press, 1999) p. 39.

14　Ren Tianyuan, *The Operation and Assessment of Venture Capital* (Beijing: Chinese Economy Press, 2000) p. 22.

15　Black and Gilson, op. cit., note 3, pp. 258–64.

16　Ministry of International Trade and Industry, White Paper, (1995) pp. 197–202.

17　Black and Gilson, op. cit., note 3, p. 246.

18　Ibid., p. 251.

19　Milhaupt, op. cit., note 7, p. 875.

20　See Black and Gilson, op. cit., note 3, p. 249.

21　Ibid.

22　Milhaupt, op. cit., note 7, p. 877.

23　Ibid. p. 877.

24　See note 18, p. 251.

25　Milpaupt, op. cit., note 7, p. 879.

26　See note 18, p. 247.

27　Ibid.

28　Ibid.

29　E. Sibbitt, 'Law, Venture Capital and Entrepreneurnism in Japan: A Microeconomic Perspective on the Impact of Law on the Generation and Financing of Venture Business', (1998) 13 *Conn. J. of Int'l L.* 61 at p. 62.

30 Ibid.
31 Ibid.
32 Milpaupt, op. cit., note 7, p. 883.
33 J. Borton, 'Venture Firms Eye on Japan's Deep Pockets', (12 August 1999) *Japan Econ. J.*, at A2, available in Lexis, News Library, Non-U.S. File.
34 Milpaupt, op. cit., note 7, p. 878.
35 Ibid.
36 Ibid.
37 Ibid.
38 Black and Gilson, op. cit., note 3, pp. 252–51.
39 Ibid.; Ronald Gilson and Bernard Black began with the plausible assumption that entrepreneurs have a preference for control. Approaching the issue principally from a demand-side perspective, they ask under what circumstances an entrepreneur would surrender control in return for the capital and non-capital assets provided by the venture capitalist. The answer they provide is that entrepreneurs do so when there is potential to regain control if the firm succeeds and the venture capitalist exits in an IPO. Because other means of exit such as sales to third parties do not return control to the entrepreneur entirely, they conclude that a developed stock market is crucial for the development of an active developed venture capital market.
40 Milhaupt, op. cit., note 7. Independent sources of funding concern the extent to which funding for innovation is liberated from potential constraints tied to existing financial structures and corporate culture. Liquidity involves an exit strategy for the venture capital provider, the existence of which is crucial to the investment decision. Incentive contractual arrangements are to motivate and align the interests of the relevant players in the venture capital investment process. Labour mobility, implicit but nonetheless crucial to the success of venture capitalism in the USA, facilitates the supply of managerial and technical expertise to operate venture business. Risk tolerance affects the willingness of venture capital participants to engage in high-risk and high-return activities.
41 C. Milhault, R. Gilson and B. Black in their respective studies came to that conclusion. See Black and Gilson, op. cit., note 3; see also Milhaupt, op. cit., note 7, p. 874.
42 C. Barry *et al.*, 'The Role of Venture Capital in the Creation of Public Companies', (1990) 27 *J. Fin. Econ.* 447; W. Sahlman, 'The Structure and Governance of Venture-Capital Organizations', (1990) 27 *J. Fin. Econ.* 473.
43 W. Megginson and K. Weiss, 'Venture Capitalist Certification in Initial Public Offerings', (1991) 156 *J. Fin.* 879.
44 Black and Gilson, op. cit., note 3, p. 255.
45 Ibid.
46 O. Williamson, 'Corporate Finance and Corporate Governance', (1988) 43 *J. Fin.* 567.
47 A. Shleifer and R. Vishny, 'Liquidation Value and Debt Capacity: A Market Equilibrium Approach', (1992) 47 *J. Fin.* 1343.
48 S. Myres, 'Determinants of Corporate Borrowing', (1977) 5 *J. Fin. Econ.* 147.

165

49 P. Gompers, 'Optimal Investment, Monitoring, and the Staging of Venture Capital', (1995) 50 *J. Fin.* 1461 at p. 1467; J. Stiglitz and A. Weiss, 'Credit Rationing in Markets with Imperfect Information', (1981) 71 *Am. Econ. Rev.* 393.
50 Black and Gilson, op. cit., note 3, pp. 253–64.
51 Milhaupt, op. cit., note 7, p. 874.
52 W. Bygrave and J. Timmons, *Venture Capital at the Crossroads* (Cambridge: Harvard Business School Press, 1992).
53 P. Gompers, 'Optimal Investment, Monitoring, and the Staging of Venture Capital', (1995) 50 *J. Fin.* 1461 at pp. 1463–64. It should be noted that the high rate of return through IPOs in the 1990s is partly affected by the bubble economy.
54 Black and Gilson, op. cit., note 3, p. 255.
55 Ibid., pp. 255–57.
56 Sahlman, op. cit., note 5, p. 500.
57 Black and Gilson, op. cit., note 3, pp. 247–49.
58 P. Gompers, 'Grandstanding in the Venture Capital Industry', (1996) 42 *J. Fin. Econ.* 133 at p. 137.
59 Black and Gilson, op. cit., note 3, p. 261.
60 <http://www.people.com.cn/GB/33831/34145/34192/2546177.html> (last visited on 23 March 2005).
61 Ibid.
62 These measures appear in the *Collection of the Laws of the PRC* (Jilin: Jilin People's Press, 1990–1992) p. 824.
63 Ibid.
64 <http://www.people.com.cn/GB/33831/33836/34152/34156/2540205.html> (last visited on 23 March 2005).
65 Ibid.
66 This Law was enacted by the Standing Committee of the National People's Congress in 1996 and appears in the *Collection of the Laws of the PRC* (Jilin: Jiling People's Press, 1996) p. 609.
67 See note 4.
68 Under the former planned economy in China, the banking industry lent not based on the rules of the market and the actual condition of the borrowers, but based on the plan of the Chinese government, which of course could not bring prosperity to the banking industry. Now the banking industry in China is changing its institutional arrangements and is busy solving the bad debt problems. See C. Andrew, 'China's Bad Loans Threaten Bank System', *Business Daily*, Bangkok, 9 November 1999; Wang Yichao, 'Dai Xianglong: China Has Confidence in Disposing Non-Performing Loans in Banks', <http://news.263.net/27/130/20010326/240089.html> (last visited on 26 March 2001); see also Fu Bin, 'A Study of the Asset-backed Securitization in Chinese Banks', *People's University of China Newspaper*, No. 4, 2000.
69 This Law appears in the *Collection of the Laws of the PRC* (Jilin: Jilin People's Press, 1995) p. 427; while the amended law in 2003 provided the State Council with the power to relax the restriction on banks so that they can own shares in other companies, so no serious change has been made.

70 Liu Shaobo (ed.), *Venture Capital Investment* (Guangdong Economic Press, 1999) p. 128.

71 Ibid.

72 Ibid., pp. 128–30.

73 The interview with directors of Capitech Venture Capital Co. Ltd in Xian revealed that the company not only pursues the goal of profit maximization but also the goal of benefitting the High-tech Development Zone of Xian as one of the shareholders is on the Management Commission of the High-tech Development Zone.

74 Wang Guogang, 'Reforming Informal Financing to Promote Economic Growth' in Zhang Shuguang (ed.), *Case Studies of China's Institutional Change* (Beijing: The Finance and Economic Press of China, 1999) pp. 459–61.

75 Ibid.

76 Fei Xiaotong, 'The Trip to Wenzhou' in Lin Bai (ed.), *A Theoretical Enquiry of the Wenzhou Model* (Nanning: Guangxi People's Press, 1987) p. 46.

77 Li Haoran, *The New Rise of Wenzhou* (Shanghai: Shanghai Social Sciences Press, 1996) p. 3.

78 Ibid., p. 4.

79 Zhang Renshou, 'Three Principles' in Lin Bai (ed.), *A Theoretical Enquiry of the Wenzhou Model* (Nanning: Guangxi People's Press, 1987) pp. 123–25; Lin Renxu, 'Five Trends' in Lin Bai, pp. 127–30.

80 Ibid.

81 Ibid.

82 Zhang Renshou and Li Hong, *A Study of the Wenzhou Model* (Beijing: China Social Sciences Publishing House, 1990) p. 128.

83 Ibid.

84 Ibid.

85 Ibid.

86 Ibid.

87 Zhang Jun, 'The Informal Financial Institutions in a Post Reform Rural Area: The Case of Wenzhou' in Zhang Shuguang (ed.), *Case Studies of China's Institutional Change* (Beijing: The Finance and Economics Press of China, 1999) p. 442.

88 See Zhang and Li, op. cit., note 82, p. 129.

89 See Zhang Jun, op. cit., note 87, p. 440.

90 Ibid.

91 See Zhang and Li, op. cit., note 82, p. 130.

92 Ibid.

93 Ibid.

94 Ibid.

95 Ibid.

96 Ibid., p. 133.

97 Ibid.

98 See Zhang Jun, op. cit., note 87, p. 442.

99 Ibid.

100 Ibid.

101 Ibid.

167

102 Ibid.
103 <http://www.chinainfobank.com> is the legal data base, Article 2.
104 The Provisions appear at *China Law and Practice* (Hong Kong: Asia Law and Practice, March 2003) p. 35.
105 Ibid., Article 6(2).
106 Ibid., Article 13(1).
107 The Regulations were promulgated by the China Securities Regulatory Commission and became effective on 1 July 2002; they appear at *China Law and Practice* (Hong Kong: Asia Law and Practice, 2002) p. 41.
108 Ibid., Article 10.
109 Provisions on FIVCIEs, see note 104, Article 10.
110 Provisions on FIVCIEs, see note 104, Article 4.
111 This Regulation was promulgated by the Ministry of Foreign Trade and Economic Cooperation, the State Administration of Taxation, the State Administration of Industry and Commerce, and the State Administration of Foreign Exchange on 7 March 2003, and appears in *China Law and Practice* (Hong Kong: Asia Law and Practice, 2003) p. 27.
112 Company Law, Article 152; this law appears in the *Collection of the Laws of the PRC* (Jilin: Jilin People's Press, 1993) p. 456.
113 F. Hayek, 'The Use of Knowledge in Society', (1945) 35 *Am. Econ. Rev.* 519.
114 A. Alchian, 'Some Economics of Property Rights' in A. Alchian (ed.), *Economic Forces at Work* (Indianpolis, IN: Liberty Press, 1997) p. 127.
115 Small Business Investment Act 15 U.S.C. 631–57 (1994 and Supp. 1998).
116 C. Milhaupt, 'The Small Firm Financing Problem: Private Information and Public Policy', (1998) 2 *J. Small & Emerging Bus. L.* 177 at p. 188.
117 Ibid.
118 E. Brewer *et al.*, 'Performance and Access to Government Guarantees: The Case of Small Business Investment Companies', (September 1996) *Econ. Pers.* 16.
119 Ibid., p.19.
120 M. McClorey, 'Are State-Sponsored Venture Capital Funds Necessary for the Development and Growth of the Kansas Economy?' (1998) 7 *Kan. J. L. & Pub. Pol'y* 152 at p. 154.
121 Ibid.
122 Ibid., p. 155.
123 Ibid., p. 156.
124 Ibid., p. 157.
125 Ibid., p. 157
126 Ibid.
127 Ibid.
128 Zvi Bodic *et al.*, *Investments* (Homewood, IL.: Irwin, 1993) pp. 26–27.
129 Ibid.
130 McClorey, op. cit., note 120, p. 165.
131 Kahsoo Ko and Hyun Young Shin, 'Venture Capital in Korea: Special Law to Promote Venture Capital Companies', (2000) 15 *American U. Int'l L. Rev.* 459.
132 Ibid., p. 468.

133 Ibid.
134 Ibid.
135 Ibid., p. 469.
136 Ibid., p. 475. A VCB must be at least three stories high and house at least six different venture capital companies at any given time.
137 Ibid., p. 479.
138 A. Saxenian, *Regional Advantage: Culture and Competition in Silicon Valley and Route* 128 (Cambridge, MA: Harvard University Press, 1994) pp. 29–82.
139 See note 4.
140 Insurance Law, Article 104 in *Collection of the Laws of the PRC* (Jilin: Jilin People's Press, 1995) p. 410.
141 See <http://www.chinaonline.com/topstories/010102/1/B100122903.asp>. Insurance companies were allowed to invest in the stock market indirectly in October 1999. In the first half of the year, the insurance industry actually invested RMB 9.15 billion (US$1.11 billion) in investment funds, up 352 per cent from the end of the last year. Zhongguo Zhengquan Bao (China Securities), 31 August 2000.
142 Decision of the Standing Committee of the National People's Congress on amending the Insurance Law.
143 Milhaupt, op. cit., note 116, pp. 189–92.
144 See D. Ellis, 'Private Equity Investment – a Time for Bottom Fishing?' (April 1998) *Asia Law* 44; see also P. Gompers and J. Lerner, 'The Use of Covenants: An Empirical Analysis of Venture Capital Agreements', (1996) 39 *J. L. & Econ.* 463.
145 Also see Milhaupt, op. cit., note 116, p. 192.
146 For an excellent treatment on the construction of a strong securities market in emerging economies, see B. Black, 'The Legal and Institutional Preconditions for Strong Securities Market', (2001) 48 *UCLA L. Rev.* 781.

Chapter 4 The case against uniformity in corporate governance

1 See A. Berle and G. Means, Jr., *The Modern Corporation and Private Property* (New York: Harcourt, 1968); G. Stigler and C. Friedland, 'The Literature of Economics: The Case of Berle and Means', (1983) 26 *J. L. & Econ.* 237; H. Demsetz and K. Lehn, 'The Structure of Corporate Ownership: Causes and Consequences', (1985) 93 *J. Pol. Econ.* 1155.
2 M. Roe, 'A Political Theory of American Corporate Finance', (1991) 91 *Colum. L. Rev.* 10; M. Roe, 'Some Differences in Corporate Structure in Germany, Japan, and the United States', (1993) 102 *Yale L. J.* 1927.
3 M. Jensen and W. Meckling, 'Theory of the Firm: Managerial Behavior, Agency Costs and Ownership Structure', (1976) 3 *J. Fin. Econ.* 305.
4 F. Modigliani and M. Millars, 'The Costs of Capital, Corporate Finance, and the Theory of Investment', (June 1958) *Am. Econ. Rev.* 48; but see Jensen and Meckling, op. cit.
5 R. La Porta *et al.*, 'Legal Determinants of External Finance', (1997) 52 *J. Fin.* 1131 at p. 1137.

6 J. Gordon, 'Corporate Governance: Pathways to Corporate Convergence? Two Steps on the Road to Shareholder Capitalism in Germany', (1999) 5 *Colum. J. Eur. L.* 219 at p. 223.

7 See R. Karmel, 'Italian Stock Market Reform', *N.Y.L.J.*, 20 August 1998, p. t 3.

8 E. Fama and M. Jensen, 'Agency Problems and Residual Claims', (1983) 26 *J. L. & Econ.* 327.

9 K. Arrow, 'The Role of Securities in the Optimal Allocation of Risk Bearing', (1964) 31 *Rev. Econ. Stud.* 97.

10 R. Coase, 'The Nature of the Firm', (1937) 4 *Economica* 386.

11 See Fama and Jensen, op. cit., note 8.

12 Demstz and Lehn, op. cit., note 1, p. 1158.

13 Berle and Means, op. cit., note 1.

14 See Gordon, op. cit., note 6, p. 220.

15 Ibid. The top six firms accounted for almost 50 per cent of the volume in public markets.

16 See S. Prigge, 'A Survey of German Corporate Governance' in K. Hopt *et al.*, *Comparative Corporate Governance – The State of the Art and Emerging Research* (Oxford: Clarendon Press, 1998) 943 at pp. 943–1043.

17 D. Neuberger and M. Neumann, 'Banking and Antitrust: Limiting Industrial Ownership by Banks', (1991) *J. Institutional and Theoretical Econ.* 147 at pp. 188–99.

18 See T. Baums, 'Corporate Governance in Germany: The Role of the Banks', (1992) 40 *Am. J. Comp. L.* 503 at p. 508.

19 Ibid., p. 510.

20 Ibid., p. 512.

21 Ibid., pp. 515–16.

22 See M. Porter, 'Capital Disadvantage: America's Failing Capital Investment System', (September to October, 1992) *Harv. Bus. Rev.* 65.

23 J. Grundfest, 'Subordination of American Capital', (1990) 27 *J. Fin. Econ.* 89.

24 See Roe, op. cit., note 2; J. Pound, 'The Rise of the Political Model of Corporate Governance and Corporate Control', (1993) 68 *N.Y.L.Rev.* 103; also see Grundfest, supra note 23.

25 J. Macey and G. Miller, 'Corporate Governance and Commercial Banking: A Comparative Examination of Germany, Japan, and the United States', (1995) 48 *Stan. L. Rev.* 73 at pp. 77–81.

26 See Roe, op. cit., note 2, p. 1937.

27 Stigler and Friedland, op. cit., note 1.

28 H. Demsetz, 'The Structure of the Ownership and the Theory of the Firm', (1983) 26 *J. L. & Econ.* 375.

29 Ibid., p. 386.

30 See La Porta *et al.*, op. cit., note 5; See also A. Demirguc-Kunt and V. Maksimovic, 'Law, Finance and Firm Growth', (1998) 53 *J. Fin.* 2107 at p. 2134.

31 See La Porta, *et al.*, op. cit., note 5; see also A. Schleifer and R. Vishny, 'A Survey of Corporate Governance', (1997) 52 *J. Fin.* 737.

32 J. Coffee, Jr., 'The Future as History: the Prospects for Global Convergence in Corporate Governance and Its Implications', (1999) 93 *Nw. U. L. Rev.* 641 at p. 644.

33 Ibid.

34 See Demsetz, op. cit., note 28, at p. 390.

35 See La Porta *et al.*, op. cit., note 5, p. 1132.

36 See L. Zingales, 'The Value of the Voting Right: A Study of the Milan Stock Exchange Experience', (1994) 7 *Rev. Fin. Stud.* 125.

37 S. Kaplan, 'Top Executives, Turnover, and Firm Performance in Germany', (1994) 10 *J. L. Econ. & Org.* 142; S. Kaplan, 'Top Executive Rewards and Firm Performance: A Comparison of Japan and the United States', (1994) 102 *J. Pol. Econ.* 510.

38 Gordon, op. cit., note 6, p. 236.

39 D. Smith, 'The Venture Capital Company: A Contractual Rebuttal to the Political Theory of American Corporate Finance', (1979) 65 *Tenn. L. Rev.* 79.

40 See Demsetz, op. cit., note 28, p. 386.

41 See Shleifer and Vishny, op. cit., note 31, p. 776.

42 M. Aoki, 'Towards an Economic Model of the Japanese Firm', (1990) 28 *J. Econ. Lit.* 1; Grundfest, op. cit., note 23; J. Charkham, *Keeping Good Company: A Study of Corporate Governance in Five Countries* (Oxford: Clarendon Press, 1994); M. Porter, 'Capital Disadvantage: America's Failing Capital Investment System', (1992) *Harv. Bus. Rev.* 65.

43 Macey and Miller, op. cit., note 25; C. Milhaupt, 'The Market for Innovation in the United States and Japan: Venture Capital and the Comparative Corporate Governance Debate', (1997) 91 *Nw. U. L. Rev.* 865; La Porta *et al.*, op. cit., note 5; Demirguc-Kunt and Maksimovic, op. cit., note 30.

44 R. Art and Minkang Gu, 'China Incorporated: the First Corporation Law of the People's Republic of China', (1995) 20 *Yale J. Int'l L.* 273 at pp. 274–75.

45 Project Group of the Chinese Academy of Social Sciences, 'Several Problems Related to the Establishment of a Modern Enterprise System', (1996) 17 (4) *Social Sciences in China* 19 at p. 20.

46 Ibid.

47 Ibid.

48 Ibid.

49 Ibid.

50 Zhou Zhengqing, 'Explanations Concerning the Commercial Banking Law of the PRC', a speech delivered at the Thirteenth Session of the Eighth Standing Committee of the National People's Congress.

51 Interview with Mr Cai, a middle-level manager with the Bank of China in Hangzhou on 25 May 1993.

52 See J. Kornai, *Economics of Shortage* (Amsterdam: North-Holland Publ. Co., 1980) for a discussion about soft budget constraints; for a discussion on the difficulty of enforcing the Bankruptcy Law in China in the 1990s, see Guanghua Yu, 'The Relevance of Comparative Corporate Governance Studies for China', (1997) 8 (1) *Australian J. Corp. L.* 49 at pp. 79–80.

53 See Xu Jingan, 'The State-share System: A New Avenue for China's Economic Reform', (1987) *11 J. Comp. Econ.* 509 at p. 514.
54 Ibid.
55 Andrew Xuefeng Qian, 'Riding Two Horses: Corporatizing Enterprises and the Emerging Securities Regulatory Regime in China', (1993) 12 *UCLA Pac. Basin L. J.* 62 at p. 63.
56 The Standardization Opinions appeared in the *Collection of the Laws of the PRC* (Jilin: Jilin People's Press, 1992), p. 650.
57 The Supplementary Measures were issued by the Commission on 24 May 1993 and available online at <http://www.chinainfobank.com>.
58 This mandatory model Articles of Association was issued by the State Economic Restructuring Commission on 30 June 1993 and appears at <http://www.chinainfobank.com>.
59 Ibid., Article 4.4.
60 Ibid., Article 4.8.
61 The Prerequisite Clauses were issued by the Securities Office of the State Council and the State Economic Restructuring Commission on 19 September 1994. An English translation appears at *China Law and Practice* (Hong Kong: Asia Law and Practice, May 1995) p. 19.
62 An English translation of this Regulation appears at *China Law and Practice* (Hong Kong: Asia Law and Practice, August 1993) p. 23.
63 The Code is available online at <http://www.hksfc.org.hk>.
64 London City Code on Takeovers and Mergers (7th edn 2002), available online at <http://www.thetakeoverpanel.org.uk>.
65 See J. Gleick, *Chaos: Making a New Science* (London: Heinemann, 1988) p. 8; also see M. Roe, Commentary: 'Chaos and Evolution in Law and Economics', (1996) 109 *Harv. L. Rev.* 641.
66 Ibid., Roe p. 643.
67 See notes 55 to 64 and the accompanying text.
68 ITS, op. cit., note 62.
69 London City Code, Section 9.1.
70 ITS, Article 48.
71 Ibid. The current price provision in the Procedures on the Administration of the Takeover of Listed Companies issued by the China Securities Regulatory Commission on 28 September 2002 follows the higher of the following two: (1) the highest price the acquirer paid during the six months prior to the date of public announcement; and (2) 90 per cent of the arithmetic mean of the daily weighted average prices of the target company's listed shares of that class during the 30 days prior to the date of public announcement. See also note 77.
72 ITS, Article 50.
73 ITS, Article 51(3).
74 ITS, Article 52(1).
75 ITS, Article 52(2).
76 ITS, Article 47(1).
77 ITS, Article 47(2). The current position is 5 per cent under the Securities Act of 1998 instead of 2 per cent.
78 ITS, Article 47(3).

79 ITS, Article 49(2).

80 Ibid.

81 ITS, Article 52(3).

82 P. Lee, 'Takeovers – The United Kingdom Experience' in J. Farrar (ed.), *Takeovers: Institutional Investors and the Modernization of Corporate Law* (Oxford: Oxford University Press, 1993) p. 192.

83 R. Austin, 'Takeovers – The Australian Experience' in J. Farrar (ed.), *Takeovers: Institutional Investors and the Modernization of Corporate Law* (Oxford: Oxford University Press, 1993) p. 144.

84 P. Davies and K. Hopt, 'Control Transactions' in Reinier Kraakman *et al.* (eds), *The Anatomy of Corporate Law* (Oxford: Oxford University Press, 2004) pp 179–80.

85 London City Code, op. cit., note 64, Section 1(a)

86 M. Jensen, 'Takeovers: Their Causes and Consequences', (1988) 2 *J. Econ. Perspectives* 21; R. Morck *et al.*, 'Alternative Mechanisms for Corporate Control', (1989) 79 *Am. Econ. Rev.* 545.

87 See R. Romano, 'A Guide to Takeovers: Theory, Evidence, and Regulation', (1992) *Yale J. on Reg.* 119.

88 See Inshuranshares Corp. v. Northern Fiscal Corp., 35 F. Supp. 22 (E.D. Pa. 1940).

89 G. Jarrell *et al.*, 'The Market for Corporate Control: The Empirical Evidence Since 1982', (1988) 2 *J. Econ. Perspectives* 49; M. Jensen and R. Ruback, 'The Market for Corporate Control: The Scientific Evidence', (1983) 11 *J. Fin. Econ.* 5.

90 See M. Eisenberg, 'The Theory of Contracts' in P. Benson (ed.), *The Theory of Contract Law* (Cambridge: Cambridge University Press, 2001) p. 206.

91 R. Nozick, 'Coercion' in Sindey Morgenbesser *et al.* (eds), *Philosophy, Science, and Method* (New York: St Martin's Press, 1969) pp. 447–53.

92 See Jarrell *et al.*, op. cit., note 89; Jensen and Ruback, op. cit., note 89.

93 L. Lowenstein, 'Pruning Deadwood in Hostile Takeovers: A Proposal for Legislation', (1983) 83 *Colum. L. Rev.* 249; M. Bradley and M. Rosenzweig, 'Defensive Stock Repurchases', (1986) 99 *Harv. L. Rev.* 1377.

94 J. Coffee, 'The Uncertain Case For Takeover Reform: An Essay on Stockholders, Stateholders and Bust-ups', (1988) *Wiscon. L. Rev.* 435 at p. 459.

95 See P. Samuelson, 'The Pure Theory of Public Expenditure', (1954) 36 *Rev. Econ. Statistics* 386.

96 S. Grossman and O. Hart, 'Takeover Bids, the Free-Rider Problem, and the Theory of the Corporation', (1980) 11 (1) *Bell J. Econ.* 42 at p. 59.

97 See F. Easterbrook and D. Fischel, 'Corporate Control Transactions', (1982) 91 *Yale L. J.* 698 at pp. 705–06.

98 Zhang Zongxin and Sun Yewei, 'The Optimization of Shareholding Structure and the Improvement of Corporate Governance in Listed Companies', (2001) 1 *Economic Review*, 36.

99 Ibid.

100 Absolute control means that the State controls more than 50 per cent of the

issued shares and relative control means that the State controls more than 30 per cent of the issued shares.

101 Zhang and Sun, op. cit., note 98.

102 Ibid.

103 Ibid.

104 Ibid.

105 Zhang Rui, 'An Legal Analysis of Negotiated Takeovers of Listed Companies', (July 2003) *Jilin University Journal (Social Sciences)* 108 at p. 109.

106 These administrative rules were jointly issued by the State Asset Administration Bureau and the State Economic Restructuring Commission on 13 November 1994. The document can be found in the legal database available online at <http://www.chinainfobank.com>.

107 Ibid.

108 Zhang Xin, 'Legislation and Regulation of Takeovers of Listed Companies', (August 2003) *Securities Market Herald* 12.

109 Chen Gong *et al.* (eds), *Principles and Cases of Corporate Mergers and Takeovers* (Beijing: Renmin University Press, 1996) pp. 63–68.

110 Ibid.

111 Hanson Trust v SCM, 774 F. 2d 27 (2d Cir. 1985).

112 This Law was promulgated on 29 December 1998 and became effective on 1 July 1999. An English translation appears at *China Law and Practice* (Hong Kong: Asia Law and Practice, February 1999) p. 25.

113 Ibid., Securities Law, Article 81.

114 Ibid.

115 Kennecott Copper Corp. v Curtiss-Wright Corp., 584 F. 2d 1195 (2d Cir. 1978); Hanson, op. cit., note 111.

116 Li Bingan, 'A Discussion of the Exemption from the Mandatory Purchase Provision', (November 2003) 18 (6) *Legal Forum* 50.

117 He Xiaogang, 'Management Buyouts: the Status Abroad, Research, and Development in China', (2003) 4 *Reform* 54.

118 Fei Yiwen and Cai Mingchao, 'An Analysis of the Takeover Effects of Listed Companies on the Shanghai Stock Exchange', (2003) 5 *World Economies* 64.

119 An English translation of the Takeover Procedures can be found in *China Law and Practice* (Hong Kong: Asia Law and Practice, November 2002) p. 43.

120 Ibid., Articles, 13, 14 and 23.

121 Ibid., Article 49(4).

122 Ibid., Article 51(4).

123 Ibid., Article 49(2).

124 Ibid., Article 49(3).

125 Ibid., Article 51(2).

126 Ibid., Article 51(5).

127 Ibid., Article 49(5) and Article 51(7).

128 Art and Gu, op. cit., note 44, p. 139.

129 General Principle 7 of the London City Code, op. cit., note 64.

130 See F. Easterbrook and D. Fischel, 'The Proper Role of a Target's Management in Responding to a Tender Offer', (1981) 94 *Harv. L. Rev.* 116.

131 See A. Schwartz, 'The Fairness of Tender Offer Prices in Utilitarian Theory', (1988) 17 *J. Legal Stud.* 165.

132 L. Bebchuk, 'The Case Against Board Veto in Corporate Takeovers', (2002) 69 *U. Chi. L. Rev.* 973.

133 M. Lipton, 'Pills, Polls, and Professors Redux', (2002) 69 *U. Chi. L. Rev.* 1037.

134 Ibid., p. 1078.

135 See, for example, 8 Del. Code Ann. § 141 (2001). Section 141 of the Delaware General Corporation Law specifies the powers of the board of directors.

136 See, for example, 8 Del. Code Ann. § 251 (2001), § 271 (2001).

137 See, for example, Cede & Co v Technicolor, Inc, 634 A2d 345, 360 (Del. 1993).

138 See, for example, Unitrin, Inc v American General Corp., 651 A 2d 1361, 1390 (Del. 1995).

139 Paramount Communications, Inc v Time Inc., 571 A 2d 1140, 1150.

140 Moran v Household International, Inc, 500 A 2d 1346, 1356 (Del. 1985).

141 See W. Allen *et al.*, 'The Great Takeover Debate: A Meditation on Bridging the Conceptual Divide', (2002) 69 *U. Chi. L. Rev.* 1067.

142 For a regulator's view, see Zhang Xin, op. cit., note 108, pp. 15–17.

143 The Hengtong case is discussed in the book referred to in note 109.

144 The Opinions were jointly issued by the State Asset Administration Commission and the State Economic Restructuring Commission on 29 August 1997 and are available online at <http://www.chinainfobank.com>.

145 Ibid., Article 17.

146 Wang Huacheng and Tong Yan, 'Management Buyouts in China: The Case of Media', (2002) 10 *Economic Theory and Management* 66; An Chunmei and Dou Zhanguo, 'An Analysis of Benefits and Risks of Management Buyouts in Listed Companies', (2002) 7 *Finance and Accounting Research* 52.

147 These Provisional Measures are available online at <http://www.chinainfo bank.com>.

148 M. Trebilcock and E. Iacobucci, Commentary: 'Public Values in an Era of Privatization: Privatization and Accountability', (2003) 116 *Harv. L. Rev.* 1422.

Chapter 5 The regulation of executive compensation

1 M. Jensen and W. Meckling, 'Theory of the Firm: Managerial Behavior, Agency Costs and Ownership Structure', (1976) 3 *J. Fin. Econ.* 305.

2 C. Loomis, 'The Madness of Executive Compensation', *Forbes* (12 July 1982) p. 42.

3 'Fat Cats and Their Cream', *The Economist* (22 July 1995) p. 19.

4 P. Cook, 'When the Boss Gets Paid Too Much', *The Globe and Mail* (28 September 1995) p. B2.

5 K. Murphy, 'Top Executives Are Worth Every Nickel They Get', *Harv. Bus. Rev.* (March–April 1986) p. 125; M. Jensen and K. Murphy, 'Performance Pay and Top-Management Incentives', (1990) 98 (2) *J. Political Econ.* 225.

175

6 Yan Zhongqin (ed.), *Employee Wages, Benefits and Social Insurance in Contemporary China* (Beijing: China Social Sciences Publishing House, 1987) pp. 75–79.

7 Ibid., pp. 80–83.

8 Ibid., pp. 91–93.

9 Ibid., pp. 106–07.

10 Ibid., p. 112.

11 Ibid., p. 108.

12 Ibid.

13 Ibid., p. 109.

14 Ibid., pp. 116–17.

15 Ibid., p. 116.

16 <http://www.chinainfobank.com>, law database.

17 Ibid., Article 3.

18 <http://www.chinainfobank.com>, law database.

19 Ibid., Article 33.

20 Gao Shusheng, *20 Years of Income Distribution System Reform in China* (Zhongzhou: Zhongzhou Ancient Book Publishing House, 1998) p. 118.

21 <http://www.chinainfobank.com>, law database.

22 Ibid.

23 Ibid., Article 23.

24 'Main Objectives and Policy Measures of Enterprise Wage Administration During the Ninth Five Year Period', available online at <http://www.china infobank.com>, law database.

25 Ibid., Part Five.

26 M. Conyon *et al.*, 'Taking Care of Business: Executive Compensation in the United Kingdom', (May 1995) 105 *Econ. J.* 701 at p. 707.

27 J. Nelson-Horchler, 'The Pay Revolt Brews', *Industrial Work* (18 June 1990) 28 at p. 30.

28 'Punters or Proprietors: A Survey of Capitalism', *The Economist* (5 May 1990) 64 at p. 73.

29 G. Crystal, 'CEO Compensation: The Case of Michael Eisner', in F. Foulkes (ed.), *Executive Compensation: A Strategic Guide for the 1990s* (Boston, MA: Harvard Business School Press, 1991) p. 353.

30 K. Murphy, 'Politics, Economics, and Executive Compensation', (1995) 63 *U. Cin. L. Rev.* 713 at p. 715.

31 26 U.S.C. 162 (m)(1), 1994.

32 26 U.S.C. 162 (m)(14)(c), 1994.

33 J. Luben, 'Firms Forfeit Tax Break to Pay Top Brass US$1 Million-Plus', *Wall Street Journal* (21 April 1994) p. B1.

34 N. Rose and C. Wolfram, 'Has the Million – Dollar Cap Affect CEO Pay', (2000) 90 (2) *Am. Econ. Rev.* (Papers and Proceedings) 197 at p. 201.

35 J. Dobrzynski, 'New Road to Riches Is Paved with Options', *New York Times* (30 March 1997) p. 1.

36 D. Johnston, 'Executive Pay Increases at a Much Faster Rate Than Corporate Revenues and Profits', *New York Times* (2 September 1997) p. D4.

37 Murphy, op. cit., note 30, p. 739.

38 K. Murphy, 'Explaining Executive Compensation: Managerial Power Versus the Perceived Cost of Stock Options', (2002) 69 *U. Chi. L. Rev.* 847 at p. 858.

39 Ibid., pp. 858–59.

40 Ibid., p. 859.

41 Ibid., pp. 859–60.

42 J. Knetsch, 'The Endowment Effect and Evidence of Nonreversible Indifference Curves', (1989) 79 *Am. Econ. Rev.* 1277.

43 Ibid.; see also J. Knetsch and J. Sinden, 'Willingness to Pay and Compensation Demanded: Experimental Evidence of an Unexpected Disparity in Measures of Value', (1984) 99 *Quarterly J. Econ.* 507.

44 E. Iacobucci, 'The Effects of Disclosure on Executive Compensation', 48 *U. Toronto. L. J.* 489 at pp. 508–10.

45 'Paying the Public Pipers', *The [Toronto] Global and Mail* (2 April 1996) p. A18.

46 Executive Compensation Disclosure, Exchange Act Release No. 33–6962, 57 Fed. Reg. 48, 126 Regulation S–K, 17 C.F.R. paras. 228, 229, 240, 249 (21 October 1992).

47 Iacobucci, op. cit., note 44 , pp. 499–500.

48 Ibid., p. 498.

49 See K. Salwen, 'The People's Proxy: Shareholder Proposals on Pay Must be Aired, SEC to Tell 10 Firms', *Wall Street Journal* (13 February 1992) p. A1.

50 J. MacIntosh, 'Institutional Shareholders and Corporate Governance in Canada', (1996) 26 *Canadian Bus. L. J.* 145 at p. 150.

51 D. Kreps, *A Course in Microeconomic Theory* (London: Harvester Wheatsheat, 1990).

52 L. Barris, 'The Overcompensation Problem: A Collective Approach to Controlling Executive Pay', (1992) 68 *Ind. L. J.* 59.

53 Iacobucci, op. cit., note 44, p. 500.

54 H. Harts, 'Does Canada Have a Problem with Executive Compensation', in E. Iacobucci (ed.), *Value for Money: Executive Compensation in the 1990s* (Toronto: C. D. Howe Institute, 1996) 59 at pp. 60–61; X. Zhou, Essays on Executive Compensation and Managerial Incentives (Doctoral Thesis, University of Toronto, 1997) p. 27.

55 Murphy, op. cit., note 30, p. 737.

56 Iacobucci, op. cit., note 44, p. 505.

57 B. Holmstrom, 'Moral Hazard and Observability', (1979) 10 *Rand J. Econ.* 74 .

58 C. Milkovich and B. Rabin, 'Executive Compensation and Firm Performance: Research Questions and Answers', in F. Foulks (ed.), *Executive Compensation: A Strategic Guide for the 1990s* (Boston, MA: Harvard Business School Press, 1991) p. 81.

59 Iacobucci, op. cit., note 44, p. 506.

60 Conyon, op. cit., note 26, p. 706.

61 Murphy, op. cit., note 38, pp. 858 and 867.

62 'The Status of CEO Annual Compensation', *Shanghai Securities News* (18 November 1998) p. 5.

63 Wei Gang, 'Senior Management Incentives and Performance of Listed Companies', (2000) 3 *Jingji Yanjio* (Economic Journal of the China Academy of Social Sciences) p. 32.

64 Yin Changlin, 'A Study on Executive Incentive Pay and Performance in Listed Companies', 1 *The Economist* (in China) (2004) p. 125.

65 Yu Aihong, 'An Empirical Study on the Remuneration of Directors and Firm Performance', (2000) 2 *Northern Economy and Trade* 14.

66 Ibid.

67 Lin He, 'The Rapid Growth of Executive Compensation: Cautioning Against Treating Listed Companies as Teller Machines', *China Securities Journal* (16 July 2004) p. 6.

68 'Remuneration of the General Manager in China's Listed Companies', *Shanghai Securities News* (18 November 1998) p. 9.

69 Liu Jianfeng, 'Executive Compensation in China's Listed Companies Increased in 2002,', *China Economic Times* (14 May 2002) p. 3.

70 Conyon, op. cit., note 26, p. 711.

71 R. Romano, 'Less is More: Making Institutional Investor Activism a Valuable Mechanism of Corporate Governance', (2000) 18 *Yale J. on Reg.* 174.

72 This Notice is available at <http://www.chinainfobank.com>, law database.

73 Ibid., Article 3(2) and 3(3) of Part IV.

74 This Governance Code is available online at <http://www.chinainfobank.com>, law database.

75 The Notice of the CSRC Concerning the Amendment of Code 2 on the Content and Format of Information Disclosure by Listed Companies (The Content and Format of Annual Report), Article 26, Part 5 of Chapter 2 (22 December 2003), available at <http://www.chinainfobank.com>, law database.

76 R. Ellis, 'Equity Derivatives, Executive Compensation, and Agency Costs', (1998) 35 *Hous. L. Rev.* 399 at p. 436.

Chapter 6 Towards a functional approach to comparative corporate governance studies

1 Research support for this project was provided by the University of Hong Kong and the Research Grants Council of Hong Kong.

2 See A. Berle and G. Means, Jr., *The Modern Corporation and Private Property* (New York: Harcourt, Brace & World, 1932); G. Stigler and C. Friedland, 'The Literature of Economics: The Case of Berle and Means', (1983) 26 *J. L. & Econ.* 237; H. Demsetz and K. Lehn, 'The Structure of Corporate Ownership: Causes and Consequences', (1985) 93 *J. Pol. Econ.* 1155.

3 M. Roe, 'A Political Theory of American Corporate Finance', (1991) 91 *Colum. L. Rev.* 10; M. Roe, 'Some Differences in Corporate Structure in Germany, Japan, and the United States', (1993) 102 *Yale L. J.* 1927.

4 M. Jensen and W. Meckling, 'Theory of the Firm: Managerial Behavior, Agency Costs and Ownership Structure', (1976) 3 *J. Fin. Econ.* 305.

5 F. Modigliani and M. Millars, 'The Costs of Capital, Corporate Finance, and the Theory of Investment', (June 1958) *Am. Econ. Rev.* 48 (arguing that in

the absence of bankruptcy costs and tax subsidies on the payment of interest the value of the firm is independent of the financial structure); but see Jensen and Meckling, op. cit., note 3, p. 33 (arguing that if agency costs are taken into consideration the value of the firms is not independent of the capital or ownership).

6 R. La Porta *et al.*, 'Legal Determinants of External Finance', (1997) 52 *J. Fin.* 1131 at p. 1137.

7 J. Gordon, 'Corporate Governance: Pathways to Corporate Convergence? Two Steps on the Road to Shareholder Capitalism in Germany', (1999) 5 *Colum. J. Eur. L.* 219 at p. 223.

8 See R. Karmel, 'Italian Stock Market Reform', (1998) 20 August, *N.Y.L.J.* p. 3.

9 E. Fama and M. Jensen, 'Agency Problems and Residual Claims', (1983) 26 *J. L. & Econ.* 327.

10 K. Arrow, 'The Role of Securities in the Optimal Allocation of Risk Bearing', (1964) 31 *Rev. Econ. Stud.* 97.

11 R. Coase, 'The Nature of the Firm', (1937) 4 *Economica* 386.

12 See Fama and Jensen, op. cit., note 8.

13 Demsetz and Lehn, op. cit., note 1, p. 1158.

14 Berle and Means, op. cit., note 1.

15 See Gordon, op. cit., note 6, p. 220.

16 The top six firms accounted for almost 50 per cent of the volume in public markets. Ibid.

17 See S. Prigge, 'A Survey of German Corporate Governance' in K. Hope *et al.*, *Comparative Corporate Governance – The State of the Art and Emerging Research* (Oxford: Clarendon, 1998) 943, at pp. 943–1043.

18 D. Neuberger and M. Neumann, 'Banking and Antitrust: Limiting Industrial Ownership by Banks', (1991) *J. Institutional and Theoretical Econ.* 147 at pp. 188–99 (reporting an average of 40 per cent as compared to about 9 per cent in the UK).

19 For more information, see T. Baums, 'Corporate Governance in Germany: The Role of the Banks', (1992) 40 *Am. J. Comp. L.* 503 at p. 508.

20 Ibid., p. 510.

21 Ibid., p. 512.

22 Ibid., pp. 515–16.

23 See M. Porter, 'Capital Disadvantage: America's Failing Capital Investment System', (September/October 1992) *Harv. Bus. Rev.* 65.

24 J. Grundfest, 'Subordination of American Capital', (1990) 27 *J. Fin. Econ.* 89.

25 See Roe, op. cit., note 2; J. Pound, 'The Rise of the Political Model of Corporate Governance and Corporate Control', (1993) 68 *N.Y.L. Rev.* 103; also see Grundfest, op. cit., note 23.

26 J. Macey and G. Miller, 'Corporate Governance and Commercial Banking: A Comparative Examination of Germany, Japan, and the United States', (1995) 48 *Stan. L. Rev.* 73 at pp. 77–81.

27 See Roe, op. cit., note 2, p. 1937.

28 Stigler and Friedland, op. cit., note 1.

29 H. Demsetz, 'The Structure of the Ownership and the Theory of the Firm', (1983) 26 *J. L. & Econ.* 375.

30 Ibid., p. 386.

31 R. Romano, 'Public Pension Fund Activities in Corporate Governance Reconsidered', (1993) 93 *Colum. L. Rev.* 795.

32 J. Coffee, Jr., 'Liquidity Verses Control: The Institutional Investor as Corporate Monitor', (1991) 91 *Colum. L. Rev.* 1977.

33 J. Macey, 'Measuring the Effectiveness of Different Corporate Governance Systems: Toward A More Scientific Approach', (1998) 10 *J. Applied Corp. Fin.* 16 at p. 24.

34 R. Gilson and R. Kraakman, 'Reinvesting the Outside Director: An Agenda for Institutional Investors', (1991) 43 *Stan. L. Rev.* 863 at p. 880.

35 R. Vanecko, 'Regulations14A and 13D and the Role of Institutional Investors in Corporate Governance', (1992) 87 *Nw. U. L. Rev.* 376 at pp. 406–08.

36 T. Smith, 'Institutions and Entrepreneurs in American Corporate Finance', (1997) 85 *Cal. L. Rev.* 1 at pp. 18–27.

37 Ibid., pp. 35–44.

38 R. Romano, 'Less is More: Making Institutional Investor Activism a Valuable Mechanism of Corporate Governance', (2001) 18 *Yale J. on Reg.* 174.

39 Ibid., p. 201.

40 Ibid., p. 195.

41 See La Porta *et al.*, op. cit., note 5; see also A. Demirguc-Kunt and V. Maksimovic, 'Law, Finance and Firms', (1988) 53 *J. Fin* 2107 at p. 2134 (arguing that firms in countries with active stock markets and well-developed legal system were able to obtain greater funds to finance growth).

42 See La Porta, *et al.*, op. cit., note 5; see also A. Schleifer and R. Vishny, 'A Survey of Corporate Governance', (1997) 52 *J. Fin.* 737.

43 J. Coffee, Jr., 'The Future as History: the Prospects for Global Convergence in Corporate Governance and Its Implications', (1999) 93 *Nw. U. L. Rev.* 641 at p. 644.

44 Ibid.

45 See Demsetz, op. cit., note 28, p. 390.

46 See La Porta *et al.*, op. cit., note 5, p. 1132.

47 See L. Zingales, 'The Value of the Voting Right: A Study of the Milan Stock Exchange Experience', (1994) 7 *Rev. Fin. Stud.* 125 (finding a high 82 per cent premium for control blocks on the Milan Stock Exchange, against an international average of 10 to 20 per cent, and a US average of 5.24 per cent).

48 S. Kaplan, 'Top Executives, Turnover, and Firm Performance in Germany', (1994) 10 *J. L. Econ. & Org.* 142–59; S. Kaplan, 'Top Executive Rewards and Firm Performance: A Comparison of Japan and the United States', (1994) 102 *J. Pol. Econ.* 510–46.

49 Gordon, op. cit., note 6, p. 236.

50 D. Smith, 'The Venture Capital Company: A Contractual Rebuttal to the Political Theory of American Corporate Finance', (1979) 65 *Tenn. L. Rev.* 79.

51 See Demsetz, op. cit., note 28, p. 386.

52 See Shleifer and Vishny, op. cit., note 41, p. 776.

53 M. Aoki, 'Towards an Economic Model of the Japanese Firm', (1990) 28 *J. Econ. Lit.* 1; Grundfest, op. cit., note 23; J. Charkham, *Keeping Good Company: a Study of Corporate Governance in Five Countries* (Oxford: Clarendon Press, 1994); M. Porter, 'Capital Disadvantage: America's Failing Capital Investment System', (1992) *Harv. Bus. Rev.* 65.

54 Macey and Miller, op. cit., note 25; C. Milhaupt, 'The Market for Innovation in the United States and Japan: Venture Capital and the Comparative Corporate Governance Debate', (1997) 91 *Nw. U. L. Rev.* 865; La Porta *et al.*, op. cit., note 5 (arguing that countries with poorer investor protections have smaller and narrower capital markets); Demirguc-Kunt and Maksimovic, op. cit., note 40 (arguing that firms in countries with an active stock market and a well-developed legal system were able to obtain greater funds to finance growth).

55 R. Romano, 'A Cautionary Note on Drawing Lessons from Comparative Corporate Law', (1993) 102 *Yale L. J.* 2021 at p. 2025.

56 See Romano, op. cit., note 37, p. 176.

57 M. Fox and M. Heller, 'Corporate Governance Lessons From Russian Enterprise Fiascoes', (2000) 75 *N.Y.U.L. Rev.* 1720 at p. 1722.

58 Ibid., pp. 1723–47.

59 Ibid., p. 1723.

60 See Stigler and Friedland, op. cit., note 1, p. 259.

61 See Zingales, op. cit., note 47.

62 See R. Lease *et al.*, 'The Market Value of Capital in Publicly-Traded Corporations', (1993) 11 *J. Fin. Econ.* 439. For information on the premium of voting shares in other countries, see Macey, op. cit., note 32.

63 See Shleifer and Vishny, op. cit., note 41.

64 B. Black, 'The Legal and Institutional Preconditions for Strong Securities Markets', (2001) 48 *UCLA L. Rev.* 781 at p. 783.

65 'Penalty Decision Regarding the Violation of Securities Regulation by Chengdo Hong Guang Industrial Ltd', *China Securities Regulatory Commission Gazette*, 8 December 1998, available online at <http://www.chinainfobank.com>.

66 'Measures Concerning the Prohibition of Speculative Trading of Shares by State Owned Enterprises and Listing Companies.' The State Council Securities Commission, the People's Bank of China and the State Economic and Trade Commission jointly issued these Measures on 27 May 1997. The Measures appear in the *Collection of the Laws of the PRC* (Jilin: Jilin People's Press, 1997) p. 498.

67 Yao Bei, 'Hong Guang: the First Case of Criminal Punishment', 15 December 2000, available online at <http://www.people.com.cn>.

68 This Regulation was promulgated by the State Council on 22 April 1993 and appears in the *Collection of the Laws of the PRC* (Jilin: Jilin People's Press, 1993) p. 480.

69 This Law was enacted by the Standing Committee of the National People's Congress on 29 December 1998 and appears in the *Collection of the Laws of the PRC* (Jilin: Jilin People's Press, 1998) p. 671.

70 Yao Bei, op. cit., note 66.

71 Luo Xiaoming, 'CSRC Investigated and Punished Energy 28', *People Net*, 20 December 2000, available online at <http://www.people.com.cn>.

72 'Public Criticisms by the CSRC on Three and Nine Medical and Pharmaceutical Co Ltd and the Relevant Persons', 27 August 2001, available online at <http://www.chinainfobank.com>.

73 The 'Guidelines of Articles of Association of Listed Companies' was issued by the China Securities Regulatory Commission on 16 December 1997 and appears in the *Collections of the Laws of the PRC* (Jilin: Jilin People's Press, 1998) p. 779.

74 'Public Criticisms by China Securities Regulatory Commission on Hubei Meierya Co Ltd and the Relevant Persons of the Company', 20 September 2001, available online at <http://www.chininfobank.com>.

75 'Penalty Decision of China Securities Regulatory Commission Concerning the Violation of Securities Law and Regulation by Shanghai Jiabao Industrial (Group) Co. Ltd', 8 October 2000, available online at <http://www.chinainfo bank.com>.

76 See note 65.

77 Ibid.

78 P. Gregory, 'Securities Fraud in the PRC', *China Law and Practice* (Hong Kong: Asia Law and Practice, March 1995) 20 at p. 21.

79 Ibid.

80 Ibid.

81 Ibid.

82 Zhengquan Shibao (Securities Times), 29 February 2000, available online at <http://www.chinainfobank.com>.

83 See Macey, op. cit., note 32, p. 19.

84 See Zingales, op. cit., note 46.

85 See Smith, op. cit., note 49; B. Black and R. Gilson, 'Venture Capital and the Structure of Capital Markets: Banks Versus Stock Markets', (1998) 47 *J. Fin. Econ.* 243.

86 See Macey, op. cit., note 32, p. 19.

87 See Schleifer and Vishny, op. cit., note 41, pp. 771 and 774.

88 See Macey, op. cit., note 32, p. 19.

89 See Baums, op. cit., note 18, p. 515.

90 See H. Manne, 'Managers and the Market for Corporate Control', (1965) 73 *J. Pol. Econ.* 110.

91 R. Romano, 'The Future of Hostile Takeover: Legislation and Public Opinion', (1988) 57 *U. Cin L. Rev.* 457.

92 For example, see M. Jensen, 'The Modern Industrial Revolution, Exit, and the Failure of Internal Control System', (1993) 48 *J. Fin.* 831 at pp. 835–47.

93 S. Rosenstein and J. Wyatt, 'Outside Directors, Board Independence and Shareholder Wealth', (1990) 26 *J. Fin. Econ.* 175.

94 R. Daniels and P. Halpern, 'Too Close for Comfort: The Role of the Closely Held Public Corporation in the Canadian Economy and Implications for Public Policy', (1995–96) 4 *Canadian Bus. L. J.* 11.

95 For a detailed discussion on the system approach to law, see L. Lopucki, 'The

Systems Approach to Law', (1997) 82 *Cornell L. Rev.* 479; for an application of the system approach to insolvency law, see L. Lopucki and G. Triantis, 'A System Approach to Comparing U.S. and Canadian Reorganization of Financially Distressed Companies', (1994) 35 *Harv. Int'l L. J.* 267.

96   For an application of the substitution theory to corporate governance, see M. Roe, 'Chaos and Evolution in Law and Economics', (1996) 109 *Harv. L. Rev.* 641 at p. 647.

97   For more information, see P. Milgrom and J. Roberts, 'Complementarities and Systems: Understanding Japanese Economic Organization', (1994) 1 *Estudios Economicos* 3; R. Gilson, 'Reflections in a Distant Mirror: Japanese Corporate Governance Through American Eyes', (1998) *Colum. Bus. L. Rev.* 203 at pp. 214 and 220–21.

98   For more information on the function of these subsystems in alleviating agency costs, see Jensen and Meckling, op. cit., note 3; Guanghua Yu, 'The Relevance of Comparative Corporate Governance Studies for China', (1997) 8 *Australian J. Corp. L.* 49.

99   Modigliani and Miller, op. cit., note 4.

100   F. Modigliani and M. Miller, Corporate Income Taxes and the Cost of Capital: A Correction', (1963) *Am. Econ. Rev.* 433.

101   See Jensen and Meckling, op. cit., note 3, p. 333.

102   R. Levine, 'Law, Finance, and Economic Growth', (1999) 8 *J. Fin. Intermediation* 8; R. Levine, 'The Legal Environment, Banks, and Long-run Economic Growth', (1998) 30 *J. Money, Credit & Banking* 596; R. Levine *et al.*, 'Financial Intermediation and Growth: Causality and Causes', (2001) 46 *J. Monetary Econ.* 31.

103   See La Porta *et al.*, op. cit., note 5.

104   W. Baumol *et al.*, *Productivity and American Leadership: The Long View* (Cambridge, MA: MIT Press, 1989) p. 13.

105   D. North, *Institutions, Institutional Change and Economic Performance* (Cambridge: Cambridge University Press, 1990).

106   For a discussion on path dependence theories, see P. David, 'Clio and the Economics of Qwerty', (1985) 75 *Economic History* 332; B. Arthur, 'Competing Technologies, Increasing Returns, and Lock-in by Historical Events', (1989) 99 *The Econ. J.* 116; L. Bebchuk and M. Roe, 'A Thoery of Path Dependence in Corporate Ownership and Governance', (1999) 52 *Stan. L. Rev.* 127.

107   For a discussion on how politics affect the role of financial institutions in corporate governance in the United States, see Roe, op. cit., note 2.

108   For more information, See Guanghua Yu, 'Towards a Market Economy: Security Devices in China', (1999) 8 *Pac. Rim. L. & Pol'y J.* 1 at pp. 1–3.

109   This Notice was issued by the State Council on 25 October 1994 and appeared in the *Collection of the Laws of the PRC* (Jilin: Jilin People's Press, 1994) p. 551.

110   Applicable only to state-owned enterprises, this law was enacted on 2 December 1986 and became effective on 1 November 1988. This law appears in the *Collection of the Laws of the PRC* (Jilin: Jilin People's Press, 1949–1989) p. 1142.

183

111 Enterprises Bankruptcy Law, Article. 37. This Law appears in the *Collection of the Laws of the PRC* (Jilin: Jilin Peoples' Press, 1949–89) p. 1142.

112 Ibid., Article 28.

113 This Law was enacted on 12 April 1986 by the National People's Congress and appears in the *Collection of the Laws of the PRC* (Jilin: Jilin People's Press, 1949–1989) p. 315.

114 *Collection of the Laws of the PRC* (Jilin: Jilin People's Press, 1949–1989) 350 at p. 358.

115 See Article 67 of the Constitution. The Constitution appears in the *Collection of the Laws of the PRC* (Jilin: Jilin People's Press, 1949–1989) p. 3.

116 The Notice, op. cit., note 109, Article 2.

117 The Notice, Article 5(2).

118 The Notice, Article 3(2).

119 The settlement fee is not the equivalent of wages owed to employees specified in the priority of distribution of bankruptcy property of the Enterprise Bankruptcy Law.

120 The Notice, Article 4(1).

121 'Supplemental Notice of the State Council on Some Issues Concerning the Experiment of Mergers, Bankruptcy, and Employee Reemployment of State-owned Enterprises in Certain Cities'. This Supplemental Notice was issued on 2 March 1997 and appears in the *Collection of the Laws of the PRC* (Jilin: Jilin People's Press, 1997) p. 545. Hereinafter Supplemental Notice.

122 Supplemental Notice, Article 5(2).

123 Ibid., Article 5(4).

124 'Bankruptcy Law in the PRC: Ten Years' Sharpening of a Sword', *Science Daily of China*, 22 January 1997, available online at <http://www.chinainfo bank.com>.

125 Ibid. An alternative explanation of why banks are not active in taking debtors to courts is that managers in banks are not doing well in screening loans, and instituting legal actions will expose bad loan decisions to administrative examination and/or those who were responsible for the bad decisions to criminal liability.

126 For more information on enforcement difficulties in this area, see Guanghua Yu, op. cit., note 97, pp. 78–80.

127 Law on Commercial Banks, Article 43(2). This Law appears in the *Collection of the Laws of the PRC* (Jilin: Jilin People's Press, 1995) p. 427.

128 See Xu Jingan, 'The Stockshare System: A New Avenue for China's Economic Reform', (1987) 11 *J. Comp. Econ.* 509 at p. 514.

129 Ibid.

130 Ibid.

131 Han Zhiguo, 'The Development of Innovation of Shareholding Economy in China', *People Net*, 26 May 2001, available online at <http://www.people.com.cn>.

132 Wu Feng, 'Ten Questions Required Quick Solutions', *People Net*, 22 September 2001, available online at <http://www.people.com.cn>.

133 Fang Yuan, 'Zhou Xiaochuan: the Securities Market Has A Big Opera Next

Year', *People Net,* 29 December 2000, available online at <http://www.people. com.cn>.

134 See Wu, op. cit., note 131.

135 This law was enacted on 29 December 1993 and became effective on 1 July 1994. The official Chinese version appears in the *Collection of the Laws of the PRC* (Jilin: Jilin People's Press, 1993) p. 456.

136 The ITS was issued by the State Council on 22 April 1993 and appears in the *Collection of the Laws of the PRC* (Jilin: Jilin People's Press, 1993) p. 480.

137 This Decision was promulgated by the Standing Committee of the National People's Congress on 28 February 1995 and appears in the *Collection of the Laws of the PRC* (Jilin: Jilin People's Press, 1994) p. 51.

138 Ibid., Article 3(1).

139 See 1997 Criminal Law, Article 160. This Law appears in the *Collection of the Laws of the PRC* (Jilin: Jilin People's Press, 1996), p. 29.

140 See Hong Guang, op. cit., note 64.

141 See, ITS, op. cit., note 135.

142 This Law was promulgated on 29 December 1998 and became effective as of 1 July 1999. The Chinese version appears in the *Collection of the Laws of the PRC* (Jilin: Jilin People's Press, 1997) p. 671. An English translation appears in *China Law and Practice* (Hong Kong: Asia Law and Practice, February 1999) p. 25.

143 Ibid., Article 202.

144 See Hong Guang, op. cit., note 64.

145 Huang Xiangyuan, 'Hong Guang Qizha An Mei Namo Rongyi Wanjie' (The Case of Fraud of Hong Guang Could Not Easily be Ended), *Securities Newspaper,* 28 December 2000.

146 Ibid.

147 Xue Li, 'Cong Hong Guang Dao Yin guang Xia, Minishi Peichange De Lu You Duochang' (From Hong Guang to Yin Guang Xia, How Far We Still Have to Go for Civil Compensation), *Shanghai Securities Newspaper,* 6 September 2001, available onlne at <http://finance-sina.com.cn>.

148 Tao Feng, 'Cong Hong Guang Dao Yin Guang Xia Kan Gumin Weiquan' (Look at the Protection of Investors from Hong Guang to Yin Guang Xia), available online at http://www.informationtimes.dayoo.com/content/2001–09/28/ content_232281/htm>.

149 'Notice of the Supreme People's Court Concerning the Temporary Non-acceptance of Securities Cases for Civil Compensation', 21 October 2001, available online at <http://www.chinainfobank.com>.

150 Ji Wenhai, 'Zhongguo Remmin Daxue Sanwei Jiaoshou Tan Zhengquan Weifa Ji Chengzhi' (Three Professors Talk about Violation of and Punishment for Illegal Acts on the Securities Markets), *Chinese Economics Times,* 17 October 2001, available online at <http://www.chinainfobank.com>.

151 'Notice of the Supreme People's Court on Certain Issues Concerning the Acceptance of Tort Cases Involving Misrepresentation on the Securities Market', 15 January 2002, available online at <http://www.chinainfobank. com>.

152 Ibid.

185

153 Ibid.
154 P. Straham, 'Securities Class Actions, Corporate Governance and Managerial Agency Problems', (1998) Working Paper, Federal Reserve of New York.
155 M. Gilson, 'Big Bank Deregulation and Japanese Corporate Governance: A Survey of the Issue', in T. Hoshi and H. Patrick (eds), *Crisis and Change in the Japanese Financial System* (Boston, MA: Kluwer Academic Publishers, 2000) p. 305.
156 See C. Milhaupt, 'Property Rights in Firms', (1998) 84 *Va. L. Rev.* 1145 at p. 1188.
157 Ibid.
158 See Wu Feng, op. cit., note 131.
159 Ibid.
160 See G. Akerlof, 'The Market for "Lemon": Quality Uncertainty and the Market Mechanism', (1970) 84 *Q. J. Econ.* 488.
161 See Black, op. cit., note 63, p. 788.
162 Securities Law, Article 202.

Index

For Product Safety Concerns and Information please contact our EU
representative GPSR@taylorandfrancis.com
Taylor & Francis Verlag GmbH, Kaufingerstraße 24, 80331 München, Germany